JUDEO-SPANISH TRADITIONAL BALLADS FROM JERUSALEM

WISSENSCHAFTLICHE ABHANDLUNGEN
BAND XXIII/1

MUSICOLOGICAL STUDIES
VOL. XXIII/1

Judeo-Spanish Traditional Ballads from Jerusalem

An Ethnomusicological Study

ISRAEL J. KATZ

THE INSTITUTE OF MEDIÆVAL MUSIC, LTD.
1653 WEST 8TH STREET, BROOKLYN, NEW YORK USA 11223, ÉTATS UNIS

1972

Internationale Standart-Numerierung der Bücher

Ausgabe Nr. 912024-97-6

Imprimé aux Pays Bas par l'Imprimerie Royale Van Gorcum & Comp., Assen

PREFACE

The study of Judeo-Spanish folklore has been, for the most part, the private domain of zealous *aficionados* whose enthusiasm and intense devotion, admirable and important in their own right, have served as an inadequate substitute for the formal training that a scholarly discipline requires. Perhaps no aspect of this rich and varied subject has been more neglected by competent specialists than the music of Sephardic balladry.

When Israel J. Katz first came to see us in 1959, he was already a graduate student with a wide background in musicology as well as an experienced professional musician. He was eager to embark upon a new career in ethnomusicology, and had come to seek our advice about the music of the Judeo-Spanish ballad répertoire as a possible area of specialization. At that time, though we were only in the early stages of our ballad project, we were acutely aware of the need to collaborate with a trained ethnomusicologist, one who could go beyond the romantic and vague generalizations that made of Sephardic music simply an extension of *cante jondo*, a kind of variant of the *flamenco* singing of Andalusian gypsies. For this reason, we applauded his decision to continue in the doctoral program at the University of California at Los Angeles. After a year of study, he left on scholarship for Israel and the opportunity to do field work among the native Jerusalem Sephardic community as well as among the Sephardim who had emigrated to Israel in recent years from various cities in the Balkans and Morocco.

During a period of two years, he lived and studied in Israel, travelling by motor scooter from community to community — Tel-Aviv, Tiberias, Bet-Shemesh, Safed, outlying agricultural settlements — always with a tape recorder and Menéndez Pidal's indispensable *Catálogo del romancero judio-español* at hand. In this way, he came to know intimately and profoundly the complex workings of a multisecular musico-poetical tradition. Through day to day contact and patient, sympathetic questioning, Katz was able to penetrate to the core of Sephardic balladry, learning in the process how a living tradition sustains itself in a seemingly unending series of variations on themes and combinations of themes, rendered with varying degrees of versatility and artistry by the numerous singers who performed for him. Regrettably, he also learned that the Judeo-Spanish ballad tradition, like all human creations, is not eternal. In fact, there is little hope that the current répertoire of ballads will be perpetuated in traditional form much beyond the present generation of singers.

As background for his work — recognizing from the outset the crucial symbiotic relationship between lyrics and music in the Hispanic *Romancero* or ballad tradition — he familiarized himself with the fundamental studies on the literary aspects of the genre. Then, with painstaking efforts and time-consuming perseverance, he gathered together every scrap of information, impressionistic or precise, concerning the music of Hispanic balladry and, specifically, the Sephardic branch of that tradition. The results of these labors have been synthesized in his richly documented historical survey of musical studies on the Judeo-Spanish *Romancero* (Chapter II, below), clearly the most inclusive and authoritative statement on the subject now available. In the main body of this book, instead of offering a *potpourri* of his findings, Katz, with the delicacy of a trained musician and the dispassionate, technical accuracy of a scholar, has lavished meticulous attention on five ballads from the fast-disappearing Jerusalem tradition. He has analyzed them in terms of Near Eastern musical theory and has demonstrated their dependence upon the musical répertoire of the great Sephardic centers at Salonika, Rhodes and Istanbul.

When, in 1953, after a lifetime devoted to the study of Hispanic epic and ballad poetry, Don Ramon Menéndez Pidal published his *Romancero Hispánico*, he realized that its two volumes were only historical *prolegomena* to the *Romancero* itself, which still awaited the critical edition it deserved. With undisguised melancholy, the revered patriarch of Hispanic scholarship saw himself as another Moses, looking down upon a Promised Land that he would never enter. It is wonderfully symbolic that in Jerusalem, the Promised Land itself, Israel J. Katz began his collection and study of musical examples from the Judeo-Spanish *Romancero*. Ahead of him lies the musicological analysis of more than one-thousand variant balladic texts, now in our possession, which were sung by Sephardic Jews from Turkey, Yugoslavia, Bulgaria, Romania, Greece, the Island of Rhodes, North Africa, and Israel.

With this book, the product of intensive field work, historical research and "in-depth" musical analyses, he has laid a solid foundation for his part in our collaborative Sephardic *Romancero* project, another step toward the balladic Promised Land that Menéndez Pidal called: *Romancero Hispánico: hispano-portugués, americano y sefardí*.

Samuel G. Armistead and Joseph H. Silverman

INTRODUCTION

It is generally accepted that in those Sephardic communities where Judeo-Spanish is still spoken, certain cultural attributes have survived in an unbroken tradition which originated in the Jewish communities of late fifteenth-century Spain. The reliques of the Castilian *Romancero* which have persisted in the intensely Spanish heritage of the Sephardic Jews are of sufficient quantity and quality to warrant an intensive study of this crucially important branch of Hispanic balladry. The importance of the Judeo-Spanish *Romancero* rests primarily upon its retention of archaïc features as well as its preservation of a goodly number of ballad themes which have long ago become extinct on the Iberian Peninsula. The numerous collections of ballad texts from Sephardic sources which have appeared since the turn of the present century attest to these facts and show, at the same time, the wide diffusion of this tradition.

On the other hand, the study of the melodies to which these ballads were sung has been almost completely neglected, except for isolated notations which have appeared in a small number of collections. The strong textual ties of the Judeo-Spanish ballads with the Peninsula moved early investigators to postulate a musical link as well. Such speculations gave rise to a number of highly romanticized generalizations concerning the origin of the Judeo-Spanish ballad melodies. These notions were never adequately challenged, nor was there any attempt at a serious study of the Sephardic ballad répertoire as it had existed in oral tradition, save for the promising start made by Manrique de Lara (d. 1929), who unfortunately left no true successor.

In the spring of 1959, I was made aware of an interesting project being undertaken by Professors Samuel G. Armistead and Joseph H. Silverman of the University of California, Los Angeles. Since the summer of 1957, they had been collecting materials from Eastern Mediterranean Sephardim residing in Los Angeles, San Francisco, and Seattle and had already formed a substantial ballad collection. Without any knowledge of their musical content, I began a preliminary search for notated melodies of Sephardic ballads.

Three sources were readily available, notably A. Z. Idelsohn's *Gesänge der orientalischen Sefardim* (Berlin-Vienna-Jerusalem, 1923), Alberto Hemsi's *Coplas sefardíes* (Alexandria, 1932-1938), and Arcadio de Larrea Palacín's *Romances de Tetuán* (Madrid, 1952). A fourth source, *Chants séphardis* (London, 1958) by Léon Algazi, was sent to me as a gift from Dr. Isaac Moyal, who at the time was President of the World Sephardi Federation.

A perusal of these works left me with certain doubts concerning their reliability. To begin with, they lacked documentation concerning the informants, their age, place of origin, and the date of collection, which should have been provided for the individual melodies. In each case, it was not entirely clear how the material had been collected, nor were there any descriptive comments about the manner of performance. The social function of the ballads within the community was also neglected, although Hemsi and Larrea Palacín do comment briefly on this latter point. The notations varied from a minimal melodic frame based upon the sung syllable to highly ornamented melodic phrases with their modalities corresponding mainly to major, minor, and Aeolian, although a few melodies were in Dorian, Phrygian, and Mixolydian. The melodies were almost completely limited to a single strophe with the quatrain structure predominating. Their time signatures, in the majority of cases, were in duple and triple time with some instances of mixed signatures. Two examples, in Idelsohn, were in *parlando rubato*. Furthermore, no attempt was made to establish the melodies' stylistic authenticity within the areas represented, nor did the notators seek out other musical variants in pursuit of a valid tune-text relationship.

However, only when I heard samplings of field recordings from the Armistead-Silverman collection did I fully realize the necessity for undertaking a study of this important ballad tradition. From these samplings, it became obvious to me that the other collections had merely scratched the surface, and that beneath these published sources lay the challenging world of an oral folk tradition that had to be investigated and described in terms of an actual field confrontation. It also became evident that a scholarly study could not be possible *without* musical variants from other important Sephardic communities of the greater Mediterranean region.

A Rockefeller Foundation Grant-in-aid and a Charles Brown Fellowship made possible a two-year field trip to Israel which enabled me not only to investigate the living Sephardic tradition but also to undertake intensive research into the musical cultures of the Middle East. Under the careful guidance of Dr. Edith Gerson-Kiwi, the eminent musicologist and long-time resident of Jerusalem, I undertook a systematic study of the varied Oriental and Middle Eastern musical cultures and became acquainted with the techniques of transcription and analysis which are so vital to field research.

Living in Jerusalem, I became familiar with the Sephardim who up until

1948 had resided in the Old City where their forebears could be traced back many generations into the Ottoman era. These were the true *Sabras*, native-born Palestinians, now Israelis. Because of their resettlement in the new city of Jerusalem, the once closely knit community had become splintered. Suffering the trials and tribulations of the new state, their spiritual cohesion had declined and consequently their traditional existence had been interrupted by standards imposed upon them by the new economy. In spite of these rather uncomfortable times, when the opportunity arose (weddings, circumcision ceremonies, *Bar Mitzvahs*, etc.), the aged women gathered and sang their traditional ballads. Their répertoire, which undoubtedly had been vigorous before Israel became a state, was already showing signs of decay. In many instances, the moribund répertoire had been reduced to mere fragments. Except for the few elders upon whose recollection this tradition rests, the ballads have found neither continued support nor reverence among the younger generations who deem them "old fashioned."

During the years 1960 to 1961, I collected some 250 ballad texts in Israel. Not only did I record from *Sabra* informants, but I also seized every opportunity to record ballad variants from among the recent immigrants from Balkan countries and from Morocco in order to expand the valuable collection made in the United States by Armistead and Silverman. My equipment consisted of a Grundig TK-35 tape recorder (220 V. 50 cycle) plus the Grundig microphone GDM 15 which has cardioid characteristics. At the outset of my field endeavors, I recorded at the speed of $7\frac{1}{2}$ ips, but later had to resort to the speed of $3\frac{3}{4}$ ips in order to conserve tape. In expediting initial interrogations of prospective informants, I found two sources particularly helpful: Ramón Menéndez Pidal's "Catálogo del romancero judío-español," from *Los romances de América* (Buenos Aires-México D.F., 1948), and Moshe Attias' *Romancero sefaradí* (Jerusalem, 1956). Later on, I received a list of *incipits* which Armistead and Silverman had prepared on the basis of their on-going field work. These source texts were used to stimulate the informants' recollections through the reading of the *incipits* of traditional ballads. Other traditional materials in addition to ballads were also recorded in order to obtain a well-rounded survey of Sephardic folklore.

Only a small portion of the ballad texts which I gathered from my aged *Sabra* informants provides the basis of the present study. I have chosen to begin the study with a brief history of the Sephardim, with special reference to the Jerusalem community, in order that the reader may understand the importance of its deeply-rooted Hispanic tradition. The following chapter offers a critical survey of the musical contributions in the field of the Judeo-Spanish *Romancero*. Here, I have attempted to bring together all the scattered musical sources and to identify all the published items collected to date. In Chapter III, where I deal with ballad analysis, I attempt, on the basis of variants collected on tape and from published sources, to identify the immediate musical predecessors of the Jerusalem répertoire in order to prove that these melodies did not originate on Palestinian soil. The transcriptions of the Jerusalem ballads included in this study are my own. In order that they may be properly understood in terms of the tradition, I have also annotated them.

I want to express my appreciation to the Charles Brown Fellowship Committee of Los Angeles for having awarded me the opportunity to study and undertake field research in Israel and to the Institute of Ethnomusicology, UCLA, for the extension of a second year through a Rockefeller Foundation Grant-in-aid. I am indebted to Professor Boris A. Kremenliev for his invaluable assistance in the musical presentation, and am especially grateful to my colleagues Professors Samuel G. Armistead and Joseph H. Silverman for their profound insights into historical, philological, and linguistic matters. I also want to thank Professors Byron Cantrell, Gilbert Reaney, Alfred Šendrey, Klaus Wachsmann, and D. K. Wilgus for their careful reading of the manuscript and helpful suggestions. My sincere gratitude to Jacqueline Thompson Elpers who assisted in transcribing the texts, to Joanne March, whose singular effort in typing the final copy attests to her remarkable ability and painstaking accuracy, and to Marcia, my dear wife, whose help with the final proofreading was but one of many testimonies to the totality of her devotion. Of course, I will not forget Dr. Edith Gerson-Kiwi's excellent tutelage during the two memorable "Jerusalem years".

TABLE OF CONTENTS

VOLUME I

Preface. V

Introduction VII

Chapter One:
The Sephardic Community of Jerusalem: An Historical Sketch 1

Chapter Two:
A Musical Survey of the Judeo-Spanish *Romancero* 20

Chapter Three:
A Musical Study of Five Ballad Tunes from the Jerusalem Répertoire 125
    A. *Arbolero* or *Vuelta del marido (i)*, MP 58 136
    B. *La adúltera (á-a)*, MP 80. 143
    C. *Landarico*, MP 82. 147
    D. *Don Bueso y su hermana*, MP 49 154
    E. *La choza del desesperado*, MP 140 158

Concluding Statement 165

Bibliography 166

Appendix I:
Published Sources Containing Melodies of Judeo-Spanish *Romances* Listed in Ramón Menéndez Pidal's *Catálogo*. 187

Appendix II:
An Inventory of the Tape-Recorded Examples and the Published Notations Utilized for the Study of the Ballad Tunes from the Jerusalem Répertoire 199

Appendix III:
Additional Ballad Themes Collected from the Jerusalem Répertoire (1959-61) 203

CHAPTER ONE

THE SEPHARDIC COMMUNITY OF JERUSALEM
AN HISTORICAL SKETCH

At the beginning of the fourth century C.E., large Jewish settlements were already scattered throughout Europe, especially in Germany and on the Iberian Peninsula where, after centuries of peaceful coëxistence, their presence became a source of concern to the powerful Christian majority. Such an attitude soon gave rise to special legislation against the Jews which was aimed at suppressing their religious influence.[1] On the Iberian Peninsula, the continual issuance of decrees by church councils occasioned waves of persecution. Jewish life on the Peninsula was almost completely stifled when, at the Third Council of Toledo (589), King Recared accepted Catholicism as the official religion of Visigothic Spain. As a result of these events, there began the first mass exodus of Jewry from the Peninsula to France and North Africa, while those remaining behind either kept steadfast to Judaism or chose to accept baptism. However, it appears that the number of converts was insignificant, judging by the rigid stipulations imposed upon the Jews, as a result of the Fourth Council of Toledo, which convened in 633. During the next century up to the time of the Arab conquest, we find a wealth of documentation concerning Jewish communities on the Peninsula, with some indication of their cultural unification, but no evidence relating to their participation in the secular arts.[2]

---

[1] Noteworthy were the canons prescribed by the Council of Elvira which met in Southern Spain (313 C.E.). These decrees foreshadowed the attitudes of subsequent church councils toward the Jews. See Jacob R. Marcus, *The Jew in the Medieval World. A Source Book: 315-1791* (Philadelphia, 1960), pp. 101-102.

[2] The most authoritative work on the Jews of the Visigothic period is Solomon Katz, *The Jews in the Visigothic and Frankish Kingdoms of Spain and Gaul* (Cambridge, 1937). Katz presents an examination of the legal conditions of Jews in Spain to 711 C.E. and in Gaul to the Carolingian period based upon canonical and civil legislative documents as his prime sources. Chapter six, pp. 73-81, briefly surveys the institutions and organizations of the Jewish communities. Katz points out (p. 76f.) that the Jews of the Diaspora considered the Jewish chief of Palestine as their supreme authority, or exilarch. However, because the Romans had prevented the Palestinian exilarch from exercising

With the Moslem invasion and the subsequent Islamic domination of Spain, Spanish Jewry entered a new phase of its history. Whereas previously, under Christian hegemony, Jewish existence was intolerable, now there began a peaceful and productive period under a new religious, economic, and political structure in which they could enjoy and participate significantly in mercantile, professional, and even agricultural pursuits.[1] Jews were even awarded titles of rank and were given responsible positions within the framework of the ruling hierarchy. In a period which followed (900-1050), often referred to as the "Golden Age of Spanish Jewry," gifted Jewish poets and scholars contributed to a literary output which has maintained its place along with other milestones of literature.[2] Moreover, because of Islam's rapid diffusion throughout the Mediterranean world, contacts were renewed with other Jewish communities in Moslem areas, particularly with the ancient community of Babylon where great institutions of learning were still flourishing. These contacts brought about a rise in Jewish cultural standards which had remained latent during the centuries of Christian rule, when such contacts had been prohibited.[3]

Since the greater portion of the Spanish Jews lived in Moslem Spain, it was not until the Reconquest was well under way in the eleventh century that the majority of Jewish communities again came under Christian control.[4] The marked Hispanization of Peninsular Jewry did not begin until the re-

his real authority, the Diaspora Jews soon turned to the exilarch of the flourishing Babylonian community. See also Shalom Albeck, ״יסודות משטר הקהילות בספרד עד השנה הרמ״ה (1180-1244)״ ['The Principles of Government in the Jewish Communities of Spain until the 13th Century']," (In Hebrew) *Zion*, XXV (Jerusalem, 1960), 85-121.

[1] For a listing of the occupations of Jews in Spain as well as Southern France and Italy before the end of the fourteenth century, see Appendix D, on page 247 of Israel Abrahams, *Jewish Life in the Middle Ages* (Philadelphia, 1896) and reprinted in 1958.

[2] Jefim Schirmann gives some interesting insights into the literary world of the Jewish poet in "The Function of the Hebrew Poet in Medieval Spain," *Jewish Social Studies*, XVI (1954), 235-252.

[3] A link with the Jews of Babylon was most natural considering the constant traffic maintained between the Caliphate of the Peninsula and the Eastern Caliphate of Mesopotamia with Bagdad as its capital. However, the customs and rituals of the Babylonian Jews had greatly influenced not only the Peninsular Jews but the Jewish world at large. The significance of North Africa's rôle in Jewish history cannot be fully appreciated without viewing it as a land bridge between Spain and Bagdad.

[4] The best and most recent books concerning Jewish life in Christian and Moslem Spain can be found in the following works: Fritz Baer, *Die Juden in christlichen Spanien*, 2 vols. (Berlin, 1929-1936), subsequently translated into Hebrew, תולדות היהודים בספרד הנוצרית, 2 vols. (Tel Aviv, 1945) and finally translated from the Hebrew into English, *A History of the Jews in Christian Spain*, 2 vols. (Philadelphia, 1961-1965); E. Ashtor, קורות היהודים בספרד המוסלמית ['*A History of the Jews in Moslem Spain*'] (in Hebrew) (Jerusalem, 1959). Other outstanding contributions are Abraham A. Neuman, *The Jews in Spain: Their Social, Political and Cultural Life during the Middle Ages*, 2 vols. (Philadelphia, 5702/1942), and José Amador de los Ríos, *Historia social, política y religiosa de los judíos de España y Portugal*, 3 vols. (Madrid, 1875-1876).

capture of Toledo in 1085.[1] During the twelfth century, the persecution of Jews in Moslem Spain particularly the Almohades — a Berber Moslem dynasty — brought new waves of Jewish emigration northward into the major cities. By the thirteenth century, when the armies of the Reconquest reached the Moslem centers of Córdova and Sevilla, the Jewish situation was perplexing indeed since both sides regarded the Jews as a threat in that their loyalty was supposedly divided between the two camps.[2] Nonetheless, learned Jews played an important rôle in the Castilian court of Alfonso X "el Sabio" (1252-1284).[3]

The mass conversion of Jews to Christianity, which began in the late fourteenth century, gave rise to further grave problems. The converts, called *Marranos* or Crypto-Jews, came to be looked upon with great mistrust by their Christian neighbors, because a significant number of them reverted to clandestine Judaic practices.[4] The riots of 1391, incited by the Christian Spaniards in the Jewish quarters — *juderías* or *aljamas* — of the major cities, are a pivotal point for Peninsular Jewish history.[5] Subsequent events held even greater perils for the *Marranos*, who, as converts, fell under the jurisdiction of the Inquisition. This tribunal, established in Spain in 1478, was set up primarily to ferret out the menacing and disloyal elements within the the Catholic faith. The religious habits of the *Marranos* furnished good reason for their being treated as heretics.[6] With the fall of Granada in 1492,

---

[1] See Mair José Benardete, *Hispanic Culture and Character of the Sephardic Jews* (New York, 1952), pp. 56-57.

[2] See Abraham A. Neuman, "Some Phases of the Conditions of Jews in Spain in the 13th and 14th Centuries," *American Jewish Historical Society Publications*, XXII (1914), 61-70.

[3] This rôle is discussed by Américo Castro in *The Structure of Spanish History* (Princeton, 1954), pp. 474-91.

[4] *Conversos* was another popular term applied to the converts. On the *Marranos*, see Cecil Roth, *A History of the Marranos* (Philadelphia, 1932), and B. Netanyahu, *The Marranos of Spain from the Late 14th to the Early 16th Century According to Contemporary Hebrew Sources* (New York, 1966).

[5] The significance of the year 1391 as the turning point for Peninsular Jewry leading to the expulsion is discussed succinctly in Benardete, *op. cit.*, pp. 27-33. Fritz Baer, *op. cit.*, Vol. II, is an excellent and expanded study of the same period. In Morocco, the Jewish quarters are known as *mellahs*, while in Tunis and Algeria they are known as *harat l'yahud* — though these terms were used principally after the sixteenth century.

[6] Concerning the *Marranos* and the Inquisition, see *Marranos in Portugal*, Survey by the Portuguese Marranos Committee, London 1922 to 1938 (London, 1938); B. Llorca, "Los conversos judíos y la inquisición Española," *Sefarad*, XIII (1948), 357-390; B. Netanyahu, "The Marranos according to the Hebrew Sources of the 15th and Early 16th Centuries," *The American Academy for Jewish Research*, XXXI (1963), 81-164; and Samuel Schwarz, "The Crypto-Jews of Portugal," *The Menorah Journal*, XII (April-May, 1926), 138-149, (June-July, 1926), 283-297.

H. J. Zimmels discusses the private lives and customs of Spanish and Portuguese

the edict of expulsion fell upon Spanish Jewry, and again in 1497 for those who had found refuge in Portugal.[1] Spain's objective — a national sovereignty based upon religious and ethnic unity — was thus apparently realized. In that same year, with the discovery of the New World, Spain emerged as one of the strongest nations in Europe.

From Spanish ports, Jews fled to France, continuing from there to various parts of Northern Europe, and ultimately to the newly established centers of the New World.[2] Other groups went to North Africa, Italy, and the Balkans. Eugene Kulischer, in a study of Jewish migrations, stated:

> It is estimated that there were in Spain 250,000 Jews who practiced their religion openly at the time of the expulsion decree. Fifty thousand, preferring to remain in Spain, embraced the Christian faith. The rest left the country. Thousands of exiles perished at sea, en route to their new [future?] homes... However, Marranos continued to leave Spain in a small but steady stream for several centuries thereafter. The largest group among the Spanish Jews, about 100,000, settled in the Turkish Empire.[3]

Marranos from numerous Jewish sources in his study of *Die Marranen in der rabbinischen Literatur: Forschungen und Quellen zur Geschichte und Kulturgeschichte der Anussim* (Berlin, 1932).

[1] Accounts dealing specifically with the expulsion can be found in: Volume II, Part One, Chapter Seventeen of William H. Prescott, *History of the Reign of Ferdinand and Isabella the Catholic* (Philadelphia, 1872), 3 vols.; Alexander Marx, "The Expulsion of the Jews from Spain," *The Jewish Quarterly Review*, XX (1908), 240-271 which was based upon two contemporaneous reports; and Valeriu Marcu, *The Expulsion of the Jews from Spain* (London, 1935).

[2] Benardete, *op. cit.*, pp. 53-85. There was a twofold wave of Jewish emigration from the Peninsula. These two waves of emigration were designated respectively as Mediæval and Renaissance by Benardete. The former composed of those who migrated to North Africa and the Eastern Mediterranean where they continued as folk societies and preserved their Hispanic culture; the latter, embracing those who migrated to various parts of Western Europe and the American Continent and whose quick Westernization had shaken off almost all traces of their Hispanic heritage.

It must be pointed out that in 1492, the greatest number of Jews went immediately to Portugal to remain there only five years. It is interesting to note that the earliest Jewish settlers in Amsterdam were *Marranos* from Lisbon who arrived there as late as 1593. Cf. Cecil Roth, *A Life of Menasseh Ben Israel* (Philadelphia, 1934), p. 16. Menasseh ben Israel established the first Sephardic Community in London in 1656 which was made up mostly of descendants of Portuguese *Marranos*.

[3] *Jewish Migrations: Past Experience and Post War Prospects*. Pamphlet series: Jews and the Post War World, No. 4 (New York, 1943), p. 18. The numerical aspect of the Peninsular Jewish population has been an interesting facet of investigation. Isidore Loeb, in his article "Le Nombre de juifs de Castille et d'Espagne au moyen âge," *Revue des Études Juives*, XIV (1887), 161, states that in the fifteenth century there was a total population of somewhere between seven to eight million inhabitants on the Peninsula, of which the Jews must not have exceeded 235,000.

In numbers concerning the expulsion, E. Ashtor, *op. cit.*, p. 440, gives 160,000 as the number of expelled Jews, of which 100,000 went to Portugal. A. Z. Idelsohn, *Gesänge*

Mention must be made of the fact that up to the time of the expulsion it was mostly *Marranos* who had fled Spain. Their main settlements were to be found in the already established communities of North Africa, particularly Western Morocco. Others settled temporarily in Naples, Genoa, Rome, and Sicily. Some of them, along with pious Jews, continued directly to the Holy Land where, ever since the fall of the Second Temple (70 C.E.), Jerusalem had remained the spiritual center for the Jews of the Diaspora. A visit to the Holy City in one's life time was regarded as a sacred duty. However, this deep-rooted wish of the multitudes was often obstructed by the hardships and hazards of the time. Thus, their most immediate concern was to resettle in surroundings where religious tolerance and economic opportunity prevailed.

Nearly a century prior to the expulsion, the Ottoman Turks, emerging as a militant political force, brought renewed vigor to Islam in the East. When the Turks captured Constantinople in 1453, the Byzantine Empire came to an end. This event opened a new chapter in Sephardic history particularly when the gates to Turkey and her immediate environs were opened to the refugees from Spain during the reign of the Ottoman King, Bayezid II (1481-1512). Yet, it was not until Selim I (1512-1520) had defeated the Mamelukes, that the Jews were allowed the freedom of movement anywhere in the conquered domains of the Ottoman Empire.[1] The Turks, now masters of the greatest portion of Mediterranean lands, were in need of the enterprising skills which the Jewish exiles were able to supply. The mass emigration of

---

der orientalischen Sefardim, (Jerusalem-Berlin-Vienna, 1923), p. 1, quoting from the Introduction of Don Isaac Abravanel's מעיני הישועה ['Wells of Salvation'] [Ferrara, 1551], gives 300,000 as the number of Jews living in Spain around the time of the expulsion, of which approximately 10,000 settled permanently in Italy. Marx, *op. cit.*, 245-46, discusses the early scholarly arguments about Abravanel's figures. However, concerning the number of Sephardic emigrants to Turkey, Idelsohn felt that a figure of 50,000 to 60,000 should not be regarded as high.

Alexandre Herculano, *Historia da origem e do estabelecimento da Inquisição em Portugal*, I (Lisbon, 1864), p. 77, gave 800,000 as an estimate of the number of Jews in Spain around 1492. Cecil Roth, "The European Age in Jewish History," in Louis Finkelstein's *The Jews: Their History, Culture and Religion* (New York, 1949), I, p. 238, states that "the number of people [affected by the expulsion] was probably about 150,000 although both contemporary chroniclers and subsequent historians exaggerated it to a fantastic degree."

Studies dealing specifically with the Jewish population of the Peninsula can be found in Isidore Loeb, *op. cit.*, 161-83, and E. Ashtor, "מספר היהודים בספרד המוסלמית" ['The Number of Jews in Moslem Spain']," (In Hebrew) *Zion*, XXVIII (Jerusalem, 1963), 34-56.

[1] Ḥaim Ze'ev Hershberg, "מראשית שלטון העותמאנים עד מסע־נאפוליון ['From the Beginning of the Ottoman Rule to Napoleon's Expedition']," *Encyclopædia Hebraica*, VI (Jerusalem, 1957), p. 489.

Spanish Jews, or Sephardim,[1] who came to the Balkans around 1516 and thereafter, united with earlier emigrant settlements and formed congregations whose religious practices followed that of the Spanish communities from which they had sprung.[2] Within a short period, the Jewish population of Istanbul increased to 30,000 souls — the largest such community in all Europe and the Near East. Salonika maintained the second largest Jewish population, although here the Jews gained a unique distinction as the predominant element in the city, due largely to the depopulation of Greeks and Turks. By the middle of the sixteenth century, Salonika became the most successful Sephardic metropolis[3]. Other Sephardic centers in the Eastern Mediterranean were founded in Izmir, Edirne, and on the Island of Rhodes.[4] It was from these centers that Palestine received continuous support and from which the greatest contingent of early Sephardic settlers came to the Holy Land.

Before the Sephardic exodus, small colonies of Ashkenazic Jews, from Central and Eastern Europe, had also settled in Greece and Turkey. Because of the pressures brought to bear upon them by the enormous influx of Sephardim, the Ashkenazim experienced hard times in trying to maintain their pristine identity. Each group had its own language: among themselves, in their homes and in secular life, the Sephardim spoke Ladino, while the Ashkenazim spoke Yiddish. Hebrew, however, was regarded by both as the sacred tongue and was used primarily for worship and other religious occasions. Had Hebrew been employed as the spoken idiom between the two groups, they would have experienced difficulty in understanding each other because of marked differences in pronunciation. Furthermore, the Hebrew scripts of each group were notably dissimilar, as were their liturgical and ritualistic practices. Circum-

---

[1] The Sephardim take their name from the word *Sepharad* found in *Obadiah* I:20, "and the captivity of Jerusalem which is in Sepharad, shall possess the cities of the south." This is one among several expressions from the Book of *Obadiah* which describes the ultimate return of the children of Israel to their former home. The Ashkenazim trace their name to *Genesis* X: 3.
[2] Idelsohn, *Gesänge der orientalischen Sefardim*, p. 2.
[3] Information regarding the emigrant Sephardic communities of Istanbul and Salonika can be found in the following works: Abraham Galante, *Histoire des juifs d'Istanbol* (Istanbul, 1942); Morris S. Goodblatt, *Jewish Life in Turkey in the 16th Century* (New York, 5712/1952); Joseph Nehama, *Histoire des israélites de Salonique* (Salonika-Paris, 1935-1959), 5 vols.; and Abraham Danon, "La Communauté juive de Salonique au XVIe siècle," *Revue des Études Juives*, XL (Paris, 1900), 206-230 and XLI (1900), 98-117, 250-65.
[4] See Abraham Galante, *Histoire des juifs d'Anatolie. Les Juifs d'Ismir (Smyrne)*, I (Istanbul, 1937); Irving Benveniste, "The Glory and Tragedy of Rhodes," *Kol-Sepharad*, II, Nos. 3-4 (London, 1966), 9-11; Simon Marcus, "לתולדות היהודים ברודוס בימי שלטון מסדר אבירי יוחנן הקדוש" ['A History of the Jews of Rhodes during the Rule of the Order of the Knights of St. John']," *Tesoro de los judíos sefardíes*, II (Jerusalem, 1959), 55-68, (In Hebrew); and I. Sonne, "Relazione sul materiale archivistico e bibliografico della Comunità Israelita de Rodi," *L'Idea Sionistica* (1931), pp. 4-5.

stances thus found the diaspora Jews to be bilingual and, in many areas, trilingual. Probably the most important factor in distinguishing the Ashkenazim from the Sephardim in Greece and Turkey was that the former were part of an individual culture while the latter had lived chiefly under Islamic domination. No matter where the Sephardim were to settle within the lands of the Ottoman Empire, they naturally would have felt more at home than their European co-religionists with regard to such matters as business practices, customs, cookery, and even dress.[1]

From 1492 to 1517, there was little traffic to Palestine. The exiles who proceeded directly to the Holy Land were people of means and high cultural standards. Egypt and Syria, functioning as corridors to Palestine from North Africa and the Balkans, became havens for the refugees, who found it practical to dwell in such important trade centers as Cairo, Alexandria, Damascus, and Aleppo. Sixteenth-century Cairo was as important culturally as was Istanbul and Salonika.

In Jerusalem, there had always been a continuous Jewish population, no matter how small. This Holy City, which had been under Islamic rule since the seventh century, derived its main cultural foundation from Islam. Only during the twelfth century (1099-1187) was Islamic rule interrupted by the Crusaders, who had established the Latin Kingdom of Jerusalem. In 1187, Saladin, the Sultan of Egypt, recaptured the Holy City and henceforth it remained mostly under Moslem control even though it was ruled by the various political dynasties: Ayyubids, Bahri Mamelukes, Burji Mamelukes, and the Ottoman Turks from 1517 up to the end of World War I.

When the great Rabbi Moses ben Nachman (d. 1270) — or Nachmanides, as he is now commonly called — was exiled by King James I of Aragón, he went to the Holy Land in 1267, and found Jerusalem in a terrible state. The Mongol invasion of 1260 had left the Holy City completely devastated. During the last three years of his life, Nachmanides founded the Sephardic community of Jerusalem and organized the Jews from Nablus and the neighboring villages as part of the official community. The community then reëstablished its ties with other settlements in Palestine and was further augmented by the continuous arrival of Jews from other parts of the Orient and Occident.[2] However,

---

[1] H. J. Zimmels' valuable contribution, *Ashkenazim and Sephardim* (London, 1958), discusses in depth the relations and differences of both groups as reflected in the rabbinical Responsa. See the comments made by Isaac R. Molho in "Some Aspects of Sephardim and Ashkenazim," *Tesoro de los judíos sefardíes*, III (Jerusalem, 1960), xvii-xxii.

[2] C. Ramos-Gil, "La lengua española en Israel," *Tesoro de los judíos sefardíes*, I (Jerusalem, 1959), xxxiii. A bibliographical sketch of the learned Rabbi can be found in the article, "Nachmanides," by Solomon Schechter in *Studies in Judaism* (New York, 1958), pp. 193-230. A letter bearing an interesting account of the Rabbi's arrival in Jerusalem can be found on p. 201.

the greatest number of Jews who emigrated to Palestine before the expulsion were those from Morocco.[1]

A decade before the Spanish expulsion, Jerusalem was suffering from the epidemics and famine which were raging throughout the Holy Land. Moreover, enormous tax burdens imposed by despotic Mameluke administrators had forced a substantial portion of the Jews to leave the city. It was during this time that the Italian Rabbi Obadiah Bertinoro appeared in Jerusalem to exert his influence in revitalizing the city's Jewish nucleus. In 1491, the Holy City had a Jewish population of 250 families of Sephardic, Oriental, Moroccan, and Ashkenazic descent. By 1495, the community numbered 130 Sephardic families alone, growing to 300 families by 1522.[2]

At the beginning of the sixteenth century, there were approximately 1000 Jewish families, or about 5,000 Jews in Palestine. The transitional period between Mameluke and Ottoman rule spiritually awakened new Messianic hopes which, together with an improvement in economic conditions, brought increasing streams of immigrants to the Holy Land.[3] From this time on, Jerusalem's Jewry was entering a brilliant period under the spiritual and intellectual leadership of such men as Obadiah Bertinoro, Yitzhak Šolal, Levi ben Habib, Moses Alošaka, and David ben Zimra.[4] With the continuous arrival of Spanish exiles, the spiritual and cultural hegemony of Jerusalem passed into the hands of the Sephardim.

Most of the new immigrants settled in Safed, situated in Northern Palestine overlooking the Sea of Galilee and very much like Jerusalem from the standpoint of physical geography. As an important commercial and industrial center, its population grew to 10,000 by the middle of the sixteenth century.[5] The city was a Sephardic stronghold, and from the standpoint of cultural and intellectual achievement, the years 1520-1580 mark the city's greatest period. To explain Safed's significance during this time, we quote David Tamar:

> Quite a number of reasons had influenced immigrants to prefer Safed to Jerusalem — material and economic reasons as well as spiritual and mystic ones. Its proximity to Meron, the burial place of Rabbi Simeon Bar Yohay, who was esteemed as the author of the Zohar, as well as the widespread expectation of the early appearance of the Messiah in the Galilee region, had much influence in favor of Safed. The latter reasons explain why there settled in this town a few chosen personalities — the great scholars, learned both in halaka [Jewish law] and Jewish mysticism; so that, within a span of a few decades it became a metropolis — a center for the study of the Torah

---

[1] Itzhak Ben-Zvi, *The Exiled and the Redeemed* (Philadelphia, 5721/1961), p. 28.
[2] Idelsohn, *Gesänge der orientalischen Sefardim*, p. 15.
[3] Herschberg, "... מראשית שלטון", p. 489.
[4] Idelsohn, *loc. cit.*
[5] Herschberg, *op. cit.*, p. 490.

and of Cabbalistic doctrines, of unrivalled importance since the termination of the Talmud...[1]

Safed's glorious age came to an end with the Druze uprisings during the late sixteenth century. Oddly enough, the victims did not seek immediate refuge to the south, but chose instead to proceed northward to Damascus where for a time they enjoyed a life comparable to that in Safed.

Cultural and economic decadence among the Sephardim in the Holy Land was already apparent in the early seventeenth century. The brief reign of Mohammed Ibn Faruk, Wali of the Sanjak of Jerusalem (1625-26), brought about horrible suffering for the Jewish population of the Holy City.[2] During the difficult times that followed, preoccupations with Messianism were increasing among the populace. Messianism had gained its momentum a century before when David Reubeni and Solomon Molko (formerly Diego Pires) aroused in European Sephardic communities new hopes for the coming of the Messiah and for the deliverance of the Holy Land from Turkish rule. Another important impetus behind this surge was the printing (in Turkey) and distribution of the Zohar among the Sephardim of the Balkans and Near East which reaffirmed their aspirations.[3] However, their greatest hope was seen in Shabbatai Zevi (b. Izmir 1626-67), who came to Jerusalem in 1662 and, after several years, was proclaimed the Messiah.[4] He was forced to leave the Holy City by the religious authorities as a result of his erratic and uncontrollable behavior. Still, Balkan Jewry never challenged his status until he converted to Islam under the duress of Turkish officials in Istanbul (1666). Shabbatai's death in the following year in a small Albanian town ended an episode which left the Jews in a state of confusion and spiritual dejection. As a result, they were subjected to derision particularly throughout the Ottoman Empire.[5]

In the last quarter of the century, when Jerusalem had entered into a period of relative calm, the Jews living in Northern Palestine became ensnared in local Arab rivalries. This situation occasioned further emigration to Jerusalem

---

[1] David Tamar, "צפת במאה הט״ז ['Safed in the 16th Century']," *Studies and Reports*, III (Jerusalem, 1960), 38. (In Hebrew.)

[2] Herschberg, *op. cit.*, p. 494.

[3] Benardete, *op. cit.*, p. 105. For two enlightening essays on the Zohar, see Gershom G. Scholem, *Major Trends in Jewish Mysticism* (London, 1955), pp. 156-243.

[4] Scholem, *ibid.*, p. 294. Shabbatai Zevi's dates were taken from Heinrich Graetz, *History of the Jews* (Philadelphia, 1956), VI, p. 538. Scholem, *op. cit.*, p. 289, gives it as 1625-1676, and Benardete, *op. cit.*, p. 119, n. 10, undoubtedly took the dates (1629-1679) from Moise Franco's *Essai sur l'histoire des israélites de l'empire Ottoman, depuis les origines jusqu'à nos jours* (Paris, 1897).

[5] Biographical sketches of Shabbatai Zevi can be found in Benardete, *ibid.*, pp. 107-110; Jacob R. Marcus, *op. cit.*, pp. 261-269; and with an interpretive and scholarly commentary by Scholem, *op. cit.*, pp. 287-324.

so that by the end of the century the Jewish population of that city numbered around 1,200.[1]

At the beginning of the eighteenth century, Jewish life in the Holy City was characterized by flourishing religious institutions built for the stream of pious Jews who came there to study the Torah. The Jewish population was supported mainly by contributions from abroad, although a number of more prominent families were receiving funds from businesses which they still maintained in their countries of origin.[2] Jewish communities in Palestine were always supported by the Jews of the Diaspora under a system called חלוקה ('distribution'). The contributions were collected by special Palestinian messengers who travelled throughout the Diaspora. The selection of messengers was handled with the utmost scrutiny, for not only was their task dependent upon a mastery of several languages, particularly Hebrew, but it was also necessary that the men should exemplify scrupulosity and be knowledgeable in religious and historical matters. Wherever they travelled they carried with them the necessary documents and were required to speak about conditions in the Holy Land.

Nonetheless, the distribution of collected funds became a constant source of discord between the Ashkenazim and Sephardim, the latter constituting the dominant Jewish population of Palestine. Not only were the practices of the Sephardim challenged, they were also accused of not sharing with any other groups. Because the Sephardim were the chief administrators of the funds, they suffered great financial losses in view of the heavy taxes imposed upon them by their immediate Ottoman rulers, under whom infidels were required to pay more than the followers of Islam.[3]

By 1741, there were 10,000 Jews in Jerusalem. Again there followed a long period of unrest (1741-70), during which many Jews left the city and the population dropped to half its size. It was not until the ascendency of 'Abd al-Hamid I as the Ottoman Sultan (1774) that Jerusalem's conditions were improved.[4]

M. J. Benardete characterized the pseudo-Messianic movement of Shabbatai

---

[1] Herschberg, *op. cit.*, p. 496.
[2] *Ibid.*, p. 495.
[3] Mordecai Kosover, "Ashkenazim and Sephardim in Palestine (A Study in Intercommunal Relations)," *Homenaje a Millás-Vallicrosa*, I (Barcelona, 1956), pp. 759-64. Moshé Burstein gives a capsule history of the ḥaluka system in *Self-Government of the Jews in Palestine since 1900* (Tel Aviv, 1934), pp. 24-26. See especially p. 25, n. 1, where he lists several valuable sources for deeper penetration into the subject.
[4] Herschberg, *op. cit.*, p. 491. However, C. H. Philips, *Handbook of Oriental History* (London, 1963), p. 44, cites 1773-1789 as the span of the rule of 'Abd al-Hamid I. Further information relating directly to eighteenth-century Jerusalem can be found in E. Šohet, "היהודים בירושלים במאה הי״ח" ['The Jews in Jerusalem during the 18th Century']," *Zion*, I (1935), 377-410. (In Hebrew.)

Zevi as the outstanding though most disturbing event of Sephardic history during the seventeenth century. In addition, he referred to the compilation and publication of the מעם לועז [*Me'am Lo'ez*] (1730) as the predominant redeeming feature of the eighteenth century.[1] This popular encyclopedia, written in Judeo-Spanish, was a compendium of Jewish lore taken from the Bible, Zohar, Talmud, and rabbinical literature to serve the needs of those lacking in Hebraïc tradition. The idea was first conceived by Rabbi Jacob ben Mahir Hulí as supplemental readings which would stimulate more interest in the prescribed weekly Biblical portions.[2] The מעם לועז became so popular that it literally renewed the ill-fated spiritual existence of Sephardic Jewry and was an important factor for the preservation of Judeo-Spanish (Ladino).

Of the Sephardic world community during these centuries, Benardete writes:

> The Sephardic world maintained some form of unity and cohesion for more than two centuries. This cohesion and unity was effectuated through immigration, commercial transactions, residence on the part of Hispano-Levantine Jews in Marranic communities; through the incorporation of Marrano Jews into the nuclei of the Near East, in Palestinian cities, in Aleppo, Damascus; and elsewhere; through the circulation of Hebrew books; through the engagement of Afro-Levantine Sephardic rabbis for the Western cities; through cooperative activities among the medieval and Renaissance Sephardim for the purpose of ransoming slaves, helping the destitute and the orphaned, and providing dowries for poor girls of Israel; and finally through the travelling shalliah ['messenger']. This analysis makes one fundamental idea stand out: namely, the unity of Sephardic Jewry in the matters of religion, philanthropy, mysticism, and messianism.[3]

Nineteenth-century Palestine up to the time of the first modern עליה [*Aliyah*] ['immigration'] was characterized by two periods. The former (1800-40) was marked by Ottoman corruption and the latter (1840-82) found the Jews entangled in the Eastern Question because of their numerical increase in the Holy Land where they were steadily achieving greater cultural and economic influence.[4]

The Jews were concentrated in the four Holy Cities: Jerusalem, Safed, Tiberias, and Hebron. In Jerusalem we find that outstanding Sephardic rabbis from Šlomo Moše Zuzin (1826-36) to Yehudah Navon (1840-41) received no governmental recognition. However, the Turkish authorities recognized Ḥaim Abraham Gagin (1842-48) as head rabbi.[5] It is important

---

[1] Benardete, *op. cit.*, pp. 100-101.
[2] *Ibid.*, pp. 114-116.
[3] *Ibid.*, p. 82.
[4] S[alo] W. Baron, "מתחילת המאה ה־19 עד ראשית ההתיישבות החדשה (1800-1882)" ['From the Beginning of the 19th Century to the Beginning of the New Settlement']," *Encyclopædia Hebraica*, VI (Jerusalem, 1957),. p. 504. (In Hebrew.)
[5] *Ibid.*, p. 507.

to note that the Turks officially acknowledged only the Sephardic community whose leader carried the Hebrew-Turkish title חכם בשי[1] [*Haḥam Baši*]. He was probably favored above other religious leaders because he knew the language and customs of the rulers of the country. The Sephardic interests were taken care of by the חכם בשי; however, he did not "necessarily wield greater religious authority than the other Rabbis ... [and his] authority was, on the whole, not very great in the Ashkenazic congregation."[2] Furthermore, during this time there was no central Jewish religious authority in the country.[3]

In 1823, the Ashkenazim established themselves as an autonomous community in Jerusalem. They came from northern and central Palestine where devastating earthquakes had destroyed their homes in Safed, Tiberias, and Nablus. As a result, Jerusalem became the largest and most important Ashkenazic settlement in the Holy Land.[4] The continuous rise in Ashkenazic population, particularly at the end of the century resulting from the pogroms in Eastern Europe, threatened the Sephardic position. This was but one more phase toward breaking away from the dominant Sephardic element, while animosities between the two groups became even greater.[5] With the influx of Europeans and Moroccans, the Sephardic population soon felt the impact of Westernization as well as a revitalization of economic well-being.

A close look at the following table containing Jerusalem's Ashkenazic and Sephardic-Oriental Jewish population from 1856 to 1939 will prove revealing:[6]

Years	Total No. Jews	Ashkenazim	Sephardim & Orientals
1856	5,700	1,700	4,000
1880	13,920	6,660	7,260
1890	25,300	13,600	11,700
1899	28,228	15,180	13,048
1913	50,000	25,000	25,000
1916	26,605	13,125	13,480
1939	80,850	42,576	38,274

[1] C. Ramos-Gil, "La lengua española en Israel," *Tesoro de los judíos sefardíes*, I (Jerusalem, 1959), xxxiii.
[2] Burstein, *op. cit.*, p. 244.
[3] *Ibid.*, p. 74.
[4] Kosover, *op. cit.*, p. 766, n. 39. Raphael Patai in *Israel between East and West: A Study in Human Relations* (Philadelphia, 1953), pp. 80-81, states that "until 1812 officially all the Jews of Jerusalem belonged to the Sephardi community ... The foundations of the Ashkenazi community in Jerusalem in 1812 were laid by the followers of the Gaon of Vilna who four years previously had settled in Safed and later moved to Jerusalem."
[5] Kosover, *op. cit.*, pp. 755-56.
[6] Patai, *op. cit.*, p. 80. Patai took the table from David Gurevich, *The Jews of Jerusalem* (Jerusalem, 1940), p. 22. See also Oscar Schmelz, "The Development of the Jewish Population of Jerusalem During the Last Century," *Jewish Journal of Sociology*, XI (June, 1969), 57-73.

Oriental Jews, comprising those communities from North Africa, the Near and Middle East, have always allied themselves with the Sephardim among whom they felt more at home. From the beginning of the nineteenth century, however, the non-Sephardi groups seceded one after another from the Sephardic community in order to establish their own autonomous structures.[1]

Around 1860, the Jews already constituted the major population of Jerusalem. The first suburb built outside the walls of the Old City consisted of dwellings for twenty families and was located on the south side of the City opposite Mount Zion. The suburb, undertaken by Sir Moses Montefiore (1784-1885), was called ימין משה ['Moses' right hand']. The Old City, surrounded by a wall built by Suliman the Magnificant in 1541, constituted an area of approximately one square mile[2] and the influx of newcomers made necessary the creation of more Jewish settlements outside the City's walls.

The old ישוב [*Yišhuv*] ['settlement'] was composed primarily of Sephardim and Oriental Jews, while the first *Aliyah* or period of immigration which began in 1882 brought exclusively Ashkenazic Jews from Russia and Romania.[3] The Sephardim had always occupied a distinctive place in the economy of Jewish life in Palestine by virtue of their Ottoman citizenship. While the old ישוב looked "upon itself as the religious «representatives» of the secular Jewish world outside, [the new ישוב, commencing with the first period of immigration, strove] to build up a self-sufficient Palestinian Jewish community."[4]

The second *Aliyah* took place between 1904 and 1914. Up to this time, more than 100,000 Jewish immigrants had entered the country. After a short while, more than half left because of intolerable political, economic and social conditions.[5] It was the four Holy Cities which attracted the early settlers; however, the immigrants of the *Aliyot* began settling in the coastal regions, particularly around Jaffa and Haifa.[6]

Subsequent *Aliyot* starting with the third (1919-23), the fourth (1924-31), and the fifth (1932-39) brought the immigrants into the rural settlements. From 1939 to 1948, immigration was at its lowest ebb, with the קיבוץ [*Kibbutz*] ('the collective settlement') coming into prominence.[7]

The Turks ruled Palestine up through the time of the First World War.

---

[1] Patai, *op. cit.*, p. 81. On pp. 82-83, Patai included a listing of the major disposition for Jerusalem's Oriental Jewish population together with the year they settled in the city.
[2] Trude Weiss-Rosmarin, *Jerusalem* (New York, 1950), p. 31.
[3] Patai, *op. cit.*, p. 58.
[4] Henrietta Szold, *Recent Jewish Progress in Palestine* (Philadelphia, 1915), p. 31. For information regarding Jerusalem at the turn of the century, Miss Szold's essay is extremely interesting.
[5] Neville Mandel, "Turks, Arabs and Jewish Immigration into Palestine, 1882-1914," *Middle Eastern Affairs*, No. 4 (London, 1965), p. 79.
[6] Burstein, *op. cit.*, p. 187.
[7] Patai, *op. cit.*, p. 71.

Under Turkish rule, Palestine was divided into two administrative units: the north formed a part of the *Wilayet* ('province') of Beirut and the south constituted the "independent" *Sanjak* ('district') of Jerusalem. The independent *Sanjaks* were under the jurisdiction of the Turkish authorities whose administrative center was Istanbul.[1]

With the British Mandate, which was conferred by the Council of the League of Nations (July, 1922) but formally began on 23rd September 1932, the Sephardim and Ashkenazim constituted officially recognized groups. Moreover, since the Mandate, a goodly number of Old City Sephardim moved to other districts in the New City, notably Zikron Moše, Meqor Barukh (Romema), Mahanei Yehuda, Nahlat Zion, Ohel Moše, Zikron Yosef, Sukkat Šalom, and Yemin Moše.[2] In 1929, when the Jewish quarter of Hebron was attacked, many of the old Sephardic *Sabras* came to settle in Jerusalem, particularly in the Old City and in Mahanei Yehuda.[3]

Up to 1948, there were about 42,000 Palestinian Jews who spoke Spanish.[4] In 1947, Jerusalem's population numbered 167,000 which included more than 100,000 Jews; the remainder could be divided almost equally between Moslems and Christians. Up to the establishment of the State, the resentment that seethed between the Jews and Arabs of the Old City brought about the curtailment of Jewish life there, and, as a consequence, the Sephardim resettled themselves in other established Sephardic sections of the City. Those who remained behind were the religious zealots, mostly Ashkenazim, who persisted in maintaining their religious institutions. Israel was declared a State on an 14th May 1948, and, when the Old City fell to the Arab Legion on 28th May, an era had ended for the Sephardim who had cherished their beloved home, within whose walls they maintained a cultural tradition, which had remained unbroken for generations. While the Old City Sephardim were scattered throughout Jerusalem, their whole cultural structure was undergoing a change as a result of the adjustments they had to make under the new government. Conditions were such that the splintered community had little or no opportunity to continue the mode of life which had been fostered for so long behind the Old City walls.

Now the aged among them live deep in the memories of the past. And, while many of them are to be found in the various old age homes throughout the city, others, who are more fortunate to be taken care of by their families, seem confused by the new Israeli generation whose attachment to the soil is far removed from the practices, traditions, and lore preserved from eras

---

[1] Burstein, *op. cit.*, p. 11.
[2] Patai, *op. cit.*, p. 95.
[3] Hanna Helena Thon, העדות בישראל [*'Ethnic Sub-groups in Israel'*] (Jerusalem, 1957), p. 34. (In Hebrew.)
[4] Ramos-Gil, *op. cit.*, xxxiii-xxxiv.

past. Still, wherever and whenever social gatherings occur, the elders continue to converse in Ladino, or *españolit*, as they refer to it, while the younger generation speaks Hebrew.[1] At a number of weddings, Bar Mitzvahs, and other social events modelled after that of the Old City, I noticed the presence of an ensemble of musicians (also Sephardim) who played popular music mainly in the Turkish style, while a vocalist among them sang Arabic songs. It was amazing to see how receptive the audience was by their participation in the Arabic vocal refrains. Conversation among the older guests was carried out in Ladino, while the younger generation spoke Hebrew; however, public announcements were made in both languages.

Up to the emergence of the State, the Sephardim were still deeply immersed in the traditional Eastern manner of life and thought. Their households and style of dress were hardly different from those of their Arab neighbors. They were conversant in Ladino, Arabic, and Hebrew, although the first constituted the language of the home. Like the Oriental Jews, they were characterized by large families at whose head sat the elder patriarch. Women were confined to the home and only the daughters of the more wealthy families were able to attend missionary schools or private institutions. The men received a traditional education which usually did not go beyond the grade school level. However, the number of schools which were established in Jerusalem around the turn of the century made possible further educational opportunities.[2] When Sephardic couples had no children, the husband was allowed to take a second wife. A strong feeling for family and strict adherence to religious observances was their greatest source of spiritual fulfillment.

The vast majority of Sephardim are merchants, craftsmen, and laborers, while very few practice law and medicine.[3] In such fields as music and art,

---

[1] A brief discussion of the salient features of *españolit* together with other interesting facts concerning Judeo-Spanish literature and publications can be found in Ramos-Gil, *op. cit.*, xxxvi-xxxix. A recent study on Ladino and its various dialects can be found in Simon Marcus, השפה הספרדית-יהודית ['*The Judeo-Spanish Language*'] (Jerusalem, 1965) (In Hebrew). Marcus includes an extensive and invaluable bibliography on the subject.

The Sephardic districts of Jerusalem have been enriched mainly by Balkan immigrants who have settled in Israel since 1948. The influx of Sephardim who came from Bulgaria, Yugoslavia, Greece, Turkey, Romania, and Morocco have brought to Israel their particular dialects of the ancient Castilian tongue.

[2] Szold, *op. cit.*, pp. 105-108, describes the various educational institutions in Jerusalem at the turn of the century. The Alliance Israélite Universelle established and subsidized a well-equipped trade school in Jerusalem in 1882.

With the Alliance Israélite Universelle, the standards of education were raised, but it "also promoted a shallow levantinism and a weakening of national consciousness which made for assimilation and feelings of inferiority." Cf. Ben Zvi, *op. cit.*, p. 21. In fact, the intensification of national education became a decisive factor in bringing about the decline of Yiddish, Ladino, and other oriental dialects in Israel.

[3] Patai, *op. cit.*, p. 90, includes a table of the occupational structure of Jewish Ethnic groups in Jerusalem in 1939, the Sephardim included, which he adapted from David

their participation is practically nil, although several members have made significant contributions in literature and journalism. The pattern of life among the Sephardim has been a hindrance to their active participation in the political affairs of the new State, and only a small number have attained high political office. Even the present leadership of the Council of the Sephardic Community in Jerusalem, was organized in 1949 along patriarchal lines, that is, around the few wealthy families.[1]

However, since the establishment of the State of Israel, there has been a renaissance in the study of Sephardic culture. Such important organizations as the World Sephardi Federation,[2] the Ben-Zvi Institute for Research on Jewish Communities in the Middle East,[3] and the Instituto de Estudios Sefardíes[4] have been instrumental in subsidizing scholarly publications in all areas of Sephardic history and culture. There also exists a number of scholarly journals which carry valuable articles concerning all aspects of Sephardic life.[5] Only recently there has appeared a definitive study of the Sephardic

---

Gurevich, *op. cit.*, [n.p.]. Another important and interesting source is D. Weinryb, "The Occupational Structure of the Second Generation of Jewish Palestine," *Jewish Social Studies*, II (1940), 279-94, 435-80.

[1] For an interesting survey of the voluntary organizations which the Sephardim themselves have organized, see Walter P. Zenner, "Sephardic Communal Organizations in Israel," *The Middle East Journal* (Spring, 1967), 173-186.

[2] The World Sephardi Federation has established its headquarters in London. Information regarding this organization can be found in *Kol-Sepharad*, I, No. 6-7 (London, 1965), pp. 16-20.

[3] Located on the campus of the Hebrew University, Jerusalem, the Ben Zvi Institute was founded in 1956. Its aims are most clearly discussed in the article by its founder, the late President of Israel, Itzhak Ben-Zvi, "Research on the Jewish Oriental Communities and the Merging of the Dispersions," *Studies and Reports*, III (1960), 1-3. Meir Benayahu, the Institute's secretary and editor of *Studies and Reports*, published a survey of the Institute's "Tasks and Activities: 1957-1960," *ibid.*, 4-11.

[4] See Richard D. Barnett and Federico Pérez Castro, co-directors, "Institute of Sephardic Studies, Madrid," *Kol-Sepharad*, II, Nos. 3-4 (London, 1966), 18-19. The First International Symposium of the Institute of Sephardic Studies held in Madrid (June 1964) is discussed by Iacob M. Hassán in "El Simposio de Estudios Sefardíes," *Sefarad*, XXIV (1964), 327-355.

[5] Of the numerous journals dealing with varied aspects of Sephardic culture, particular attention is called to the following which are rich in subject matter concerning the Sephardim of the Eastern Mediterranean and Israel:

a. במערכה [Ba' Ma'arakah]. A monthly published by the Council of the Sephardic Community in Jerusalem. (Jerusalem, July, 1961-   ). In Hebrew.

b. עדות [Edoth]. A quarterly for folklore and ethnology. (Jerusalem, Oct., 1945-1948.) Hebrew with English summaries.

c. *Le Judaïsme séphardi*. Published by the World Sephardi Federation. (London, July 1932-   and Nouvelle Série, May, 1951-   .) Articles in English, French, and Spanish.

community of Jerusalem which is particularly rich in materials covering the last one-hundred years.[1]

The practices and customs of the Sephardim of the Old City were most closely patterned after those of Salonika.[2] In fact, it was mainly through their contacts with Balkan Sephardim that their cultural heritage was maintained. This

d. קרית ספר [Kiryat sefer]. Quarterly bibliographical review of the Jewish National and University Library. (Jerusalem, 1924-   .) In Hebrew.
e. *Kol-Sepharad*. Published by the World Sephardi Federation. (London, September 1958-   .) English, French, and Spanish.
f. לוח ארץ־ישראל [Luaḥ Ereẓ Yisrael]. Edited by Abraham Moses Luncz. (Jerusalem, 1895-1916). In Hebrew.
g. מזרח ומערב. Mizraḥ u-Ma'arav. Edited by Abraham Elmaleh. (Jaffa-Tel Aviv, 1919-1932). In Hebrew.
h. מחברת [Maḥbereth]. Also cited under the French title *Les Cahiers de l'Alliance Israélite Universelle*. Edited by Abraham Elmaleh. (Jerusalem, 1951-   .) Hebrew and French.
i. *Sefarad*. Originally cited as the "Revista de la Escuela Estudios Hebraicos," 1941-1944 and later as the "Revista del Instituto Arias Montano de Estudios Hebraicos y Oriente Próximo." (Madrid, 1945-   .) Spanish.
j. ספונות [Sefunot]. Annual for research on the Jewish Communities in the East. Published by the Ben Zvi Institute. (Jerusalem, 1956-   ). In Hebrew with English Summaries.
k. שבט ועם [Ševet v' Am]. A compilation of articles by well known Sephardim who participated in the World Sephardi Congress in Jerusalem (1960). (5 vols. in Hebrew.)
l. מחקרים ופעולות [Meḥakrim u-pa'alot] ['*Studies and Reports*']. Information on the projects being sponsored by the Ben Zvi Institute. (Jerusalem, 1959-   .) In Hebrew, French, and English.
m. *Tesoro de los judios sefardies* [אוצר יהודי ספרד] [*Oẓar Yehudey Sefarad*]. Edited by Isaac R. Molho. (Jerusalem, 1959-   .) In Hebrew, French, Spanish, and English.
n. ידע־עם [*Yeda 'Am*]. Journal of the Israeli Folklore Society. (Tel Aviv, June 1950-   .) In Hebrew.
o. ציון [*Zion*]. A quarterlyf or research in Jewish History. Published by the Jewish Historical Society of Israel formerly Historical-Ethnographical Society of Palestine. (Jerusalem, 1935-   .) Mention must be made of the recent establishment of the American Society of Sephardic Studies (1968). Dr. Isaac Jack Lévy, Dept. of Foreign Languages and Literatures, University of South Carolina, Columbia, South Carolina is the Society's Executive Secretary. The Society has published its first annual, Series I (1968-1969) under the auspices of the Sephardic Studies Program, Yeshiva University, New York. Yeshiva University has also initiated a Bulletin entitled, *The American Sephardi* (December, 1966-   ) which is published semi-annually for American Sephardic Congregations.

[1] Jacob Yehoshua, ילדות בירושלים הישנה ['*Childhood in Old Jerusalem: Description of Sephardic Life of the Past Century*']. Jerusalem: Ruben Mass, 1965-66. 2 vols. (In Hebrew.) Under the name Yeshaia, Mr. Yehoshua participated in the Symposium on Sephardic Studies in Madrid (1964), see Iacob M. Hassán in *op. cit.*, p. 11.

[2] Much of the information concerning the Sephardim of the Old City was confirmed by Isaac R. Molho, with whom I met on various occasions during my stay in Israel. Cf. also Michael Molho's *Usos y costumbres de los sefardies de Salónica* (Madrid-Barcelona, 1950) and the introduction to Moshe Attias' *Romancero sefaradi* (Jerusalem, 1961).

legacy consists of a vast body of Judeo-Spanish literature, together with proverbs, folktales, and an unbroken chain of oral tradition rendered in poetry and song from their rich Spanish inheritance.[1] As all their social and religious events called for music, their répertoire of songs which cover the life span from birth to death, the honored Sabbath, and the numerous holidays of the Jewish calendar, is most extensive. Songs, especially among the women, have formed an integral part of their confined household life. It is the Sephardic woman whom we hold in high esteem and admiration for her preservation of the ancient folksongs which have been sung by the exiles for more than five centuries. Included in their répertoire are the cherished ballads from the Spanish *Romancero*. However, through the centuries, the recollection of ballads has steadily dwindled and even in Jerusalem, only a few of them have remained as a vestige of their former popularity.

A study of the remnants of the Jerusalem ballad répertoire is the subject of this investigation. The brief historical survey which I have presented cannot hope to explore all the exciting by-roads over which the Sephardic exiles have travelled during the past centuries.[2] How a segment of these people came to settle in Jerusalem, and what cultural affinities they have maintained with their Balkan predecessors in such notable communities as Salonika, Istanbul, and Rhodes has, I believe, been firmly established here. The reasons for the preservation of the Spanish ballad tradition among the

---

[1] Concerning Judeo-Spanish literature, see: Henry V. Besso, "Judeo-Spanish Literature," *Le Judaïsme séphardi*, No. 23 (December 1961), 1016-1022; *Ladino Books in the Library of Congress*. A Bibliography compiled by Henry V. Besso (Washington, D.C., 1963) (Hispanic Foundation Bibliographical Series No. 7); Michael Molho, *Literatura sefardita de oriente* (Madrid-Barcelona, 1960); and A. Yaari, *Catálogo de libros en ladino* (Jerusalem, 1934).

Information about Judeo-Spanish proverbs can be found in Henry V. Besso's "Introduction to a Bibliography of Sephardic Proverbs, "*Le Judaïsme séphardi*, No. 18 (April 1959), 882-827.

Poetry is discussed by Nehamia Allony in "לחקר שירת ספרד וכינוסה ['An Investigation of Sephardic Poetry and its Gathering']," *Tesoro de los judíos sefardíes*, II (1959), 118-127. (In Hebrew.)

The subject of Sephardic folklore is treated in: Solomon Gaon, "Folklore of the Sephardim in the Balkans. Études sépharadiques," *Le Judaïsme séphardi*, No. 2 (1953), 64-66, and No. 3 (1954), 104-109; Michael Molho, "Consideraciones sobre folklore sefardí," *Davar*, No. 76 (Buenos Aires, May-June, 1958), 61-76; Raphael Patai, "Sephardi Folklore," *The World of the Sephardim* (New York, 1960), pp. 22-36; Baruch Uziel, "הפולקלור של היהודים "הספרדים" ['Folkore of the Sephardic Jews']," *Rešumot* (Tel Aviv, 1930), 359-397, and "למען הפולקלור של היהודים הספרדים" ['For the Sake of Sephardic Folklore']," *Ševet v'Am*, I (1959), 102-105.

[2] As a helpful guide for illustrating the Sephardic Diaspora, I have provided the reader with a map (p. 22) of the Mediterranean region upon which I have indicated those important Western and Eastern communities to which the Sephardic exiles emigrated. (See page 4 note 3 *supra*).

Sephardim can only be understood in terms of their history. While this subject constitutes only a small segment of Sephardic culture, it has managed to attract a goodly number of faithful investigators. Before studying the musical aspects of the Jerusalem répertoire, I consider it useful to survey all the studies dealing specifically with the music of the Judeo-Spanish *Romancero*.

CHAPTER II

A MUSICAL SURVEY OF THE JUDEO-SPANISH *ROMANCERO*

With the discovery of the New World and the expulsion of the Jews from Spain in the last decade of the fifteenth century, Spanish culture was diffused to two distant corners of the World: to that vast area which was to become Hispanic America and to the Hispano-Judaic emigrant communities of North Africa and the Eastern Mediterranean. Music and poetry as an integral part of this Hispanic heritage had already developed into national genres, notably the *villancico*[1] and *romance*[2] which enjoyed wide popularity. We have only to contemplate the rich poetic creativity of the *cancionero* period (late fourteenth to early sixteenth century)[3] and the collections of the sixteenth-century *vihuelistas* to ascertain how vital these musical-poetical forms were to the Spanish genius.[4]

---

[1] For the best sources concerning the origins and development of the *villancico*, the following are recommended: Isabel Pope, "The Musical Development and Form of the Spanish *Villancico*," *Papers of the American Musicological Society for 1940* (AMS, Inc., 1946), 11-22, and "The Musical and Metrical Form of the Villancico," *Annales Musicologiques*, II (1954), 189-214; Pierre Le Gentil, *Le Virelai et le villancico: Le Problème des origines arabes* (Paris, 1954), 279pp; and Antonio Sánchez Romeralo, *El Villancico*, (Madrid, 1969), 623 pp.

[2] Fundamental treatment of the *romance* can be found in Ramón Menéndez Pidal, *Romancero Hispánico (hispano-portugués, americano y sefardí)* (Madrid, 1953), 2 vols. For a brief and well written account in English, see Colin Smith, *Spanish Ballads* (New York, 1964), 217 pp. For a concise musical history of the *romance*, see Miguel Querol's contribution to *Die Musik in Geschichte und Gegenwart*, XI (1963), col. 845-848. See also Higinio Anglés, "Das spanische Volkslied," *Archiv für Musikforschungen*, III, No. 3 (Leipzig, 1938), particularly pp. 346-348.

[3] See Charles V. Aubrun, "Inventaire des sources pour l'étude de la poésie castillane au XVe siècle, "*Estudios dedicados a Ramón Menéndez Pidal*, IV (Madrid, 1953), pp. 297-330 and Francisca Vendrell de Millás, "Los cancioneros del siglo XV," *Historia general de las literaturas hispánicas*, II (1951), pp. 55-70.

[4] See Eduardo Martínez Torner, "Los vihuelistas del siglo XVI," *Temas folklóricas: Música y poesía* (Madrid, 1935), pp. 21-31; Miguel Querol Gavaldá, "Importance histori-

The Spanish *Romancero*, existing over the length and breadth of the Hispanic world wherever Spanish, Portuguese, or Catalan are spoken, is a uniquely important manifestation of the essential unity of Hispanic culture. Since the early nineteenth century, the *Romancero* has been the subject of serious scholarly investigation by Hispanists.[1]

However, one very important aspect of Spanish balladry was much neglected until the turn of the present century, when Spanish scholars first took notice of the folkloristic heritage of the Sephardic Jews of North Africa and the Eastern Mediterranean. Here indeed a substantial portion of the *Romancero* was — and is — still preserved in living oral tradition in a spoken idiom dating back to fifteenth-century Spain, if not earlier.[2]

In 1906-1907, Ramón Menéndez Pidal (1869-1968) published his *Catálogo del romancero judío-español*.[3] This imposing catalog includes selections of over 140 *romances* extant in various Sephardic centers. According to Menéndez Pidal, the catalog was twofold in purpose:

> ... primero, dar una idea de la riqueza y carácter del romancero judío-español: segundo, promover y facilitar la búsqueda y publicación de nuevas variantes que vengan a completar el conocimiento de la tradición de los judíos españoles ...[4]

The first objective established the catalog as a potential "Child Canon" for Sephardic balladry, although it will be seen that many subsequent collectors

---

que et nationale du romance," *Musique et Poésie au XVIe siècle* (Paris, 1954), pp. 299-324; and Daniel Devoto, "Poésie et musique dans l'œuvre des vihuelistes (notes méthodologiques)," *Annales Musicologiques*, IV (1956), 85-111.

[1] Important as a bibliographical source is M. García Blanco's "El Romancero," in *Historia general de las literaturas hispánicas*, II (1951), pp. 1-51. Studies concerning the *Romancero* in Hispanic America can readily be found under their respective country headings in Merle E. Simmons, *A Bibliography of the Romance and Related Forms in Spanish America* (Bloomington, 1963), 396 pp.

[2] In "Notes on Judeo-Spanish," *Proceedings of the Leeds Philosophical Society*, VII (1955), p. 194, Cynthia Crews wrote: "Jews left Spain speaking fifteenth-century Spanish, although even then, no doubt, they had certain peculiarities of speech that were specifically Jewish. They continued with this language which sounds somewhat similar to modern Portuguese, owing to the preservation of the same consonant sounds, which although existing in Old Spanish are now lost and survive only in Portuguese."

A recent contribution to the study of the various Judeo-Spanish dialects is Simon Marcus, השפה הספרדית־יהודית [*'The Judeo-Spanish Language'*] (Jerusalem, 1965), 181 pp.

[3] First published in the journal, *Cultura Española*, IV (1906), 1045-1077; V (1907), 161-199. Subsequently reprinted in *El romancero: teorías e investigaciones*, (Madrid, 1928), pp. 101-183, and in *Los romances de América y otros estudios* (Buenos Aires-México, 1948), pp. 121-188. Henceforth Sephardic ballads will usually be referred to by the title used in the *Catálogo*. I have, however, taken certain liberties in altering some of the titles for the sake of clarity. In the case of ballads which do not appear in the *Catálogo*, a thematically descriptive Spanish title has been devised.

[4] *Catálogo*, p. 121.

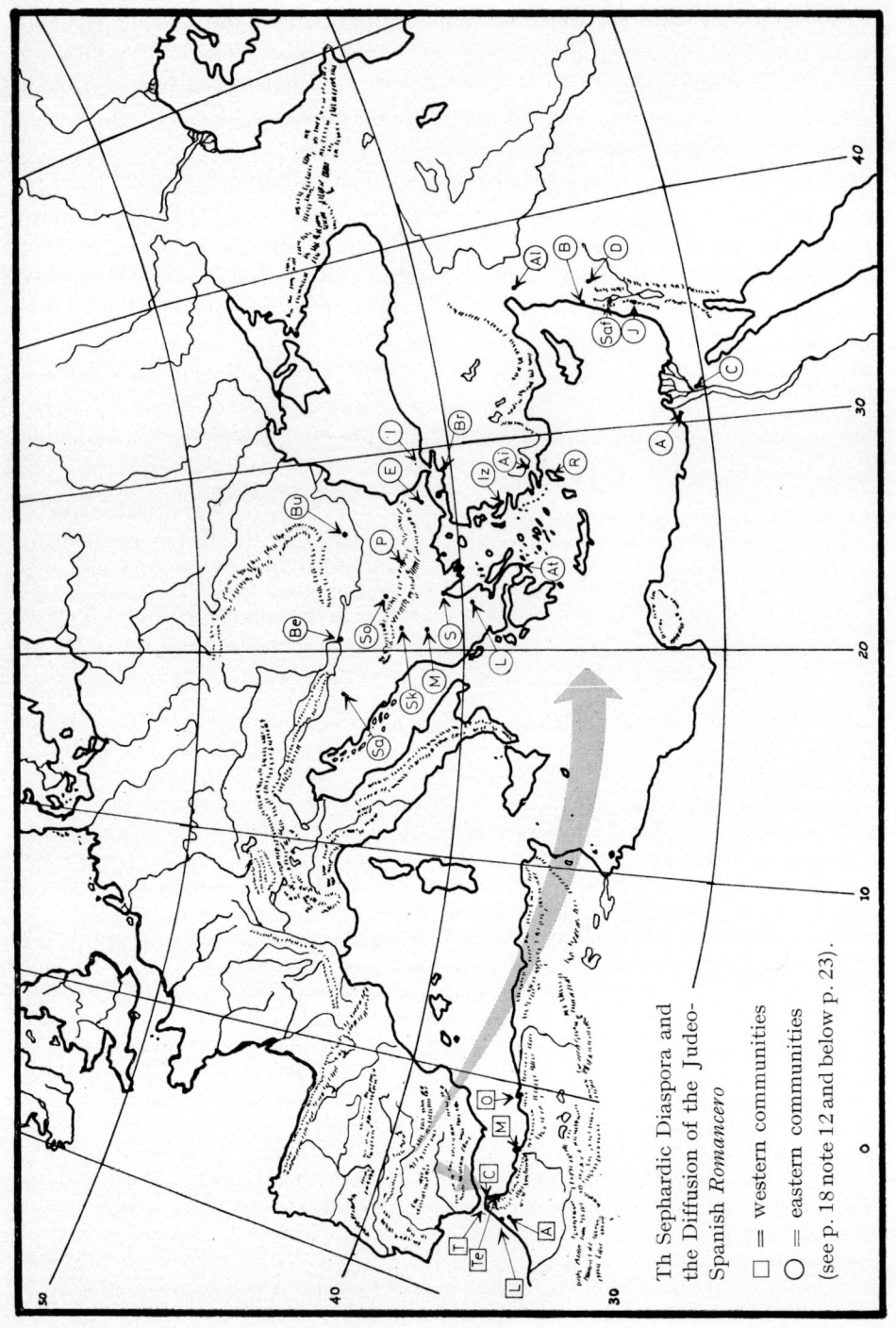

The Sephardic Diaspora and the Diffusion of the Judeo-Spanish *Romancero*

☐ = western communities
◯ = eastern communities
(see p. 18 note 12 and below p. 23).

did not choose to follow its arrangement.[1] The second objective was not proposed in vain. The *Catálogo* stimulated substantial interest among students of the *Romancero* to investigate its Sephardic branch in the light of poetry,

[1] Historically speaking, F. J. Wolf and C. Hofmann's *Primavera y flor de romances* (Berlin, 1856) was the first edited collection of ballads to serve as a basis for modern editions of the Spanish *Romancero*. Menéndez y Pelayo reprinted and enlarged this work in Vols. VIII and IX of his *Antología de poetas líricos castellanos* (Madrid, 1899). Durán's massive collection, *Romancero general* (Madrid, 1828-1832) includes both erudite and traditional poems in *romance* verse.

On the other hand, Menéndez Pidal fashioned his *Catálogo* from almost all the known Sephardic versions published up to 1906 in scholarly journals. He also included a goodly number of ballads from private, unedited collections, particularly that of José Benoliel (1857-1928) from Tangier. Subsequent contributions to the Sephardic branch of the *Romancero* have uncovered numerous ballads not included in the *Catálogo*. Moshe Attias' רומנסירו ספרדי (Jerusalem, 1956), later reïssued with the addition of a Spanish translation of the Introduction (Jerusalem, 1961), threw new light on the ballads of the Balkan and Near Eastern tradition and did much to bring up to date the bibliography of successive Sephardic collections. Attias did not organize his texts according to Menéndez Pidal's traditional classification, but, taking his cue from Bénichou in enlisting the aid of a synoptic chart, he cross-referenced his ballads with hitherto unknown Eastern Sephardic collections as well as with the *Catálogo*, and important Moroccan Peninsular collections. In a review of this work, S. G. Armistead and J. H. Silverman ("A New Sephardic *Romancero* from Salonika," *Romance Philology*, XVI [1962]), 59-82) discuss not only the value of Attias' contribution, but make important corrections to his study and add further bibliographical cross-references.

It is important to note that S. G. Armistead and J. H. Silverman's *Judeo-Spanish Traditional Ballads from the Eastern Mediterranean Area* (in progress) and *Judeo-Spanish Traditional Ballads from Morocco* (in progress) will supersede the *Catálogo* by accomodating all the new materials gathered to date and will add an elaborate cross-cultural index of Sephardic themes, relating them to the ballads of the major European ballad traditions. A more extensive bibliography of analogs in the Peninsular tradition will also be included. I plan to collaborate in this endeavor by contributing a musicological study and musical transcription of the ballads included in these two collections. The materials to be edited were collected collaboratively in the United States, Israel, and Morocco between 1957 and 1969.

The letter designations for the various communities are as follows:

A	Alcazarquivir	C	Ceuta	O	Orán
A	Alexandria	D	Damascus	P	Plovdiv
Ai	Aiden	E	Edirne	R	Rhodes
Al	Aleppo	I	Istanbul	S	Salonika
At	Athens	Iz	Izmir	Sa	Sarajevo
B	Beirut	J	Jerusalem	Saf	Safed
Be	Belgrade	L	Larache	Sk	Skopje
Br	Bursa	La	Larissa	So	Sofia
Bu	Bucharest	M	Melilla	T	Tangier
C	Cairo	M	Monastir	Te	Tetuán

history, philology, and folklore. Spanish investigators placed much emphasis upon post-exile Judeo-Spanish culture in its relation to the Peninsula. Yet, although the *Catálogo* makes several important illusions to music,[1] its publication did not stimulate further investigations of the musical aspects of Sephardic balladry.

Several interesting publications pertaining to the music of the Judeo-Spanish *Romancero* had, however, appeared before the publication of the *Catálogo*. In 1857, *The Ancient Melodies of the Liturgy of the Spanish and Portuguese Jews*,[2] prepared by Rev. D[avid] A[aron] de Sola (1796-1860), Cantor of London's Bevis Marks Synagogue from 1815 to 1816,[3] was published

---

[1] Menéndez Pidal writes (pp. 136-138): "Entre los judíos, el romancero es más estimado y conocido aún de las clases educadas, bastando preguntar por él para que se le encuentre, aunque sufre también la concurrencia de las canciones de moda ... En Adrianopolis ... las letanías rimadas llamadas «juncos» que se modelan sobre cantos profanos, algunos de ellos romances españoles ... En Salónica parece que los romances son cantados todavía con frecuencia ... son romances cantados por nuestras madres cuando acunan a los niños y cuando velan a las paridas de noche, ...[y] hay romances «para novias» ... que «los cantan a las novias, con candelas y luces encendidas en las manos, cuando las encierran con los novios en la cámara de desposada la primera noche de boda». Los bailes populares, imitados de los turcos, y especialmente de los europeos, no son ya ocasión de canto de romances, y, en general, la decadencia del género es perceptible; ..." Leo Wiener collected his *romances* in Sofia from "cantores de profesión en las bodas." "Los romances de origen bíblico son tan populares como los otros, y por una curiosa superstición, cuando se principian a cantar es obligatorio acabarles; las judías antiguas no bromean con estas cosas, y tiene gracia el tono y aire solemnes que asumen cuando cantan estos romances."

[2] London: [Wertheimer and Co.], 1857, iv. 23 pp. plus sixty-two additional pages containing seventy-one melodies, the last melody being composed by the Rev. de Sola. A photographic reproduction of the *Ancient Melodies* ... was brought out by the Committee of Management of the famous synagogue [Bevis Marks] together with additional melodies harmonized for four voices by the late E. R. Jessurun, Choirmaster of Bevis Marks. See *Sephardi Melodies: being The Traditional Liturgical Chants of the Spanish and Portuguese Jews' Congregation, London*. London: Oxford University Press, 5691/1931.

E. R. Jessurun also collected and prepared the musical examples for the *Book of Prayer of the Spanish and Portuguese Jews' Congregation, London* (London: Oxford University Press, 5718/1958), pp. 246-359. However, in this edition Jacob Hadida revised and supplemented the musical examples for the daily and occasional services.

[3] The Bevis Marks Synagogue of the Spanish and Portuguese Jews in London still remains the center for the Sephardim in England. Its present structure dates back to 1700. Its history can be found in Moses Gaster, *History of the Ancient Synagogue of Spanish and Portuguese Jews, The Cathedral Synagogue of the Jews in England, situate in Bevis Marks. A Memorial Volume to Celebrate the 200th Anniversary of its Inauguration, 1701-1901.* (London, 5661/1901); Paul Goodman, *Bevis Marks in History: A Survey of the External Influences of the Congregation Sahar Asamaim Bevis Marks, London* (London, 5694/1934); and, Cecil Roth, "The Bevis Marks Synagogue," *Le Judaïsme Séphardi*, No. 9 (Dec., 1955), 392-94. See also Abraham de Sola, *Biography of David Aaron de Sola, Late Senior Minister of the Portuguese Jewish Community in London* (Philadelphia, 1864).

in an effort to preserve "the poetical parts [hymns] of the Sephardic liturgy... combined with their melodies... from future decay and oblivion..."[1] These melodies, which Rev. de Sola heard in Amsterdam and London, were sung by him to Mr. Emanuel [Abraham] Aguilar (1824-1904), pianist and composer, who harmonized them so that they could be sung "in parts," and conveniently employed keyboard notation to facilitate further their performance.[2] A most promising attempt at a preface for these melodies was presented by the Rev. de Sola under the title "An Historical Essay on the Poets, Poetry and Melodies of the Sephardic Liturgy."[3] Though informative and succinct, this preface nevertheless attests to the author's lack of knowledge concerning the *Romancero*. In a portion of this essay, de Sola reconstructs for us the manner in which the hymns of the celebrated Hebrew poets — Šlomo Ibn Gabirol (1021?-1055?), Judah Halevy (1075?-1140?), and others — were adapted to popular secular tunes and also commented upon rabbinical opposition to this practice.[4] In an elaborate note, he explains the *incipits* in Israel Najara's (1555-1628) זמירות ישראל [*Zemirot Yisrael*] (Venice, 1599-1600), indicating those poems which were to be sung to particular *romance* melodies as well as demonstrating how liturgical poems were patterned after secular models with regard to structure and sounds.[5]

---

[1] De Sola, *The Ancient Melodies of the Liturgy of the Spanish and Portuguese Jews*, p. 11.

[2] Of the seventy-one melodies, two are for 5 voices, forty for 4 voices, six for 3 voices, one for a duet, nineteen for solo voice and keyboard accompaniment, three for solo voice and chorus, and one for solo voice unaccompanied. All the Hebrew texts are printed in transliteration. Tempo indications are given in Italian together with metronome markings.

[3] De Sola, *ibid.*, pp. 1-16. A photocopy of pp. 1-16, together with the title page of *The Ancient Melodies...* appears in a booklet which accompanies the Folkways Records Album No. FR 8961, *Music of the Spanish and Portuguese Synagogue*. John Levy, who recorded the music for this album at the Bevis Marks Synagogue, stated as his reason for reproducing the essay: "the book is out of print and quite unobtainable... it would be of interest to reproduce some of its pages for the sake of the valuable information given therein." Unfortunately, in his attempt to make this essay available, Levy did not reproduce the valuable footnotes inserted on the lower portion of the pages comprising the essay. Furthermore, he failed to include the lower half of page 16 and page 17 which make up the remainder of the essay.

For a popular rendition of this essay, see Rev. Francis L[yon] Cohen (1862-1934) "Folksong Survivals in Jewish Worship," *Journal of the Folk-Song Society*, I, No. 2 (London, 1900), 32-38, 52-59. This article, originally read as a paper before the Folk-Song Society on Nov. 23, 1899, contains much of the material, obviously taken from de Sola, together with several of the musical examples with some alterations. However, the essay is remarkably informative in its presentation and takes care to correct some of de Sola's errors. The Rev. Cohen was considered an authority on cantillation and synagogal music.

[4] De Sola, *op. cit.*, pp. 13-16.

[5] De Sola, *ibid.*, p. 13, n. 12. The dates given for Najara were taken from Alfred Šendrey's *Bibliography of Jewish Music* (New York, 1951), p. 399. Idelsohn, *Jewish Music*, p. 362,

Certainly one would have expected this learned Sephardi to correct the spelling of *Fassi abassi Silvana* to read correctly *Paseábase Silvana* (MP 98). Particularly puzzling is the translation of the Hebrew רומנסי [*romance*] by the word *romaic*.[1] Furthermore, the Rev. de Sola was not able to differentiate between the titles of popular Spanish songs (*canciones*) and *romances*, employing the former term as a generic form for all the Spanish titles.[2] Such errors notwithstanding, the essay is important in that it demonstrates how strong an influence the melodies of the *Romancero* had had upon the structure of the Hebrew poems which were composed and adapted to liturgical purposes during the sixteenth century by poets of the exile generation. Concerning the the melodies of his collection, Rev. de Sola writes:

> The age and time of composition of each melody varies considerably, and cannot always be accurately ascertained. To guide us in this respect, we must in the first place ascertain by whom the hymns, to which the melodies are attached, were written, and the time the various authors of them flourished, which has been stated above in every instance in which it could be ascertained; because the greater part of these hymns and melodies were adopted either in the life time, or soon after the death of the poets who composed the hymns. The fact of the melodies [which at the time could not be written down, but were orally acquired and transmitted], being the same in every Sephardic congregation, however, widely separated and without communication with each other, affords ample proof of their antiquity, genuineness, and general adoption, and no doubt they have reached us nearly in their original form.[3]

gives Najara's dates as: Safed, 1550 Gaza, 1620. Hanoch Avenary, in his article "Jüdische Musik," published in *Die Musik in Geschichte und Gegenwart*, VII (1958), col. 250, agrees with Šendrey, but later in "Études sur le cancionero judéo-espagnol (XVIe et XVIIe siècles)," *Sefarad*, XX (1960), p. 3, gives Najara's birth year as 1545. Nonetheless, it is startling to note that de Sola, *op. cit.*, p. 7, alludes to Najara as having lived in the fourteenth century.

[1] De Sola, *ibid.*, p. 13, n. 12.

[2] Scholarly and popular interest in the *romance* as a generic form waned during the seventeenth and eighteenth centuries. As a result of the enthusiasm of German and Austrian Romanticists (Jakob Grimm, F. J. Wolf, C. Hofmann, et. al.) in the early and mid-nineteenth century, the many latent national genres were revived, bringing about, among other things, the rediscovery of the *Romancero*. De Sola, having no knowledge of these literary events, was ignorant of the corpus of balladry making up the *Romancero*.

[3] De Sola, *op. cit.*, p. 15. On page 16, we find de Sola's subdivisions of the melodies contained in his work. These subdivisions consist of: the first, "whose origin is supposed to be prior to the settlement of the Jews in Spain"; the second, those "composed in Spain, and subsequently introduced by the Israelites into the Iberian Peninsula"; and the third, though not given as such, to accomodate the melodies which were not included in the first and second groups but were to be considered as belonging to a later period.

Idelsohn, on the other hand, was of the opinion that the tunes in de Sola's work were "mostly adopted tunes of Dutch origin from the 17th and 18th centuries, only less than half of them being traceable back to Spain." See *Jewish Music in Its Historical Development* (New York, 1929), pp. 338-339.

Abraham Danon (1857-1925), like de Sola, studied the *incipits* of Najara's זמירות ישראל. But, Danon, in 1895, went a step further by identifying eighteen *romances* among the Spanish *incipits*, thus affirming the strong influence of the *Romancero* upon Sephardic poets after the expulsion.[1] Furthermore, Danon explained that it was still common practice among the Jews of "le temple du Portugal" (the most important synagogue in Adrianopolis — now Edirne —) to intone rhymed litanies during the Sabbath morning service "à titre d'exercice musical, d'après les modulations arabes appelées מקאמאת «séances»."[2] These collections of rhymed litanies or *joncs* (in Spanish *juncos*), as they were called, were in reality nothing more than a selection of liturgical poems incorporated into the Sabbath liturgy. Such was the unedited collection of poems composed by Israel Najara entitled שארית ישראל [*Še'erit Yisrael*], also modelled upon secular melodies.[3] According to Danon, this *junco* was contained in a MS of octavo size, consisting of 148 leaves in cursive Judeo-Spanish characters, transcribed by several unnamed copyists without any indication of date.[4] The collection included no less than forty ballad *incipits*.

Moshe Attias (1898-   ), the Israeli scholar, commented upon Danon's discovery of the use of ballad tunes as the musical vehicle for liturgical poetry:

> Una explicación más aceptable es que la infecundidad en la creación de nuevas melodías obligó a los poetas a componer sus poesías según las melodías cantadas por el pueblo. Danón mismo relata que la melodía de varias de las poesías fue copiada de canciones turcas y griegas. Por otra parte, los feligreses en las sinagogas de las comunidades

---

[1] Abraham Danon, "Recueil de romances judéo-espagnoles chantées en Turquie," *Revue des Études Juives*, XXXII (1896), 102-123, 263-275; XXXIII (1896), 122-139, 255-268.
[2] *Ibid.*, p. 104. In note 4, Danon remarks that *jonc* " . . . est le mot tchonq, qui en persan signifie «harpe», en turc, d'après le Lehdjéi-Osmani, «harmonie appelée soupir». Dans un Diwan turc ms. j'ai trouvé ce mot répété à fin de chaque distique de certaines poésies." More probably the Judeo-Spanish term derives from Turkish *cönk* 'anthology; miscellany'.
[3] The date of the MS, שארית ישראל, has been difficult to establish. See Danon, *ibid.*, p. 104, and W. Bacher, "Les Poésies inédites d'Israël Najara," *Revue des Études Juives*, LVIII (1909), 241-269; LIX (1910), 96-105, 231-238; LX (1910), 221-234. It is to be noted, that to Najara is attributed the printing of the first Hebrew songster in the Orient, זמירות ישראל, which was printed in Safed in 1587. A second and enlarged edition appeared in Venice, 1599-1600.

Further information concerning Najara's life and works can be found in: A. Z. Idelsohn, *Gesänge der orientalischen Sefardim* (Berlin-Jerusalem-Vienna, 1923), German edition, pp. 10-14 and the Hebrew edition, pp. 7, 20-27; "ר׳ ישראל נגירה ושירתו" ['R. Israel Najara and his Poetry']," *ha-Šiloah*, XXXVII (Berlin, 1919), 25-36; and *Jewish Music*, 362-363. See also Samson Bernfeld, "נעים זמירות ישראל" "ה־מאסף" XIII, No. 2 (Warsaw, 1887), 18-25; Max Herman Friedländer, *Pizmonim, Hymnum de R. Israel Najara* (Vienna, 1858); M. D. Gaon, "ר. ישראל נגירה ז״ל ומירותיו" ['R. Israel Najara and his Poetry']," *Mizrah u-Ma'arav*, V, No. 3 (Jerusalem, 1930), 145-63; and Theodor Fuchs, "Prilog muzici sefardskih živdova u Turskoj," *Omanuth*, I (Agram, 1936-37), 157-164.

[4] Danon, "Recueil de romances . . .," 104-105.

sefardíes en el oriente saben bien que algunas de las melodías de las canciones que se cantan en las grandes festividades han sido extraídas de las romanzas y de otras canciones populares[1].

Among the Sephardim, liturgical poetry is represented by the metrical and rhymed hymn known as the פיוט [*piyyut*]. This form, whose earliest appearance dates from the sixth century in the Byzantine Empire, was intensely cultivated in eleventh- and twelfth-century Spain.[2] When the Sephardic ritual became fixed and established on the Iberian Peninsula, the great Hebrew poets enriched the liturgy with poetic contributions based upon existing melodies, mainly from secular sources. This practice, known as *contrafactum*,[3] was opposed by the rabbinical authorities who tried in vain to keep the "profane melodies" outside the synagogue. However, this practice was widely cultivated especially after the expulsion of the Sephardim from Spain, and it was mainly through the mediation of the חזן [*hazzan*] ['cantor'] that these melodies made their way into the synagogue.[4]

In 1960, Hanoch Avenary (1908-   )[5] published two important musicological studies concerning the Judeo-Spanish *contrafactum incipits* in the collections of Hebrew poetry. In the first, entitled "Études sur le cancionero judéo-tspagnol (XVIe et XVIIe siècles),[6] Avenary utilized the *incipits* to indicate

---

[1] *Romancero sefaradí* (Jerusalem, 1961), pp. 341-340.
[2] Hanoch Avenary, "Jüdische Musik," *Die Musik in Geschichte und Gegenwart*, VII (1958), col. 235-236, 238-242. For more information concerning the *piyyut* and its development, see A. Z. Idelsohn, *Jewish Liturgy and its Development* (New York, 1932), pp. 34-46; Jefim Schirmann, "Hebrew Liturgical Poetry and Christian Hymnology," *The Jewish Quarterly Review*, XLIV (Oct., 1953), 123-161; and Eric Werner, *The Sacred Bridge* (New York, 1959), pp. 234-246.
[3] Willi Apel, *Harvard Dictionary of Music* (Cambridge [USA], 1955), p. 183.
[4] The *piyyutim* as developed by the Hebrew poets in Spain employed Arabic meters and were also sung to well known Arabic tunes which were strophic in form. According to Idelsohn, *Jewish Music*, p. 127:

> The custom of adopting tunes from local Arabic or other music made a breach in the unity of Synagogue song, for until the rise of the *piyyut* (poetry) the traditional modes prevailed in the worship of all communities in the Diaspora. But since poets arose in various localities who composed poems, they selected local tunes for their products, or composed tunes in the style of the music of the people of their environment.
>
> Nonetheless we find a number of tunes common in the various Sephardic communities in the East and the West, though with some variations ... Whether these common tunes originated in the Orient and from there were carried by *chazzanim* ['cantors or precentors'] to the scattered Sephardic congregations, or originated in Spain before the expulsion in 1492, it is impossible to find out with certainty.

[5] Avenary, an eminent musicologist presently residing in Tel Aviv, had long been known to the scholarly world as Herbert Löwenstein.
[6] *Sefarad*, XX (1960), 377-94. This work was reviewed by Margit Frenk Alatorre in *Nueva Revista de Filología Hispánica*, XIV (1960), 312-18.

the musical wealth of the Eastern-Mediterranean Sephardim in the sixteenth and seventeenth centuries. He explained how vital these materials were for clarifying the history of the Sephardic folksong and pointed out that the *incipits* could very well serve to establish the chronology of the Spanish *romance*, among other genres, particularly since certain *incipits* were printed in the Near East decades before the printing of the first *Romanceros* on the Iberian Peninsula. Avenary even found five additional collections of *piyyutim* from Ottoman sources of the sixteenth and seventeenth centuries from which he was able to add thirty ballad *incipits* to Danon's original investigation.

In his second article, "מנגינות קדומות לפזמונים ספרדים (המאה הט״ז)" ['Ancient Melodies for Sephardic Hymns of the Sixteenth Century'],"[1] he traced the sources of four *incipits* to three *villancicos* and one *romance* in the *Cancionero musical de Palacio* (c. 1500). In the latter case, the *incipit*, Doliente estaba Alixandre was traced to the three-voiced *romance*, *Morir se quiere Alexandre*.[2] However, Avenary's method was based primarily on the identity of texts without investigating the tunes collected from the existing tradition.

According to de Sola, Danon, Attias, and Avenary we are given to understand that the Sephardim were able to maintain and preserve a substantial portion of their pre-exile ballad repertoire in the *piyyut contrafacta* of *romance* melodies. However, the questions remain: To what extent were the original tunes of the Spanish inheritance preserved in oral tradition? To what extent was this musical heritage affected by cultural factors native to the lands where the exiles settled?

The ballads which the exiles carried with them were those which were in vogue in Spain and Portugal at the time of their expulsion. In succeeding generations, the ballads were replenished by the later arrival of *Marranos* who brought with them *pliegos sueltos* ['broadsides'] containing the then-current *romance* texts. The period from 1500 to 1550 marked the heyday of the broadsides on the Peninsula leading up to the printing of *Cancioneros de romances*, or *Romanceros*, which were collections of *romances* compiled from the earlier broadside tradition. The first collection of ballads is considered to be the famous *Cancionero sin año* printed by Martín Nucio in Antwerp around 1549. Colin Smith remarks that "the printing of the old ballads with their music began in 1535-1536 in the music-books of Luis Milán and Luis de Narváez, and continued up to that of Francisco de Salinas in 1577. In these books, however, the ballads figure no more than occasionally among many other types of lyrics and tunes."[3]

---

[1] *Tesoro de los judios sefardies*, III (Jerusalem, 1960), 149-53.
[2] Listed in the *Cancionero musical de Palacio* as item No. 111 (Higinio Anglés' edition, Barcelona, 1947-'51, 2 vols.). The ballad is also cited in the *Catálogo* as No. 44, *Muerte de Alejandro*.
[3] Colin Smith, *Spanish Ballads*, pp. 19-20. This subject is discussed in greater depth by Miguel Querol and Daniel Devoto. See page 20, note 4.

Other than the *incipits* mentioned above we do not possess any musical notations for Sephardic ballads until relatively recent times. This lack of musical documentation which spans four centuries has made the task of studying the Sephardic ballad répertoire a rather difficult one. Musically speaking, this répertoire represents two — Moroccan and Turkish (or possibly three, with Greek) — musical style traditions located at opposite ends of the Mediterranean basin. However, the major division in Sephardic balladry is between the East — Greece, Turkey, and the Balkans — and the West — Morocco and other settlements in North Africa.

For a reconstruction of the *romancero* musical tradition emanating from Spain, we must eventually undertake a comparative study of the now moribund Judeo-Spanish ballad répertoire preserved by Sephardim from Eastern and Western Mediterranean communities. This undertaking will be based upon the taped field recordings of S. G. Armistead, J. H. Silverman, and I. J. Katz, made between 1957 and 1969.[1] Our collaborative archive, which numbers more than 1,350 variant texts, represents over 200 different narrative themes from such countries as Greece, Turkey, Yugoslavia, Bulgaria, Romania, Israel, and Morocco, and constitutes one of the largest and most important extant collections of Judeo-Spanish ballads. Working also with the sources surveyed in this chapter, we proposed as our ultimate aim to work backwards in time toward a comparative study with the known musical sources of fifteenth- and sixteenth-century Spain. Only through such a formidable undertaking can we hope to identify those features of the Sephardic répertoire which are of Spanish origin as well as to clarity those extranious influences which have altered their performance in oral tradition.

Probably the oldest printed notation of a Judeo-Spanish ballad appeared in a Viennese journal in 1897.[2] It is a transcription of the ballad *Una ramica de*

---

[1] The collaborative research of Armistead, Silverman, and myself is discussed in, "A Judeo-Spanish *Romancero*," *Ethnomusicology*, XII (January, 1968), 72-85.

[2] *Der Urquell* (Eine Monatschrift für Volkskunde), ed. Friedrich S. Krauss (New Series) I, "Heft" 8 (Vienna, 1897), p. 206. This ballad, also known to Danon, *op. cit.*, 127-128. subsequently became item No. 107 of the *Catálogo*.

The first printing of a Judeo-Spanish ballad text was that which dealt with the classical theme of *Virgilios*, MP 46, and which appeared in the *Boletín de la Institución Libre de Enseñanza* (1885), p. 24. It was communicated by Enrique (Ḥaim) Bejarano (1850-1931), the Chief Rabbi of Turkey. Five years later, a second ballad dealing with the assassination of Giovanni Borgia, the first Duke of Gandia and son of Pope Alexander VI, by his brother Cesare in 1497 appeared in A. Sánchez Moguel "Un romance en el dialecto de los judíos de Oriente," *Boletín de la Real Academia de la Historia*, XVI (1890), 497. The ballad was later cited as *La muerte del Duque de Gandía*, item No. 14 in the *Catálogo*.

It is interesting to note that these first printed texts along with the first published notation were collected in the Eastern Mediterranean. Only with the appearance of the *Catálogo* in 1906-1907, do we learn of the first Sephardic ballads from the Moroccan tradition.

ruda collected by Joseph Passy in Philippopolis — now Plovdiv, Bulgaria — and inaccurately designated as a *Spaniolisches Volkslied*.[1] The melody is reproduced here:

Example 1: *Una ramica de ruda*

[musical notation]

U-na ra----mi-ca de ru -- da   i--ja mi-_-_-- a quen   te la dio   o la di-o.

[Translation: "A little branch of rue, my daughter, who gave you a little branch of rue?"]

However, it was not until the turn of the present century when the collection of Sephardic *romance* melodies was undertaken as a serious endeavor. The collectors of these melodies were primarily interested in preserving an oral tradition which they felt had too long been neglected. The melodies, the manner in which they were collected, and the thoughts which the collectors may have nurtured about the Sephardic musical legacy will be examined in this chapter.

Among the musicological giants who have worked in the field of Sephardic balladry, the most deserving of high recognition is Manual Manrique de Lara, who devoted his later years to the pursual of ballad melodies wherever his military duties carried him. It is with him that the contemporary history of the musical study of the Sephardic *Romancero* begins.

MANUEL MANRIQUE DE LARA (1863-1929)

A little more than a year prior to the publication of the *Catálogo*, at one of the Sunday gatherings in the home of Marcelino Menéndez y Pelayo (1856-1912), the initial meeting of Ramón Menéndez Pidal and Manual Manrique de Lara took place. Already a marine captain of prominence, Manrique de Lara was steadily gaining a national reputation as a composer.[2] Here, in the company of famous scholars, at the very time when Menéndez y Pelayo was completing his important *Tratado de los romances viejos*, much was discussed about the

---

[1] The melody was taken down by Passy, however, J. Benaroya made the final notation which appears here. The index reference for J. Beranoya appearing in Šendrey's *Bibliography of Jewish Music*, p. 392, is a misspelling of Benaroya; however, Šendrey gives it correctly on p. 361.

[2] Among his other accomplishments, he was proficient as a painter and literary critic. He studied composition with Ruperto Chapí and at the turn of the century he was known for such works as: *El ciudadano Simón* (1900), a *zarzuela* in three acts; *Sinfonía en mi menor en estilo antiguo* (1892, but first performed in Madrid, 1915); the first part of the Symphonic trilogy, *La Oriestada* (performed in 1890 under Bretón). In 1917, he was accorded membership in the Academia de Bellas Artes. His inaugural address was entitled: *Orígenes literarios de la Trilogía Wagneriana*.

Romancero that stirred his imagination. This was an opportune time to seek out ideas for a new operatic venture which Manrique de Lara had in mind. For his subject, he had chosen the Cid, and who but Menéndez Pidal himself could give the composer more valuable assistance?[1]

It was Manrique de Lara's wish to confront the living tradition so that he could retrieve some of the ancient melodies for his operatic scores. During his frequent trips to the various cities of Spain (Sevilla, Cartagena, Cádiz), he was not successful in collecting sung versions of traditional ballads. Menéndez Pidal assured him that the tradition was extant in many areas on the Peninsula and he took it upon himself to introduce Manrique de Lara to the exciting world of oral tradition as well as to initiate him in actual fieldwork.[2] We learn of this first attempt in Menéndez Pidal's own words:

> Le invité a que pasásemos juntos un par de días veraniegos en los pinares de las Navas del Marqués, en la provincia de Ávila, y cuando allá fuimos, en julio de 1905, se mostró sorprendido al ver cómo a aquellas gentes no había que preguntarles por romances o canciones antiguas en general, sino por versos determinados de tal o cual romance que provocaban el recuerdo del interlocutor. Éste era, al parecer, el gran secreto que me daba buenos resultados, y que Manrique tomó como una revelación, dando por fracasado su procedimiento que consistía en informarse del cura, del maestro y demás conspicuos de los pueblos sobre los cantos populares que allí se usaban. El resultado en las Navas era extraordinario. Todos con quien hablábamos tenían en su memoria algunos romances que copiábamos Manrique y yo, faltándonos manos para transcribirlos.[3]

This first encounter with the tradition was a revelation to Manrique de Lara, indeed far greater than he would have surmised. From that time on, he continued to collect the oral treasures wherever he traveled. In 1911, he was commissioned by the Centro de Estudios Históricos of Madrid to travel to the Sephardic communites of the Near East for the purpose of collecting the then current répertoire of songs and texts. From June through November of that year, he visited such cities as Sarajevo, Sofia, Bucharest, Belgrade, Larissa, Istanbul, Izmir, Rhodes, Beirut, and Damascus.[4] He seems also to have

---

[1] R. Menéndez Pidal, *Cómo vivió y cómo vive el Romancero* (Valencia, 1947), p. 71.
[2] *Loc. cit.*
[3] *Ibid.*, pp. 71-72. Eight months after their first adventure, Menéndez Pidal in his essay, "Los romances tradicionales en América," *Cultura Española*, I (Madrid, Feb.,1906), 94, acknowledged the work of Manrique de Lara, stating that he was "estudiando la música del romancero antiguo y moderno." Menéndez Pidal even included one of Manrique de Lara's early transcripciones, *El villano vil*, though not from a Sephardic source.
[4] Cf. R. Menéndez Pidal, *Romancero Hispánico*, II, 331. From Jesús Bal y Gay's article entitled "Espagne" in *Folklore Musical* (Paris, 1939), p. 64, we learn that Manrique de Lara, along with Eduardo Martínez Torner and Bal y Gay, was working on the *Romancero musical* under the direction of Ramón Menéndez Pidal. This work was sponsored by

travelled to Jerusalem,[1] a fact that is most vital to this study; however, we will refer to the significance of this point later on. Manrique de Lara's Balkan and Near Eastern venture would have been prolonged had it not been for an impending epidemic of cholera and the outbreak of the Italo-Turkish War, 5th October 1911. Both events severely impeded his freedom of movement and he was forced to cease his work in the midst of a most promising field trip.[2]

In 1915, Manrique de Lara had the opportunity to collect numerous ballads from Sephardim residing in the Spanish zone of Morocco.[3] In the following year, he engaged in collecting both in Spain (Sevilla and Cádiz) and Morocco (Tetuán, Alcazarquivir, and Larache).[4] For the year 1918, we have indications of his having collected in Spain (Huesca, Palencia, and in the province of León).[5] Another two years in Morocco (1919-1920) found him residing in Larache and serving as colonel of a marine infantry battalion.[6] In December

---

the Centro de Estudios Históricos (Madrid). It appears somewhat strange that Bal, writing the article in 1935, did not mention Manrique de Lara's death in 1929.

Musical transcriptions from the Balkan trip can be found in M. Manrique de Lara, "Romances españoles en los Balkanes," *Blanco y Negro*, Año 26, Madrid, 2nd January, 1916, No. 1285. The four transcriptions published here are assigned no geographic origin; however, Vicente T. Mendoza in *El romance español y el corrido mexicano* (México D.F., 1939) reproduced the four transcriptions together with indications of their origin. Thus, we know that the examples from Sofia and Belgrade (p. 36) and from Istanbul and Salonika (p. 37) have been properly identified. While these transcriptions were given with piano accompaniment, the example from Salonika can be found without accompaniment in E. López-Chavarri (1881-   ), *Música popular española* (Barcelona, 1958), p. 107, and hastily written out, with errors in copying, in Gonzalo Castrillo, *El canto popular castellano* (Palencia, 1925), p. 65.

Texts only are to be found in R. Menéndez Pidal, *Romancero tradicional*, II (Madrid, 1963), from the following cities: Izmir (pp. 209-10), Rhodes (pp. 211-212), and Salonika (p. 213).

[1] In Manrique de Lara's own words, as cited by Manuel Ortega in *Los hebreos en Marruecos* (Madrid, 1919), p. 234. However, the source and date of this information are not given.
[2] *Romancero Hispánico*, loc. cit. For a short résumé of the Balkan trip, see Manrique de Lara, "Romances españoles . . ."
[3] *Romancero Hispánico*, II, 332. This and successive trips were also sponsored by the Centro de Estudios Históricos. Cf. *Romancero traditional*, I (1957), for texts collected at this time: Tangier (pp. 178-179) and Tetuán (p. 180). When Manrique de Lara returned from Morocco that year, he met with Menéndez Pidal. See *Romancero Hispánico*, II, 369, n. 6.
[4] The following areas are represented in *Romancero tradicional*, I (1957): Cádiz (p. 161), Sevilla (pp. 162, 245, and 246), Tetuán (pp. 177 and 179), Alcazarquivir (p. 181), and Larache (p. 181). Only the latter example is given with its musical notation.
[5] Cf. *Romancero tradicional*, I (1953), p. 72, for a text from León, and *ibid.*, II (1963) for texts from Huesca (p. 36) and Palencia (p. 280).
[6] *Romancero Hispánico*, II, 332.

of 1923, now a brigadier general, he returned to the Balkans in the official capacity of Chairman of the Mixed Commission for the Exchange of Greek and Turkish Populations.[1]

Manrique de Lara was the first serious minded musician to investigate the music of the flourishing Sephardic tradition. His truly magnificent contribution in collecting a massive sampling of the cherished traditional melodies was a feat which elevated him well above his musical predecessors. He worked diligently to notate as many melodic variants and versions of existing ballads as could be found. Whenever possible, he took care to return to particular singers in order to get two or more renditions of certain ballads. In his field notations, Manrique de Lara cited carefully the name, age, and location of each informant, plus, in some instances, personal remarks concerning the rendering.[2] However, he did not indicate the date of each encounter nor was there any effort on his part to organize the material according to the Menéndez Pidal *Catálogo*, although he certainly was acquainted with that work. After his death in 1929, the complete collection of notated manuscripts became the property of Ramón Menéndez Pidal.

John Brande Trend in 1926 made mention of Manrique de Lara's work and added that "his results have not yet been published but they will be awaited with considerable interest . . ."[3] The fruit of his labor, a collection of several thousand texts, a good portion of which have been musically transcribed, still remain unedited and unpublished except for those isolated and scattered tunes mentioned above.[4]

A perusal of the twenty-two published notations of ballads collected by

---

[1] *Romancero Hispánico*, II, n. 57.
[2] *Ibid.*, I, pp. 395-96.
[3] J. B. Trend, *The Music of Spanish History to 1600* (London, 1926), p. 109f.
[4] Evidence of the state of Manrique de Lara's work was clearly indicated in the *Catálogo de la Exposición Bibliográfica Sefardí Mundial* (Madrid, 1959), p. 142, where displayed as item No. 841, the annotation reads: "Romances recogidos de la tradición oral en diversos países por Manrique de Lara (Letra y música) y enviados a don Ramón Menéndez Pidal." A note above this citation indicates that the materials have remained unedited.

Estimates concerning the number of items in this collection are not conclusive; nevertheless several sources indicate the number of ballads collected at various stages of his work. Manrique de Lara, "Romances españoles . . .," stated that by 1916 he had already collected more than 300 melodies and 80,000 lines of text. From E. Martínez Torner, "El cancionero sefardí," *Temas folklóricos: Música y Poesía* (Madrid, 1935), p. 53, we learn that more than 600 *romance* melodies collected by Manrique de Lara were on file at the Centro de Estudios Históricos. Gilbert Chase, in *The Music of Spain*, 2nd. ed. (New York, 1959), p. 336, n. 4, mentions that Manrique de Lara collected several thousand songs among the Sephardic communities of the Near East.

Manrique de Lara from Sephardic informants reveals certain inherent characteristics in his musical transcription:[1]

1. All examples are in the treble clef and notated in vocal style.

2. Key signatures seem to have been employed in order to keep the melody within the framework of the staff without resorting to excessive use of leger lines.

3. Concerning the time signatures: eleven pieces employ 6/8, three 2/4, one 3/4, one 3/8, and one 4/4 (*La buena hija*, Tetuán). One example (*La mujer engañada*, Istanbul) contains 2/4 and 3/4 throughout in alternate measures. Three examples (*La mujer engañada*, Salonika, *Landarico*, Belgrade, and *El huérfano*, Damascus) alternate between 6/8 and 9/12 [*sic*! I suggest that Manrique de

---

[1] Notated music for the Sephardic ballads can be found in the following sources:
(1) *Romancero Hispánico*, I (1953).
　From Tetuán: *¿Por qué no cantáis la bella?*, MP 57 (p. 398); *Garcilasso*, not listed in the *Catálogo*, cf. F. J. Wolf and C. Hofmann's *Primavera y flor de romances* (Berlin, 1856), No. 93 (p. 398); *Duque de Bernax*, MP 53 (p. 399); *La infantina*, MP 114 (p. 399).
　From Tangier: *Ximena pide justicia*, MP 3 (p. 399).
　From Alcazarquivir: *La jactancia del conde Vélez*, not in the *Catálogo* (p. 399).
　From Larache: *Conde Alarcos*, MP 64 (p. 400).
　From Bucharest: *Las cabezas de los siete infantes de Lara*, MP 2 (p. 400).
　From Sofia: *Mujer guerrera*, MP 121 (p. 400); *Juicio de Paris*, MP 42 (p. 400).
　From Belgrade: *Landarico*, MP 82 (p. 401); *El conde Olinos*, MP 55 (p. 401).
　From Istanbul: *El sueño de doña Alda*, MP 21 (p. 401); *Don Bueso y su hermana*, hexasyllabic, MP 49 (p. 401).
　From Beirut: *Rosa Florida y Montesinos*, MP 26 (p. 402).
　From Damascus: *Conde Claros y la Princesa acusada*, MP 24 (p. 402).
(2) Manrique de Lara, "Romances españoles ..."
　From Salonika and Istanbul: *La mujer engañada*, hexasyllabic, MP 74.
(3) *Romancero tradicional*, I (1957).
　From Larache: *El hijo vengador*, MP 119 bis (p. 181).
(4) Catalán, Diego. "A caza de romances raros en la tradición portuguesa," III Colóquio Internacional de Estudos Luso-Brasileiros (Lisbon, 1957); *Actas*, I (Lisbon, 1959).
　From [Tetuán]: *La buena hija*, MP 119 (Lám. 1, between pp. 448 and 449).
　From Tetuán: *El huérfano*, MP 122 (Lám. 1, between pp. 448 and 449).
　From Damascus: *El huérfano*, MP 122 (Lám. 2, between pp. 464 and 465).
(5) Katz, Israel J. "A Judeo-Spanish Romancero," *Ethnomusicology*, XII (January, 1968), 72-85.
　From Larache: *La infantina*, MP 114, and *Conde Alarcos*, MP 64.

The ballad notations of Manrique de Lara included in the recently published *Romancero tradictional*, Vol. III, have not been included in the present study. For purely informative reasons, it should be noted that three of the ballad melodies, representing the theme *La vuelta del Navegante*, were collected in Sarajevo (May-June, 1911); seven melodies, representing *La vuelta de hijo maldecido*, MP 124, were collected in such centers as Sarajevo (1911), Belgrade (1911), Beirut (1911-1912?), and Tangier (August, 1915).

Lara meant 9/8]. Only in one instance is there a ballad without a time signature (*El conde Olinos*, Belgrade).

4. Tempo markings are given in Italian with such designations as: Allegretto poco mosso, Andtemosso, Andante con espres[s]ione, Allegro moderato, etc. The tempo indication given for the ballad without a time signature is Andte Modto *ad libitum* with the sign √ ? to mark the cæsura in the melodic line.

5. The strophic pattern employed for all but one transcription is the quatrain, composed of four melody sections. The one example which does not conform to this pattern is basically a distich or couplet, which was written out as a sestet, ABABAB (*Rosa Florida y Montesinos*, Beirut). Furthermore, it can be argued that the two ballads (*Las cabezas de los siete infantes de Lara*, Bucharest, and *El conde Olinos*, Belgrade) are in distichs, even though they are considered textually as quatrains, ABAB. Of the quatrain structures, thirteen are ABCD and four are AABC, the second melody section being a repetition of the first. Two examples from Damascus, *Conde Claros y la Princesa acusada* and *El huérfano*, have a peculiar quatrain structure $A^{x+y}\ A^{x+z}\ A^{x+y}\ A^{x'+w}$. While the former is alluded to as the tune of a ballad sung by the false Messiah Shabbetai Zevi (1626-1676),[1] Manrique de Lara made no mention of the melodic similarity between both ballads. In fact, it is also startling to note that he employed different time signatures for them, especially when they were collected in the same city. Nevertheless, this may well serve to illustrate how ballad tunes were frequently interchanged within a given répertoire. Both examples are given below:

Example 2: *Las cabezas de los siete infantes de Lara*

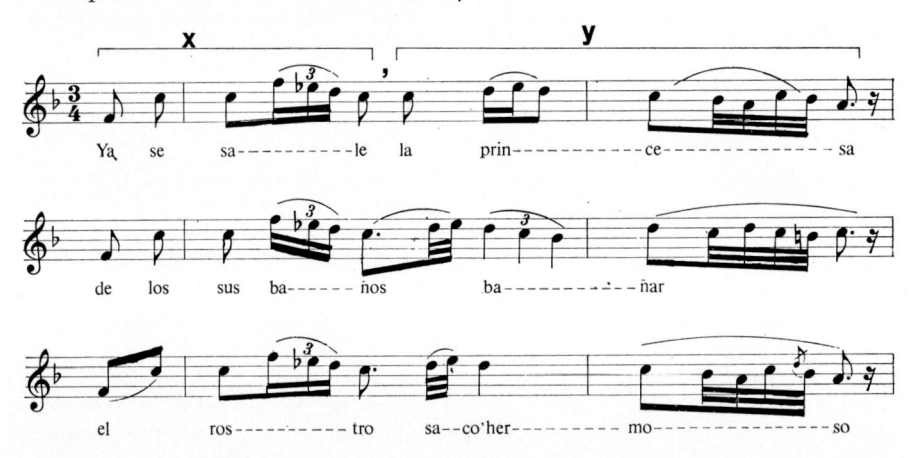

[1] *Romancero Hispánico*, I (1953), p. 402, and II, pp. 222-226. See also Ramón Menéndez Pidal, "Un viejo romance cantado por Sabbatai Çevi," *Mediæval Studies in Honor of J. D. M. Ford* (1948), pp. 185-190.

más que ro- - - - - - - sa   en el ro- - - - sal.

[Translation: Now the princess comes forth from bathing in her baths. As she came forth, her face was more beautiful than a rose on a rose bush.]

Example 3: *El huérfano*

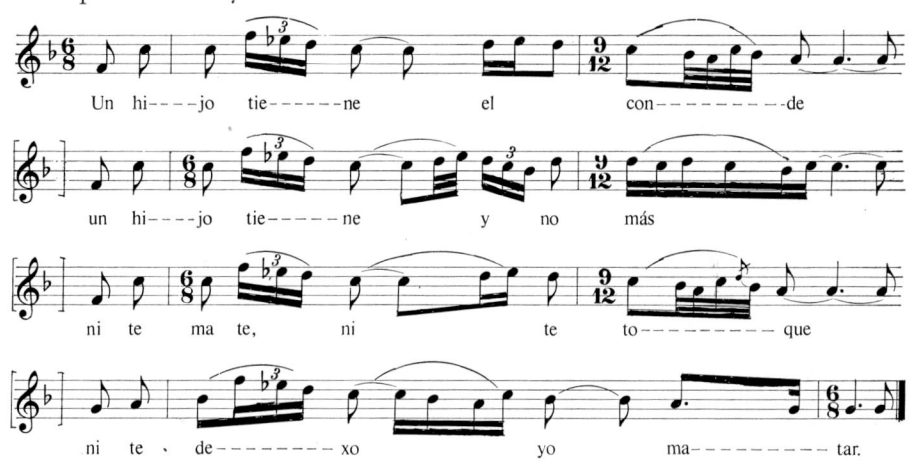

Un hi- - - -jo tie- - - - - -ne   el   con- - - - - - - -de

un hi- - - -jo tie- - - - - ne   y   no   más

ni te ma te,   ni   te   to- - - - - - - - que

ni te · de- - - - - - - xo   yo   ma- - - - - - - - - tar.

[Translation: The count has but one son, one son he has and no more. "May You not be killed, nor even touched, nor will I let you be killed."]

6. As to modal structure, eleven ballads are in the major mode, six in the minor, four are Mixolydian (*El conde Olinos*, Belgrade; *El sueño de doña Alda*, Istanbul; *Conde Claros y la Princesa acusada* and *El huérfano*, Damascus) and one in Phrygian (*La jactancia del conde Vélez*, Alcazarquivir). The tonal centricity of these modes places fourteen in the authentic category and eight in the plagal. Nine melodies end on the *finalis*, seven on the fifth degree, four on the second degree, and two on the third. Chromatic alterations occur in in the following ways: raising the seventh degree in minor melodies; giving some minor coloring (as in the example, *Juicio de Paris*, from Sofia); rendering the melodic and harmonic aspects of the minor mode; and functioning as upper and lower auxiliaries in embellishing passages.

7. Three examples exceed the octave with an ambitus of a major 9th. Twelve have the range of an octave, four a minor 7th, and three a major 6th.

8. All the melodies are basically diatonic, with some triadic inferences normally outlining the triad of the *finalis*, or tonic. Leaps of a 4th occur in most of the examples. Leaps of a 5th can be found only in three examples. In two of them, the leaps occur after the first melodic section and in the third example

after the third melodic section. A leap of a minor 7th, which occurs between the third and last melody sections, is found in the text of *La jactancia del conde Vélez* from Alcazarquivir.

9. Rhythm, a basic and vital musical parameter, is undoubtedly one of the most fascinating aspects of balladry. One could indicate by various subscripts the corresponding rhythms underlying each melodic section. The process would however be most deceptive since the smallest rhythmic units play a more important rôle here than do the melodic units which generally are employed for pieces of a larger scale. Although the rhythms affixed by the transcriber in the field are, in the majority of instances, more accurate than the melodic lines themselves, it would seem rather superficial to classify the rhythmic structures in their melodic-structure context without delving farther into the specific motif structure as well. If we were to carry this procedure even further, eventually the relationship of ballad rhythmic structures within a given time signature would have to be shown. I have chosen to avoid this category, except for exact reïterated patterns which are employed in two or more of the corresponding melody sections.

The ballad *¿Por qué no cantáis la bella?* from Tetuán represents such an example. The first two melody sections are based on the rhythm (a), while the latter two are based on a slight variant of (a), which may be indicated as (a′):

The example *Las cabezas de los siete infantes de Lara* from Bucharest, alluded to above, which is basically a distich, is based on the following rhythm corresponding to each hemistich:

The first melody section of *Juicio de Paris* from Sofia is broken up into two rhythmic units; however, it does not divide the sung syllables evenly as one would expect, but conforms to the following pattern:

Dur--------mien---do   es---ta------ba   Pa---ri-----si

For other examples, see the pattern employed for the first, second, and fourth melody sections of *Landarico* (Belgrade), the first and second melody sections of *El sueño de doña Alda* (Istanbul) and *La mujer engañada* (Salonika and

Istanbul), and the patterns employed for the first, second, third, and fourth melody sections of *El hijo vengador* (Larache).

10. The underlying text is fully punctuated with syllables accurately divided. However, because of space limitations some texts were inaccurately placed. For example, the last two measures of *La infantina* (Tetuán) should read:

[pa]dre ma-dre te------ ni---------a

And beginning with the last beat of the sixth measure of *Landarico* (Belgrade), the text underlay should be as follows:

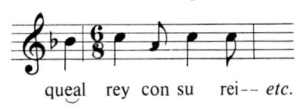

queal rey con su rei-- *etc.*

The elisions in Manrique de Lara's texts are not indicated at all. Refrains, such as *"y nuevo amor"* occur in two ballads, *La mujer engañada* (Salonika and Istanbul), while the textual interjection *"iah-ah!"* can be found in *Rosa Florida y Montesinos* (Beirut). Although Manrique de Lara indicated with a comma (as seen in Example 2 above) the pauses and cæsuras in several of his examples, he was not consistent in this practice.

The musico-textual strophe is basically made up of four hemistichs, each hemistich corresponding to a musical phrase. All but three are based on the hemistich of octosyllables, the exceptions being *Don Bueso y su hermana* (Istanbul) and *La mujer engañada* (Salonika and Istanbul).

11. All ornaments are written out in full, although there is a special regard for grace notes and grace-note pairs which are indicated with a lighter hand. In the majority of cases, ornamental figures appear on the ultimate or penultimate syllable in each hemistich. Ties and slurs are indicated.

12. There are a number of errors which must be corrected:
a. In the fourth measure of *Garcilasso* (Tetuán), the last two notes should be sixteenths, and the last eighth-note rest of the last measure should be omitted.
b. For *Duque de Bernax* (Tetuán), changing the figuration in the seventh measure to:

would make the note *a-flat*[1] even less effective in the modal coloring by functioning as a sprite upper auxiliary.

c. The rhythm of the sixth measure of *La infantina* (Tetuán) should be corrected to read:

d. For *La mujer de Juan Lorenzo* (Bucharest), the last measure should read:

e. For *El hijo vengador* (Larache), the syllable of the fourth measure should be properly placed to read:

ga------na

f. For *El huérfano* (Tetuán):
   (1) the first note b^1 is a sixteenth-note.
   (2) measure 1: the last note is an eighth.
   (3) measure 2: a slur is missing under the notes b^1 which comprise the second and third beat; the note preceding the last eighth-note is a sixteenth.
   (4) measure 4: the second and third note are sixteenths; the first note above the slur is an eighth; and the note preceding the last eighth-note is a sixteenth.
   (5) measure 6: the last two notes are a sixteenth and an eighth respectively.
   (6) measure 7: the second and last notes are eighths.

g. For *El huérfano* (Damascus): the corrected version is given in Example 3 above.

h. For *La buena hija* (Tetuán): the corrected version is given here because of the excessive number of notational errors:

Example 4: *La buena hija*

Andante

Pa- se – á – ba- see el buen Ci-----di por la su guar-dia po-- li----------da; mi--ran-
do- lees-- ta   lain-- fan------------- ta don-de   su   ca---sa ga--rri--------da.

[Translation: The good Cid was strolling through his fine guard house (fortress) the princess was looking at him from her splendid house.]

13. From the standpoint of ornamentation alone, it is quite apparent that those gathered examples of Manrique de Lara's transcriptions exhibit marked differences for the figurations employed in the ballads of North Africa and in those of the Eastern Mediterranean.

14. Manrique de Lara called attention to the fact that in Morocco the ballads are sung in a most unusual manner. After the first four hemistichs, the singer repeats the melodic strophe, this time beginning with the third and fourth hemistichs which now correspond to the first and second melodic phrases. This manner of rendering is continued throughout the entire piece.[1]

15. Most discerning is Manrique de Lara's practice of indicating rests at the beginning of a number of ballads: e.g., ¿*Por qué no cantáis la bella?* (Tetuán), *Garcilasso* (Tetuán), and *Ximena pide justicia* (Tangier). Whether or not the two former ballads were printed without their accompaniments (which, incidentally were given for *La mujer engañada* [Istanbul and Salonika]), is not known; however, Manrique de Lara may be considered the first to set accompaniments to these melodies.

While the bulk of Manrique de Lara's notations remains unpublished, it is most difficult to appraise his valuable contribution on the basis of the scant sources indicated above. E. Martínez Torner, who undoubtedly studied much of his collection, made the following observations:

> Las melodías transcritas por Manrique de Lara son, en su casi totalidad, de abolengo español y no pocas viven aún hoy en nuestro pueblo. Presentan muchas el aspecto exterior del canto andaluz, con extraordinaria riqueza melismática, y abundan en ellas la tonalidad y los ritmos característicos de la música de Andalucía, cuya estética, dicho sea de paso, aún no ha sido revelada.[2]

Even though Torner's remarks were based upon his own knowledge of Hispanic folk music, there are grave questions concerning their validity. Manrique de Lara, himself, did not leave a legacy of published writings concerning his field endeavors, and it may very well be that, along with his handwritten musical notations, will be found manuscripts, log books, diaries, and other valuable sources of information which may bring to light his own views concerning the tradition. Be that as it may, Manrique de Lara's magnificent labor of love in collecting a massive sampling of early twentieth-century Sephardic balladry has provided future generations of investigators with the unique and precious raw materials for future research.

---

[1] Manrique de Lara, *op. cit.* See also *Romancero Hispánico*, II, 369, n. 9. Daniel Devoto demonstrates how this method of rendering was in vogue among the sixteenth-century *vihuelistas* in "Poésie et musique dans l'œuvre des vihuélistes," *Annales Musicologiques*, IV (1956), 92-93.

[2] "El cancionero sefardí," pp. 53-54.

ANTONIO BUSTELO (d. 1927?)

Contemporary with Manrique de Lara's tour of duty in Larache, the impressive study *Los hebreos en Marruecos* by Manuel L. Ortega first appeared in print.[1] There was need for such a social and political history of Moroccan Jewry, especially at a time when Spain's foothold in northern Morocco was becoming firmly established. Spain's active Moroccan adventure began with the Spanish-Moroccan War (1859-1860) and resulted in the acquisition of Tetuán. In the latter part of 1904, France and Spain began their partition of Morocco into zones of influence which brought about the French and Spanish Protectorates in 1912. Entering the second decade of the twentieth century, an enlightened Spain could now reëxamine the rôle of the Sephardim and come to revere the deep-rooted Hispanic culture which they had faithfully preserved since their expulsion.

In part two of his book, Ortega devoted a chapter to "Viejos romances de Castilla."[2] Very appropriately he added the descriptive sub-heading "De la España que fué. — El espíritu de la Edad Media vive en las canciones de los hebreos marroquíes." The twenty-two melodies and texts included in this chapter were taken from the private collection of Antonio Bustelo. The only information we have regarding Bustelo is contained in an elaborate note written by Ortega:

> Uno de los españoles que más han trabajado por la Patria en Marruecos dentro de su esfera de acción, es el músico mayor militar D. Antonio Bustelo. A él debemos la música de estos maravillosos romances, que hemos entresacado de la copiosa colección que posee, recogida con paciencia benedictina de labios de las viejas hebreas de los Mel-lah marroquíes. El señor Bustelo, sin gozar de subvenciones oficiales, impulsado únicamente por el arte y por el patriotismo, ha desarrollado una labor de recopilación de la música árabe y hebrea, que, en justicia, debe premiar nuestro Gobierno.[3]

Larrea Palacín, who collected Sephardic ballads thirty years later in Tetuán, informs us that it was a woman from the Benchimol family of that city who sang *romances* for Bustelo and Ortega, and that these are the ballads which appeared in Ortega's book:

---

[1] Madrid: Editorial Hispano Africana, 1919. It should be noted that one year before this publication, two ballad melodies, which were notated by D. Juan Berruezo de Mateo, Músico Mayor del Batallón Cazadores de Llerena, núm. 11, appeared in Africano Fernández, *España en Africa y el peligro judío* (Santiago, 1918), p. 306, n. 1. The ballads can be identified as MP 12, *La mujer de Juan Lorenzo* (for "Hermosa", p. 304) and MP 49, *Don Bueso y su hermana* (for "Mi hermana", p. 305). The latter ballad is linked with the octosyllabic Peninsular tradition.
[2] *Ibid.*, pp. 233-261.
[3] *Ibid.*, p. 235, n. 2.

A esta familia [Benchimol] perteneció la señora que cantó a los señores Bustelo y Ortega los romances publicados en el libro ya citado, y de ese dictado queda el recuerdo de la generosidad con que el señor Ortega gratificó a la informadora.[1]

When E. Martínez Torner attempted to work out a system for classifying some 600 *romance* melodies,[2] he made mention of the fact that thirty-six of these melodies had been collected by Bustelo in Tetuán, and added that all of these melodies would be included in the *Romancero General* which Ramón Menéndez Pidal had been preparing.[3] To date, only two volumes have been completed and these deal with specific historical ballad themes which undoubtedly were absent from Bustelo's collection.[4] Since it is known that among the MSS notations of Manrique de Lara there are a number of *romance* melodies which were copied from Bustelo's collection, we may yet see a still greater number of Bustelo's transcriptions when they are eventually published in the *Romancero General*.

Antonio Bustelo's contribution to the Ortega study has been well acknowledged. Bustelo was an ambitious man and could not confine himself to the strict duties of his military position. He was also extremely interested in Arabic music and was one of the first to transcribe the music of the classical *nawbas* into modern notation.[5]

There are four editions of Ortega's *Los hebreos en Marruecos*, which appeared in 1919, 1919, 1929, and 1934.[6] Doubtless because of the popularity of the

---

[1] A. Larrea Palacín, *Romances de Tetuán*, Tomo I (Madrid, 1952), p. 10. Larrea referred to the third edition (Madrid, 1929) of Ortega's book.
[2] "Ensayo de clasificación de las melodías de romance," *Homenaje a Menéndez Pidal*, Tomo II (Madrid, 1925), pp. 391-402.
[3] *Ibid.*, p. 391, n. 2.
[4] Three volumes of this work have already been published under the general heading *Romancero tradicional*. Vol. I (Madrid, 1957) deals with the "Romanceros del Rey Rodrigo y de Bernardo del Carpio," Vol. II (Madrid, 1963) with the "Romanceros de los Condes de Castilla y de los Infantes de Lara," and Vol. III (Madrid, 1969) the "Romances de tema odiseico."
[5] P. Patrocino García-Barriuso, *La música hispano-musulmana en Marruecos* (Larache, 1941), pp. vii-viii. A photograph of Bustelo can be found on p. viii.

The *nawba* [*nauba*], which originated in Moslem Spain during the Abbasid dynasty (somewhere between the eighth and thirteenth centuries), grew out of the practice of individual performances at designated times by minstrels at the court. As each performance was unique, owing to the particular vocal techniques and musical form employed in each suite or cantata — the usual designations for *nawba* — the varied performances became integral movements. These movements, primarily vocal in content, were soon preceded by instrumental preludes, and in the fifteenth century the *nawba* began with an elaborate overture called a *basrau*.

[6] First edition, see p. 42, note 1. The second edition, see ibidem, has "2. edición" impressed on the back side of the paper cover. The third edition was printed in Madrid: Compañía Ibero-Americana de Publicaciones, 1929, and the fourth edition, Madrid: Talleres Tipográficos, 1934. The citation for the second edition can be found in the *Dictionary Catalog of the Klau Library Cincinnati* (Boston, 1964), XIX, p. 368.

book a second edition was brought out in the first year of publication. Without delving into all the revisions which differentiate these editions, I wish to note that it is important to bear in mind, first of all, that these revisions occurred primarily between the 2nd and 3rd editions. The 4th edition was merely a reprinting of the third. As far as Chapter VI of Part Two, "Viejos romances de Castilla," is concerned, the major differences existing between the 2nd and 3rd editions can be itemized under the following headings: pagination, type-setting, ballad texts, and ballad melodies.

A. *Pagination*: for the 2nd edition, pp. 233-261; for the 3rd, pp. 207-236.
B. *Type-setting*: the change of type face is quite obvious. A bolder type face, perhaps an 11-point pica, is apparent in the 2nd edition, while the 3rd edition employs a standard 10-point pica plus cursive type for titles.
C. *Ballad texts*: the texts have been altered somewhat in the 3rd edition. No mention is given of the editor for the 3rd edition, though the changes were undoubtedly aimed at rendering the texts more readily understandable. Capitalization, applied to the first word of every line in the 2nd edition, was limited to the standard usage of capitals for proper nouns and at the beginning of sentences in subsequent editions. Punctuation was thoroughly revised from the 2nd to the 3rd edition, and words which were pushed together in the second edition were spaced according to standard practice in the 3rd edition. Close scrutiny of the texts of both editions indicates that important changes occurred in spelling, as well as in the addition and omission of words. The omission of accent marks seems to have been occasioned by the weak impression made during the printing of both editions. Since the texts have been utilized by scholars, who may or may not have been aware of these textual changes in the particular edition they cited, I list all the alterations:[1]

                Second edition   *Third edition*

1. *Pregonadas son las guerras* (= *Mujer guerrera*)

Page 236:	Page 210:
line 6: cualquiera	line 6: cualquier
lines 22, 24, 32, 36, 46: barón	lines 22, 24, 32, 36, 46: varón
line 27: cavellos	line 27: cabellos
line 44: calló	line 44: cayó

[1] Concerning the texts, Paul Bénichou remarked "la transcripción es, desde el punto de vista de la lengua, bastante desigual en la exactitud; pero la colección resulta utilísima por la rareza de los textos de romances marroquíes publicados hasta hoy." See "Romances judeo-españoles de Marruecos," *Revista de Filología Hispánica*, VI (1944), 42. One must bear in mind that Bénichou used the fourth edition only, while Larrea Palacín and Attias utilized the third edition for their important studies. These scholars were unaware of the discrepancies existing among the various editions.

2. *Paseábase Güezo* (= *El rey envidioso de su sobrino*)

    Page 237:
    lines   3, 7: Bara
    line   16: Y de quién es Granada?»
    line   18: Si queries tomadlas»
    line   33: viene
    lines   35, 41: D. Güezo
    line   39: Mientras se aprontan

    Page 211:
    lines   3, 7: vara
    line   16: y de quién Granada?
    line   18: si queréis tomarlas."
    line   33: biene
    lines   35, 41: don Güezo
    line   39: mientras que se aprontan

    Page 238:
    line   61: Hay
    line   69: Leváis

    Page 212:
    line   61: Ahí
    line   69: lleváis

3. *Escuchis, señor soldado* (= *Vuelta del marido*[é])

    Page 238:
    line   38: bergel

    Page 213:
    line   38: vergel

4. *Alabóse el conde Velo* (= *La jactancia del conde Vélez*)

    Page 239:
    line   13: vencierais
    line   21: De seda y borcados
    line   27: De sedas y brocados

    Page 213:
    line   13: vencieras
    line   21: de sedas y de brocados
    line   27: de sedas y de brocados

    line   34: joyar

    Page 214:
    line   34: joyas

5. *Las ricas bodas se hacen* (= *Grandes bodas hay en Francia*)

    Page 240:
    line   10: ¿Conde, u que miráis ahí?
    line   22: No sabrán adonde yo fuí.
    line   25: algolfa
    line   27: Al bajar de las escaleras
    line   32: Conde, o ¿que lleváis ahí?
    line   33: pagecito
    line   35: page

    Page 214:
    line   10: Conde, ¿qué miráis ahí?
    line   22: no sabrán adonde fuí.
    line   25: algorfa
    line   27: Al bajar las escaleras
    line   32: Conde ¿que lleváis ahí?
    line   33: pajecito
    line   35: paje

    line   42: volvelda

    Page 215:
    line   42: volvedla

6. *En la ciudad de Toledo* (= *Diego León*)

    Page 241:
    line   4: barón
    line   6: intinción
    line   23: bara
    line   24: baradas

    Page 215:
    line   4: varón
    line   6: intención
    line   23: vara
    line   24: varadas

    line   42: rebés

    Page 216:
    line 42: revés

7. *Por las torres de Gibraltar*

    Page 242:
    line   14: rronllíle

    Page 216:
    line   14: ronllíle

8. *Sépase por todo el mundo* (= *El capitán burlado*)

   Page 243:
   line   8: no pasa

   Page 217:
   line   8: non pasa

   Page 218:
   line   45: «Sepáis D. Fernando y amigo:

   line   45: "Sepáis, don Fernando amigo:

9. *Un hijo tiene el Rey David* (= *Amnón y Tamar*)

   Page 244:
   line   16: guisare

   Page 218:
   line   16: giusara

   line   24: trugieron

   Page 219:
   line   24: trujieron

10. *Cantar de Aliarda* (= *Aliarda*)

    Page 245-246
    There are no textual alterations.

    Page 219-220

11. *Este ser villano* (= *La mujer engañada*)

    Page 247:
    line   15: descalsia
    line   16: vevía
    line   23: muger
    line   31: Seré
    line   32: Como ser solía.

    Page 221:
    line   15: descansia
    line   16: bebía
    line   23: mujer
    line   31: cerré
    line   32: como hacer solía.

    line   68: El que orca hace;
    line   70: orca
    note 1, line 4: Que yo no lo quería

    Page 222:
    line   68: el que la horca hace;
    line   70: horca
    note 1, line 4: Que yo no quería

12. *Estábase Moriana* (= *El veneno de Moriana*)

    Page 248:
    line   1: Estávase

    Page 222:
    line   1: Estábase

    line   21: ojitas
    lines 25, 26, 29, 30: veváis
    line   27: Que siete años habían siete.

    Page 223:
    line   21: hojitas
    lines 25, 26, 29, 30: bebáis
    line   27: Omitted here because of a sequential error, but transposed to line 24.

    Page 249:
    line   65: Ya sacan a Don Güezo

    Page 223:
    line   65: Ya le sacan a Don Güezo,

13. *Desdichada fué Calmena* (= *La mala suegra*)

    Page 249:
    line   14: Guarismo a la puerta avate
    line   25: desbainada
    line   28: page
    line   29: Albir seas,

    Page 224:
    line   14: Guarismo a la puerta bate
    line   25: desvainada
    line   28: paje
    line   29: Albricias,

14. *La Reina xerifa mora* (= *Hermanas reina y cautiva*)

    Page 251:
    line   46: labó

    Page 225:
    line   46: lavó

15. *De Valencia pido* (= *El rapto*)

    Page 251:
    line   5: Buestras

    Page 226:
    line   5: vuestras

    Page 252:
    line   35: Sacarí

    Page 227:
    line   35: Sacaré

16. *Cercada está Santafuente* (= *Búcar sobre Valencia*)

    Page 253:
    line   74: Se ponen los de la Pascua

    Page 226:
    line   74: se pone los de la Pascua

17. *Ya se va la blanca niña* (= *La lavandera de San Juan*)

    Page 254:
    line   2: labar
    line   3: laba
    line   5: Mientras los paños sensuga
    line   15: segita

    Page 229:
    line   2: lavar
    line   3: lava
    line   5: mientras los paños ensuga
    line   15: sejita

    Page 255:
    line   38: Me dites pie chiquititos;
    line   39: Zapatos de cordobar.

    line   38: me dites pies chiquititos;
    line   39: zapatos de cordobán;

18. *Xuliana en su castillo* (= *Moriana y Galván*)

    Page 256:
    lines 25, 33: hierva
    line   26: beviendo
    line   31: page
    line   54: salvage

    Page 230:
    lines 25, 33: hierba
    line   26: bebiendo
    line   31: paje
    line   54: salvaje

    line   59: salvage

    Page 231:
    line   59: salvaje

19. *Quien quiera tomar consejo* (= *Catalina*)

    Page 257:
    line   4: Lo que a mí me contensió.

    Page 231:
    line   4: lo que a mí me acontesió,

    Page 232:
    line   20: barón
    line   35: Cavalgó
    line   37: Cavalgó y se fué a vuscar;
    line   46: vuscar

    line   20: varón
    line   35: cabalgó
    line   37: cabalgó y se fué a buscar.
    line   46: buscar

20. *Un hijito la Princesa* (= *El huérfano*)

    Page 258:
    line   4: page

    Page 232:
    line   4: paje

    Page 233:
    line   9: Que si el Rey le dá la mula,

    line   9: que si el Rey la da las armas,

Page 259:
line 39: pagecito
line 42: Yo la tengo
line 47: page
line 54: cavalgare

line 39: pajecito
line 42: yo las tengo
line 47: paje
line 54: cabalgare

21. *Estábase la Delgada* (= *Delgadina*)

Page 260:
line 9: «Nunca Dio,
line 26: Peinándose a las sus canas:
line 31: «Yo te la diera de mi vida de mi alma,
line 32: *Omits*: «Yo te la diera ...

Page 234:
line 9: "Nunca Dios
line 26: peinándose las sus canas:
line 31: "Yo te la diera, mi vida,
line 32: yo te la diera, mi alma;

22. *A cazar iba el caballero* (= *La infantina*)

Page 261:
line 44: busquedad

Page 236:
line 44: búsqueda

D. *Ballad melodies*: all musical notations of the 2nd edition appear to be engravings of Bustelo's original field notations. It is not certain, however, that this was really the case. In many instances it is difficult to ascertain note values because of the weak impressions made in the process of printing the 2nd and 3rd editions. All the notated examples bear a hand-written tempo indication in the upper left hand corner of the first staff preceding the soprano clef, and they carry the author's signature "Antonio Bustelo" or "Bustelo" written in an oblique position immediately after the double bar. One such notation was printed upside down, i.e., *Ya se va la blanca niña* (p. 254).[1]

---

[1] Even Idelsohn, who took four of the ballad tunes from Ortega's 1919 edition (in the order: pp. 244, 237, 239, and 269), did not notice this striking phenomenon. Cf. his *Gesänge der marokkanischen Juden*, Vol. V of the *Hebräisch-orientalischer Melodienschatz*, pp. 15-16.

However, in Idelsohn's work (p. 16), the lithographed copies of Bustelo's *romances* contain errors which must be rectified. In the first melody (from Ortega, p. 244), measures 12 through 17 were omitted. The eighth-note pattern in the second measure should be a dotted-eighth followed by a sixteenth. Slurs were omitted from measure four to the first note of the following measure, and for measure nine to the first note of the following measure. Measure seven should have a tie connecting the pitches b^1.

In the third melody (from Ortega, p. 239), the second note of the third measure should be d^1, not e^1, as shown. The enclosed ($\#$?) located above the penultimate measure does apply to the second note.

A number of slurs are missing in the fourth melody (from Ortega, p. 269): In measure 2, spanning the first and second beats; measure, 3, the second and third beats; measure 4, the entire measure; measure 7, the first and second beats; measure 10, second and third beats; measure 11, second and third beats; measure 12, the second and third beats con-

In the 3rd edition, we find lithographed musical examples. Moreover, even though the print is now much larger and clearer, we do find occasional discrepancies in the notations of both editions, and in many cases, this 3rd edition clarifies many of the notational problems encountered in the former editions. Tempo indications, now set in type, are placed at the top left-hand corner above the clef, and Bustelo's signature is completely removed. Even the stems are placed in better accord with contemporary notational practices.

There are numerous notational errors in both editions and there remain some questions concerning note values in particular measures. These discrepancies follow:

1. *Mujer guerrera* (2nd edition, p. 236; 3rd edition, p. 210)
2nd edition only:
measures 6, 7, and 14: the notes with weak or no stem impressions are quarters.
Both editions:

measure 9: there are two possibilities in solving the note values of this measure. The rhythm can either be ♩ ♫♩ or ♪♫♩.

In the 2nd edition, there is no stem on the second note, while in the 3rd edition a quarter-note is shown, but the following notes are not indicated as a triplet.

tinuing over to the first note of the following measure; measure 15, the eighth-note pattern; and in the penultimate measure, the third beat extending over to the last note of the melody. The eighth-note pattern of measure 7 should be a dotted-eighth followed by a sixteenth-note. The rhythm for measure 8, ♩ ♫♩ should read ♩. ♫ with a slur over the eighth-note pattern extending over to the first note of the following measure. And in measure 11 the rhythm ♩ ♩ ♫ should be corrected to read ♩ ♫. ♩.

Furthermore, Gerson-Kiwi, who quoted *Romance* No. 9, MP 37 (p. 244) from Ortega's 1919 edition, went a step further by attempting to underlay the tune with its accompanying text. This example was included among others in her contribution to the scholarly *Die Musik in Geschichte und Gegenwart*, Vol. VII (1958), col. 273, in an article entitled "Jüdische Volksmusik." Here is an instance where, had Gerson-Kiwi looked in the 3rd or 4th edition of *Los hebreos en Marruecos*, other clues would have yielded a more accurate text underlay. Besides, it is quite incomprehensible how Gerson-Kiwi arrived at an altered version of Bustelo especially since the text was clearly printed after the melody. Gerson-Kiwi should also have collated the notations of this ballad, as it appeared in the

measure 12: a somewhat similar condition exists in this measure. However, in both editions, the last note is given as a quarter-note without indicating the preceding pattern, i.e., ♩.♫♩, a as triplet figure.

last measure: there appears to be an empty last measure for which the dotted-quarter note *e* would be most appropriate. The 3rd edition does not indicate this situation.

1919 and successive editions, besides utilizing Larrea Palacín's transcription of this same ballad (cf. *Romances de Tetuán*, I, p. 130).

Gerson-Kiwi included the same example in a survey entitled "The Legacy of Jewish Music Through the Ages" which was reprinted in four different sources: 1) בתפוצות הגולה [*'In the Dispersion'*], V, No. 4 (Winter, 1963) [Jerusalem: World Zionist Organization], p. 61; 2) *In the Dispersion: Surveys and Monographs on the Jewish World*, No. 3 (Winter 1963-1964) [Jerusalem: World Zionist Organization], p. 160; 3) published as a booklet which was presented at the Sixteenth Internatonal Folk Music Conference (Jerusalem, 1963); and 4) *Journal of Synagogue Music*, I, No. 1 (February 1967/Adar I 5727), 14. (Published by the Cantors Assembly of America, New York).

The following transcriptions represent Gerson-Kiwi's and that which I suggest as a possible solution for Bustelo's version of *Amnón y Tamar*:

[Translation: King David has a son called Hablor «=Amnón» by name. He fell in love with Tamar even though she was his own sister.]

2. *El rey envidioso de su sobrino* (2nd edition, p. 237; 3rd edition, p. 211)
2nd edition only:
measure 5: the rhythm should read ♩. ♪♩ (b^1, a^1, and b^1 respectively), not as in the 3rd edition where the rhythm is given ♩. ♪ 𝄾 .
measure 6: due to over-inking, the third note is a half-note.
measure 8: second note is a dotted-quarter.
measure 9: second note is a dotted-quarter.
measure 10: the first note given here as b^1, is shown in the 3rd edition as a^1. Also, the quarter-note stem is omitted for the first note, and the value of the second note is a dotted-quarter.
last measure: due to over-inking, the second note is a half-note.

3. *Vuelta del marido (é)* (2nd edition, p. 238; 3rd edition, p. 212)
2nd edition only:
measure 4: the last two notes are united as an eighth-note pair, whereas in the 3rd edition, these notes are given as individual eighth-notes.
measure 5: the second note of the ornamental figure following the fourth note is b^1.
measure 6: the slur is missing under the first *f*-sharp.
measure 7: the second note of the ornamental figure following the first note is a^1.

4. *La jactancia del conde Vélez* (2nd edition, p. 239; 3rd edition, p. 213)
2nd edition only:
measure 8: correct rhythm should be ♩ ♩. ♫ .
measure 12: the correct note is g-sharp as shown in the 3rd edition.
measure 13: the natural (♮) before the second note is omitted here, but not in the 3rd edition.

5. *Grandes bodas en Francia* (2nd edition, p. 240; 3rd edition, p. 214).
2nd edition only:
measure 1: the second and third notes should be e^1 and d^1 respectively.
measure 4: the second note is a half-note.
measure 8: the last note is a half-note.

6. *Diego León* (2nd edition, p. 241; 3rd edition, p. 215)
2nd edition only:
measure 2: the note is a dotted-quarter.
measure 6: same as for measure 2.
measure 14: the second note should be an *e* as given in the 3rd edition.

measure 17: the second note *e* appears as an illegibly impressed eighth-note, thus giving the overall rhythmic scheme for the measure as: ♪♪♫ . However, in the 3rd edition this note does not appear at all, so that the rhythm is given as: ♪♫ .

measure 18: a *g♯* is preceded and followed by an unidentified typographical mark. In the 3rd edition, it is shown as *g*-natural, a dotted-quarter note.

measure 19: this measure is most unclear. The first typographical mark which may be due to over-inking is followed by a succession of three eighth-notes (*d*, *f♯*, and *a¹*). The 3rd edition, on the other hand, interprets this as an eighth-rest followed by two connected eighth-notes with the respective pitches *f*-natural and *a¹*. A *g*-natural in place of *f*-natural is suggested.

3rd edition only:
measure 22: the second eighth-note should be *e*.

7. *Por las torres de Gibraltar* (2nd edition, p. 242; 3rd edition, p. 216)
2nd edition only:
measure 8: stem missing for the first half-note.
measure 9: the note following the quarter-rest should be *d¹*.

8. *El capitán burlado* (2nd edition, p. 243; 3rd edition, p. 217)
2nd edition only:
measure 4: no slur is indicated in this measure, whereas it occurs in the 3rd edition.
measure 17: the stem for the first quarter-note is missing.
measure 23: the first note should be a dotted-quarter.

9. *Amnón y Tamar* (2nd edition, p. 244; 3rd edition, p. 218)
2nd edition only:
measure 11: no slur is indicated for this measure, whereas it encompasses all the notes in the 3rd edition. Also, the stem is missing from the first note of the second group.
measure 12: stem is missing from the first quarter-note.
measure 15: slur is missing from the triplet figure. It is shown in 3rd edition.
measure 16: triplet indication is missing, whereas it is shown in 3rd edition.
Both editions:
measure 20: slurs are missing for the triplet figures.

10. *Aliarda* (2nd edition, p. 245; 3rd edition, p. 219)
2nd edition only:
measure 2: the three connected eighth-notes are a triplet. The following note, with a missing stem, is a quarter.
measure 3: the figuration beginning on the third beat can be clarified rhythmically as ♩ ♫ ♩. ♪ (a^1, b^1, a^1, g, and f). The slur should continue up to the fourth beat.
measure 5: the first note should be a quarter-note. The ornament following the last quarter-note consists of two sixteenth-notes (f^1 and e^1), and should be placed over the bar line with a slur connecting them to the first eighth-note d^1.
measure 6: the figuration beginning on the third beat is identical with that given for measure 3 above. It is followed by a quarter-note.
measure 7: there seems to be an illegibly impressed sharp before the last quarter-note. This is not indicated in the 3rd edition.
measure 8: a bracket which underlies this measure in the 3rd edition does not appear here.
measure 9: the last note is a quarter.
measure 11: the last note is a half-note.
measure 13: cf. measure 8 above. In addition, the last note d should be c as indicated in the 3rd edition.
measure 15: the last four notes are indicated as a grouping of four eighth-notes whereas in the 3rd edition this is indicated as two groups of two eighth-notes each.

11. *La mujer engañada* (2nd edition, p. 246; 3rd edition, p. 221)
2nd edition only:
measure 6: should be a quarter-note followed by two quarter-note rests, as shown in the 3rd edition.
measure 8: the correct rhythm for this measure should read ♩ ♩. ♪ to agree with 3rd edition.
measure 11: rhythm should agree with measure 8 above.
measure 12: this note is the dotted-half note g.

12. *El veneno de Moriana* (2nd edition, p. 248; 3rd edition, p. 222)
2nd edition only:
measure 5: the first note is a half-note.
measure 11: the second note should be a dotted-quarter.
measure 12: the first note should be a dotted-quarter.
measure 13: the third note should be a dotted-quarter.

measure 14: the first note should be a dotted-quarter.
last measure: this note is a dotted-half note.
3rd edition only:
measure 7: an eighth-rest is missing before the last eighth-note.
measure 10: a quarter-rest is missing after the first quarter-note.
measure 12: the first note is a dotted-quarter.
measure 14: the last eighth-note given as an *f*-natural should be an *f*-sharp as shown in the 2nd edition.

13. *La mala suegra* (2nd edition, p. 249; 3rd edition, p. 224)
2nd edition only:
measure 8: the first note is an ornamental note or a kind of anticipatory note preceding the first eighth-note *e*. It was undoubtedly meant to be sung on the beat, giving this and the following note the value of sixteenth-notes.
Both editions:
measure 9: an eighth-rest should follow the first note.

14. *Hermanas reina y cautiva* (2nd edition, p. 250; 3rd edition, p. 225)
2nd edition only:
measure 9: the first quarter-note is *d*.

15. *El rapto* (2nd edition, p. 251; 3rd edition, p. 226)
There are no notational errors.

16. *Búcar sobre Valencia* (2nd edition, p. 252; 3rd edition, p. 227)
2nd edition only:
measure 21: the last eighth-note is *c*.
last measure: the quarter-note is *b*.

17. *La lavandera de San Juan* (2nd edition, p. 252; 3rd edition, p. 229)
2nd edition only: the melody was printed upside down.
measure 2: sixteenth-rest must be inserted between the eighth-rest and the sixteenth-note.
measure 3: same as above.
measure 4: the figure on the second beat is a triplet.
measure 5: same as measure 4 above.

18. *Moriana y Galván* (2nd edition, p. 255; 3rd edition, p.230)
2nd edition only:
measure 6: the first note is a quarter.
measure 10: the rhythm is given as ♪♪♪ while in the 3rd edition it is shown as ♪♪♪ .
measure 12: the figure on the first beat is a triplet.

measure 15: last eighth note given as a^1; in 3rd edition given as g.
measure 16: same as measure 12 above.
3rd edition only:
measure 3: what appears as a dot after the first note is misleading. The rhythm should read ♩♪ (c^1 and d^1 respectively).

19. *Catalina* (2nd edition, p. 257; 3rd edition, p. 231)
2nd edition only:
measure 5: the note d is a dotted-quarter.
measure 8: the note values are given here as ♩♪ while in the 3rd edition they are reversed.
measure 14: the pitches should be d, b, and a respectively.
measure 15: the note following the eighth-rest is a.
measure 16: the second note is an eighth.
Both editions:
last measure: an eighth-rest should follow the first note.

20. *El huérfano* (2nd edition, p. 258; 3rd edition, p. 232)
2nd edition only:
measure 3: the first note is a dotted-quarter.
measure 9: pitches given as e, d, b; whereas in 3rd edition indicated as d, c, b.
measure 10: pitches should be b, a, and a, respectively, to agree with 3rd edition.
measure 13: a slur is indicated under the second, third, and fourth eighth-notes, whereas in the 3rd edition, the slur is omitted.
3rd edition only: time signature, $\frac{3}{4}$, is missing.

21. *Delgadina* (2nd edition, p. 259; 3rd edition, p. 235)
2nd edition only:
measure 2: shows second quarter-note as g, whereas in the 3rd edition it is shown as a^1.
measure 3: all eighth-notes are connected by one stem. In the 3rd edition, the notes are divided into three pairs of eighth-notes.
last measure: the last dotted-quarter note is c.

22. *La infantina* (2nd edition, p. 261; 3rd edition, p. 235)
2nd edition only:
measure 2: the last note is a quarter.
measure 8: the first note is a dotted-quarter.
last measure: the note is a half-note while in the 3rd edition it is inaccurately given as a dotted-half.

In view of the textual and notational inconsistencies which exist between the original and subsequent editions of *Los hebreos en Marruecos*, it is remarkable that this work has been used as a "standard reference" for Sephardic balladry in one or another of its editions. Even the common allusion to Bustelo's if not at times to Ortega's "twenty-two" romances, is erroneous.[1] The fact of the matter is that there are only twenty-one ballads in this collection;[2] the seventh item, *Por las torres de Gibraltar*, is actually a narrative song, also strophic and in quatrain form.

Taking into account the above corrections for the musical notations, we can draw the following observations from Bustelo's transcriptions:

1. All twenty-one *romance* melodies were notated in the treble clef and in vocal style.

---

[1] See page 44, note 1. In addition, among those who cited the 1919 edition were E. Gerson-Kiwi (*Die Musik in Geschichte und Gegenwart*, VII (1958), col. 278), A. Z. Idelsohn (*Jewish Music*, p. 516, n. 13 and *Gesänge der marokkanischen Juden*, p. 1, n. 5, where he attributed the twenty-two ballads to Ortega), and A. Šendrey (*Bibliography of Jewish Music*, p. 65, item No. 1449). The 3rd edition was cited by M. J. Benardete (*Hispanic Culture and Character of Sephardic Jews*, p. 184), M. García Blanco (*Historia General de las literaturas hispánicas*, II, p. 47), and S. Marcus (השפה הספרדית־יהודית, p. 172, item No. 457), while the 4th edition was mentioned by R. Menéndez Pidal (*Romancero Hispánico*, II, 332)· In the latter case, Menéndez Pidal attributed the ballads to Ortega instead of Bustelo.

[2] It is important to bear in mind that the titles given in many of the collections were usually those transmitted to the collector by the informant, or in the majority of instances, those represented by the first lines. I have chosen to bring all these titles within the framework of common themes, so that they may be readily located for comparative studies. See page 21, note 3.

The ballad texts for which melodies are present can be identified as follows: *Mujer guerrera*, MP 121 (2nd ed., p. 236; 3rd ed., p. 210); *El rey envidioso de su sobrino*, hexasyllabic, MP 123 (2nd ed., p. 237; 3rd ed., p. 211); *Vuelta del marido* (é), MP 59 (2nd ed., p. 238; 3rd ed., p. 212); *Grandes bodas hay en Francia*, MP 95 (2nd ed., p. 240; 3rd ed., p. 214); *Diego León*, MP 63 (2nd ed., p. 241; 3rd ed., p. 215); *El capitán burlado*, MP 117 (2nd ed., p. 243; 3rd ed., p. 217); *Amnón y Tamar*, MP 37 (2nd ed., p. 244; 3rd ed., p. 218); *Aliarda*, MP 102 (2nd ed., p. 245; 3rd ed., p. 219); *La mujer engañada*, hexasyllabic, MP 74 (2nd ed., p. 246; 3rd ed., 221); *El veneno de Moriana*, MP 86 (2nd ed., p. 248; 3rd ed., p. 222); *La mala suegra*, MP 70 (2nd ed., p. 249; 3rd ed., p. 224); *Hermanas reina y cautiva*, MP 48 (2nd ed., p. 250; 3rd ed., p. 225); *El rapto* (*i-a*), hexasyllabic, MP 94 (2nd ed., p. 251; 3rd ed., p. 226); *La lavandera de San Juan*, MP 134 (2nd ed., p. 254; 3rd ed., p. 229); *Moriana y Galván*, MP 61 (2nd ed., p. 255; 3rd ed., p. 230); *Catalina*, MP 67 (2nd ed., p. 257; 3rd ed., p. 231); *El huérfano*, MP 122 (2nd ed., p. 258; 3rd ed., p. 232); *Delgadina*, MP 99 (2nd ed., p. 259; 3rd ed., p. 234); and *La infantina*, MP 114 (2nd ed. p. 261; 3rd ed., p. 235).

The ballad *Búcar sobre Valencia*, MP 6, is preceded by *Garcilasso*, Wolf and Hoffman, *Primavera y Flor*, No. 93, which does not appear in the *Catálogo* (2nd ed., p. 252; 3rd ed., p. 227); and *La jactancia del conde Vélez* is also not listed in the *Catálogo* (2nd ed., p. 239; 3rd ed., p. 213).

2. Key signatures were employed which would keep the melodies in the confines of the staff; two exceptions however, *Catalina* and *El huérfano*, resort to the second leger line below the staff. Bustelo was favorable to signatures containing sharps: three sharps for eight melodies, two for six melodies, and one for two melodies. Only in one instance did he employ flats: two flats for *La infantina*. The remaining four melodies are without key signatures.

3. For time signatures: seven melodies employed 2/4, six 3/4, five 3/8, and three have the accepted designation for common time. This distribution seems rather peculiar, especially after one has witnessed the preponderant use of 6/8 for all those ballads collected in Morocco by Manrique de Lara.

4. Tempo markings are indicated in Italian with a distribution ranging from slow to fast as follows: Andante for six examples, Moderato for five, Allegretto for nine, and Allegro for one.

5. Since not all the editions underlay the texts, it must not be presumed that Bustelo failed to carry out this duty, either for the ballads in those editions or for his own personal collection. Without the advantage of text underlay, it would be risky indeed to attempt to establish formal structures for these ballads, based upon a tune-textual relationship. Here, if we take Bustelo's phrasing as a possible indication of syllable placement, we are still faced with those instances where a surplus or lack of notes leave us baffled. In this regard, we can only venture a guess concerning their formal structure. However, any attempt to solve these formal problems should be based upon a thorough comparison of thematic-melodic variants in other published Moroccan collections.

Seventeen examples appear unquestionably as quatrains with the following distribution: twelve with the formal structure ABCD, of which *La jactancia del conde Vélez* carries the form $AB^{w+x}C^{w+y}D^{w+z}$; three AA'BC, and one $AAB^{x+y}C^{x+z}$ (*El rapto*). Those examples which are difficult to judge may be classified with regard to their melody sections: ABCDD' for *Mujer guerrera*; AABC[DEF] for *Diego León*; AA'BCDC' for *Aliarda* (see Example 5); and ABCDA'B' for *Moriana y Galván*.

An interesting feature may be noted in the opening melodic sections of five ballads. These sections could almost be set in some order which would suggest that they all spring from a common source; at its head the first example, *La lavandera de San Juan*, a simple triadic melody. *Mujer guerrera* can be considered as an extension of the first example, while in *Vuelta del marido*(é), although the opening motit is repeated, the profile is maintained except for the final note. The fourth melody, *La jactancia del conde Vélez*, could be a minor variant of *Mujer guerrera*. Finally, *Amnón y Tamar*, although in a different mode, still shows a basic kinship through its contour.

Example 5:

Andante   a. La Lavandera de San Juàn

Moderato   b. Mujer guerrera

Andante   c. Vuelta del marido

Andante   d. La Jactancia del Conde Vélez

Andante   e. Amnón y Tamar

6. As to their modal structure, fourteen are in the major mode, three in the minor (*Búcar sobre Valencia, La infantina,* and *La jactancia del conde Vélez*), three are Aeolian (*El veneno de Moriana, Grandes bodas en Francia,* and *El rey envidioso de su sobrino*), and one is Mixolydian (*La mala suegra*). Notice that *Diego León*, which is predominantly in the major mode, has Mixolydian tendencies with its use of g-natural in measures 18 and 19. Moreover, twelve of these are plagal modes and end on the fifth degree. The remainder, in the authentic mode, end on the *finalis*. The example *El rey envidioso de su sobrino* may be considered in the category of the "gapped scale," since the note g, which would function here as the sixth degree of the tune's Aeolian modality built upon the *finalis* b^1, is missing. By arranging the pitches of this melody in an ascending order of pitch, we obtain:

However, should we now rearrange this order so that all the pitches are properly connected, at the same time omitting the octave repetitions, we have in effect the traditional hexachord , which may reveal the historical importance of this melody.

7. Concerning the ambitus of the melodies in question, the octave prevails in thirteen examples. Those which exceed the octave are *Búcar sobre Valencia, La mujer engañada,* and *El rey envidioso de su sobrino* (major 9th); *Delgadina* and *La lavandera de San Juan* (minor 10th); *Grandes bodas en Francia* and *Aliarda* (major 10th); and *Catalina* (major 11th).

8. The melodies are basically diatonic in character, with some triadic features normally outlining the triad of the *finalis*. However, the triadic quality of *La lavandera de San Juan* is quite remarkable, above and beyond the first melody section which was given above.

Example 6: *La lavandera de San Juan*

Thirds can be found in all but one example (*Vuelta del marido* [é]). Intervals of the 4th occur in thirteen examples, while 5ths are found in seven examples. Four melodies contain leaps of a 6th (*Moriana y Galván, La mala suegra, Mujer guerrera,* and *El rey envidioso de su sobrino*). The leap of an octave can be found in two examples (*Moriana y Galván* and *Aliarda*). Somewhat startling is the opening of *El rey envidioso de su sobrino* with its double 4ths, here seen with the leap of a minor 6th in the fourth measure:

Example 7: *El rey envidioso de su sobrino*

9. Rhythmically speaking, the most stereotyped pattern is that which accompanies *Vuelta del marido* (é). The ballad deals with a knight who, returning from the battles against the English, is reunited with his wife after a brief period of interrogation leading up to their happy reunion. Here we are confronted by a martial pattern which pervades the whole ballad:

10. As pointed out above, because Bustelo's ballads were not printed with their texts underlaid, we cannot discuss the text-tune relationship. Even if one should attempt to underlay the texts properly, it should be borne in mind that Bustelo's notations leave us without the clues necessary for such an undertaking, inasmuch as we cannot state with assuredness whether these are instrumental or vocal notations. And, of course, it goes without saying, that the mistakes in notation outlined above should by no means be considered final, especially were we to rely upon the slur indications for the placement of text syllables.

11. In many instances, the lack of properly underlaid texts makes it quite impossible to guess which syllables in a particular hemistich carried its melismatic figurations. However, certain ballads, such as *Amnón y Tamar* and *Aliarda*, appear to be quite ornamental in character.[1] The latter example may prove useful:

Example 8: *Aliarda*

It is questionable whether Bustelo employed the indication $\overline{|\quad 5\quad}$ in its literal sense. I suggest that he may have meant 5/4 for those measures so indicated.

Bustelo also utilized the grace note and grace-note pairs as well as triplets, ties, and slurs. The riddle of the Bustelo ballads is yet to be solved. Nonetheless, the melodies were copied by a professional musician well steeped in the European tradition. We can only hope that Bustelo's ballad collection will some day come to light.[2]

A. Z. IDELSOHN AND EUGÈNE BORREL: A CLARIFICATION

Abraham Zevi Idelsohn (1882-1938) was the first musicologist to attempt a systematic study of the sacred and secular music of the Jewish people, utilizing the comparative method with significant analytical procedures. It was his aim "to give a description and an analysis of the elements and characteristics

---

[1] The notation for *Amnón y Tamar* can be found under note 66 *supra*.
[2] For additional insights into the Bustelo ballads, see Israel J. Katz, "The Enigma of the Bustelo Ballads in Manuel L. Oretega's *Los Hebreos en Marruecos*," to appear in the *International Folk Music Council, Yearbook* (1971).

of Jewish music, in their historical development, from the earliest times of its appearance as a Semitic-Oriental song, throughout the ages and countries."[1] The realization of this purpose was the product of twenty-five years of laborious field research, the materials of which comprised the monumental *Hebräisch-orientalischer Melodienschatz*,[2] printed in ten volumes over a period of nineteen

---

[1] *Jewish Music*, preface, p. iii.
[2] The enigma of the publication of the *Hebräisch-orientalischer Melodienschatz* in German, English, and Hebrew editions has never been fully clarified. Even Idelsohn led us to believe that this work was to be printed as a trilingual enterprise.

From an investigation of the matter, I conclude that only the German edition was completed. It was brought out in volumes printed in the following order:

  I: Gesänge der jeminischen Juden (1914), 158 pp.
  II: Gesänge der babylonischen Juden (1922), 140 pp.
  III: Gesänge der persischen, bucharischen und dahestanischen Juden (1922), li, 68 pp.
  IV: Gesänge der orientalischen Sephardim (1923), 280 pp.
  V: Gesänge der marokkanischen Juden (1929), 119 pp.
  VI: Der Synagogen-Gesang der deutschen Juden im 19. Jahrhundert (1932), 234 pp.
  VII: Die traditionellen Gesänge der süddeutschen Juden (1932), 181 pp.
  VIII: Der Synagogen-Gesang der osteuropäischen Juden (1932), 143 pp.
  IX: Der Volksgesang der osteuropäischen Juden (1932), 211 pp.
  X: Gesänge der Chassidim (1932), 72 pp.

The English edition, the *Thesaurus of Hebrew Oriental Melodies*, contained only the following volumes:

  I: Songs of the Yemenite Jews (1925), 117 pp.
  II: Songs of the Babylonian Jews (1923), 140 pp.
  VI: Synagogue Songs of the German Jews in the 18th Century (1932), xxvi, 234 pp.
  VII: The Traditional Songs of the South German Jews (1933), lix, 181 pp.
  VIII: The Synagogue Song of the East European Jews (1932), xxxiv, 143 pp.
  IX: Folk Song of the East European Jews (1932), xlii, 211 pp.
  X: Songs of the Chassidim (1932), xxix, 72 pp.

The eminent musicologist Dr. Alfred Šendrey, in his most valuable *Bibliography of Jewish Music* (New York, 1951), p. 21, listed the full citation for the German edition yet did not mention those volumes which appeared in English.

The Hebrew edition, אוצר נגינות ישראל ['*Oẓar Neginot Yisrael*'], comprises only the following:

  I: נגינות יהודי תימן ['Neginot Yehudai Teman'] (1924), x, 117 pp.
  II: נגינות יהודי בבל ['Neginot Yehudai Bavel'] (1922), ix, 140 pp.
  III: נגינות יהורי פרס, בוכרא ודגיסטן ['Neginot Yehudai Paras, Boḥara, u-Dagestan'] (1922), viii, 68 pp.
  IV: נגינות יהודי ספרדי המזרח ['Neginot Yehudai Sefaradai ha-Mizraḥ'] (1923), xv, 280 pp.
  V: נגינות יהודי מרוקו ['Neginot Yehudai Marokko'] (1928), xi, 119 pp.

Šendrey, *loc. cit.*, item No. 439, cites a Hebrew edition of *Ozar Neginot Yisrael* (1922-28), 3 vols., 5 parts, which he found at the New York Public Library. He also listed 1929 as the year of publication for the fifth volume of the Hebrew edition.

Idelsohn's *Jewish Music and its Historical Development* was published when the first five of his ten volumes were already issued, and on p. 344 of this edition, we learn that volume VI of the German edition was still in press.

A recent reprinting (1965) of the *Hebräisch-orientalischer Melodienschatz* has been issued,

years (1914-1933), and culminating in an interpretive work which has long been considered the basic contribution to the field, *Jewish Music in Its Historical Development* (New York, 1929).[1] This unique endeavor was outstanding not only because it treated the musical practices of the various Oriental and East-European Jewish communities, but also in that it contained documented historical and cultural materials together with invaluable musical transcriptions made with the aid of a recording apparatus. In Idelsohn's own words, concerning the collecting and processing:

> The entire collection [was] copiled by the method of recording traditional tunes phonographically, transcribing the music from the plates, comparing the phonographical records with the performance by various people of one and the same tune, in order to ascertain those characteristics of each tune common to all traditions.[2]

However, we are concerned here mainly with the fourth and fifth volumes of the *Hebräisch-orientalischer Melodienschatz*, i.e., the *Gesänge der orientalischen Sephardim*[3] and the *Gesänge der marokkanischen Juden*,[4] respectively. An investigation of both works shows that the differences between the Eastern- (Balkans, Near East) and Western-(Morocco) Sephardic traditions were already apparent to Idelsohn. The musical notations of the fourth volume were taken from Palestinian informants representing such countries as Serbia, Bulgaria, Greece, Turkey, etc., while those of the fifth volume are representative of informants from Morocco.

A perusal of the fourth volume shows how Idelsohn compared his collected field materials with musical notations published in other prominent collections of Sephardic music in order to designate their common scales and melodic

---

together with a reprinting of the seven-volume English edition and volumes I-IV only of the Hebrew edition. Available through B. M. Israël, Amsterdam.

Concerning the publishers for the editions listed above, Benjamin Harz (Jerusalem, Berlin, and Vienna) was responsible for the first five volumes while F. Hofmeister (then Leipzig) printed volumes six through ten. Breitkopf und Härtel made the musical plates for all the volumes.

[1] Subsequently the work has undergone two reprintings: the first, by the Tudor Publishing Company (New York, 1948); and the second, issued in paperback, by Schocken Books, Inc. (New York, 1967).

[2] *Ibid.*, p. 344. For an interesting synopsis of this work, see Idelsohn's "Phonographierte Gesänge und Aussprachsproben des Hebräischen, der jemenitischen, persischen und syrischen Juden," *Sitzungsberichte der kaiserlichen Akademie der Wissenschaften in Wien*, 175. Band 4. Abhandlung (Vienna, 1917), 119 pp. Idelsohn, *Jewish Music, op. cit.*, erroneously cites this as volume 171.

[3] Idelsohn, *loc. cit.*, explains that the Hebrew edition of Vol. IV is enriched with more folkloristic materials, while the German edition presents more musical research studies. Šendrey obviously took the cue from Idelsohn, *loc. cit.*, when he listed an English edition of Vol. IV in his *Bibliography of Jewish Music*, p. 21. See page 61, note 2.

[4] See page 61, note 2.

structures. Furthermore, he took particular care to compare these materials with those from Spanish sources dating back to the fifteenth century. Realizing the need for background information for an understanding of the basic concepts of Near Eastern music, he included a chapter on Arabic music and concluded this imposing work with a discussion of the parallels between the Spanish and Slavic folksong.

Idelsohn acknowleged the presence of Castilian *romances* preserved among the Oriental Sephardim and added that they even created new songs — texts as well as melodies — in their new environment, especially in such communities as Salonika and Istanbul.[1] In his *Jewish Music*, he called attention to the *romances* in Ortega's *Los hebreos en Marruecos* (1919 edition),[2] and published four of the melodies from that collection in volume five of the *Melodienschatz*.[3] However, Idelsohn was unaware of the works of Max Leopold Wagner[4] and J. Subak[5] and such distinguished Turkish scholars as Abraham Danon[6] and Abraham Galante.[7] Also startling is the omission of the noted lexicographer Salomon Israel Cherezli (d. 1937),[8] among the notable Sephardim who lived in Jerusalem in the latter part of the nineteenth century and during Idelsohn's residence there.[9] Most assuredly, Idelsohn was totally ignorant of the *Catálogo*. Had he known of it, he certainly would have pursued the music of Sephardic balladry at a time when the tradition in Jerusalem was still in its heyday.

Of the twenty-three secular songs included at the end of volume four,

---

[1] Vol. IV, p. 50.
[2] P. 516, n. 13.
[3] P. 16.
[4] M. L. Wagner, "Beiträge zur Kenntnis des Judenspanischen von Konstantinopel," *Kaiserliche Akademie der Wissenschaften. Schriften der Balkankommission. Linguistische Abteilung. II. Romanische Dialektstudien*. Heft III (Vienna, 1914).
[5] J. Subak, "Vorläufiger Bericht über eine ... Forschungsreise nach der Balkanhalbinsel zur schriftlichen und phonographischen Aufnahme des Judenspanischen," *Balkan-Kommission der kais. Akademie der Wissenschaften in Wien: Anzeiger der philosophisch-historischen Klasse*, Heft IV (Vienna, 1910).
[6] A. Danon, "Recueil de romances judéo-espagnoles chantées en Turquie," *Revue de Études Juives*, XXXII (1896), 102-123, 263-275; XXXIII (1896), 122-139, 255-268.
[7] A. Galante, "Quatorze romances judéo-espagnoles," *Revue Hispanique*, X (1903), 594-606.
[8] Cherezli is known for his *Nouveau petit dictionnaire judéo-espagnol-français*, 2 vols. (Jerusalem, 1898-1899). He was also fond of the *Romancero* and engaged in collecting ballads among the Sephardic residents of Jerusalem. In 1960, I was able to purchase a collection of his ballads in MS from his son, Aḥinoam Cherezli, and presented these to my colleagues, S. G. Armistead and J. H. Silverman, who published them in "Judeo-Spanish Ballads in a MS by Salomon Israel Cherezli," *Studies in Honor of M. J. Benardete* (New York, 1965), pp. 367-387.
[9] The list of distinguished Sephardim can be found in Vol. IV, pp. 15-16.

under the English-Hebrew-German titles, "Spanish Songs — שירים בהספניולית — Spanische Lieder," three can be identified as ballads.[1] However, a most precarious situation has arisen here, since two of the ballads in question were also purported to have been collected by the French musicologist, Eugène Borrel (1876-1962).[2] The problem can be outlined in the following manner:

1. Around the year 1918, Borrel, serving in the capacity of military interpreter, made an expedition to Salonika where he had an opportunity to hear "mélodies israélities."[3] Borrel collected several melodies from a male and a female singer and made his notations the subject of a communication which he presented to the Société Française de Musicologie on 17th December 1920. This communication was finally published in the *Revue de Musicologie*, VII, No. 12 (Nov., 1924), 164-168.[4]

2. Idelsohn's melodies, published as items 476 through 500 at the end of volume four, *are direct copies* of Borrel's notations with some deviations in editing.[5] Nonetheless, it is curious that Idelsohn's volume four appeared in 1923, a year before Borrel's communication was printed. Even more striking is the fact that Idelsohn, who always took care to acknowledge his sources, omitted references for these melodies other than mentioning that they were of Salonikan origin.[6]

3. How then can one account for this situation, when Idelsohn had for long been cited as the sole collector of the melodies in question? There is reason to believe that Idelsohn came upon these musical notations through a third party who had copied out the melodies either at the time or shortly after Borrel's communication to the *Société de Musicologie*. If these melodies were not made known to Idelsohn while he was in Jerusalem, then we may speculate

---

[1] *Ibid.*, pp. 275-280. The three melodies which contain ballad texts are identified as: *El sueño profético*, MP 68 (Item No. 499, p. 280), which is identical to MP 129. *El villano vil*, MP 139 (Item No. 500, p. 280); and a ballad not listed in the *Catálogo*, *La sentencia del bajá* (Item No. 480, p. 275).
[2] The first two ballads listed above.
[3] Isaac Molho asserts that he together with Borrel collected *romances* from Jewish singers in Salonika, and that these were published after the war. See "מקורותיו והוקריו של הרומאנסירו ['The Sources and Scholars of the Romancero']," *Les Cahiers de l'Alliance Israélite Universelle*, IV (Jerusalem, 1955), 108.
[4] Through the kindness of Henri Guilloux, a personal friend of the late Eugène Borrel, I have in my possession the original galley proof for the "Mélodies Israélites," which was to have been corrected by Borrel before its inclusion in the 1924 issue of *Revue de Musicologie*. In note 1 of this proof, Borrel mentions the communication and the date of its presentation, but the note did not appear in the final printing.
[5] Only four of the five melodies from Borrel's article appear in Idelsohn's work. Idelsohn No. 497 is Borrel's item IV (p. 167). Likewise No. 498 corresponds to item III (pp. 166-167); No. 499 to item I (p. 166); and No. 500 to item II (p. 166).
[6] Vol. IV, p. 51.

that he must have come upon them after he left Palestine in 1921 and took up temporary residence in Berlin, where he began the preparations for printing his monumental *Hebräisch-orientalischer Melodienschatz* with the publisher Benjamin Harz. There were numerous opportunities for him to make contact with participants of the Society's meetings, since up to the time of the printing of volume four he had made several visits to Paris and other important European cities.[1] Whether or not he came in contact with Borrel is difficult to establish; however, Idelsohn most certainly would have commented upon such a meeting.

Still, the fact remains that Idelsohn placed these melodies at the end of his collection, and, judging by their notation, they are quite obviously out of character with the Spanish songs preceding them. Why Idelsohn did not include Borrel's fifth melody is explained by the fact that Borrel included his fifth example only at the time of publication in 1924.[2]

Nonetheless, Idelsohn may have edited these melodies to suit his own notions of the tradition as he knew it. I shall reproduce here only the notations of the two *romances* included in the *Gesänge der orientalischen Sefardim*, placing Idelsohn's deviations above Borrel's transcriptions. It seems highly improbable that both men could have interviewed independently the same informant. Variation is the rule and essence of oral recitation. Even if these melodies had been transcribed twice and on the same day, there would undoubtedly have been much more variation than is manifested in the mirror-like correspondence between the Idelsohn and Borrel transcriptions.

Example 9: *El sueño profético*

Idelsohn No. 499

Borrel No. 1

Hay el rey de Francia   Tres hi----jas te--ni--------a.

---

[1] This information was made available to me by A. Irma Cohon, who worked closely with Idelsohn from the time he had first settled in Cincinnati, Ohio, in 1924 up to 1937, the year before his death, when as an invalid he was transported to Johannesburg, South Africa, to be with his family.

[2] Borrel, *op. cit.*, p. 165, added the fifth melody, "Reina de la gratia," for comparative purposes. It was dictated to him in Izmir around 1900 by a Jewish musician, Santo Chikiar.

la u-na la-vra- - - - - - - - - - - -va Y la   o-tra   cu- - - - si- - - - - - - - - - a.

[Translation: Oh, the King of France had three daughters; one was weaving, the other was sewing . . .]

Borrel took notice of the melismatic formulæ on the last syllable of each hemistisch, which led him to believe that the tune may have been of Mozarabic origin. Considering the question of modality, he found it "rather strange," but ventured to say that it could have been influenced by Anatolian music.[1] Idelsohn, on the other hand, attributed to this melody the modal designation of a popular Arabic melody-type, the *Hidjaz* maqam. However, his key signature should have been given as [music notation] instead of [music notation] to conform to his own description of this maqam.[2] A careful look at the above example will bear out the fact that Idelsohn did not adhere to the key signature in its literal sense. Only in the last line do we see it unfold in the final melody section, especially in the eighth-note pattern after the third *fermata* where the characteristic augmented-2nd interval is present. The *fermata* signs above the final note of each melody section were probably added by Idelsohn.

The second melody, which Borrel labelled as the "deuxième mode grégorien en *la* avec cadence iastienne [Istrian],"[3] was not commented upon at length by Idelsohn except for the mention that it had "Greek coloring" along with the other examples from Salonika.[4] Again, we may take notice of the errors present in Idelsohn's examples. In spite of the suggested attempt by Idelsohn to revise these melodies in part, the notational and textual errors were undoubtedly the result of poor copying.

Example 10: *El villano vil*

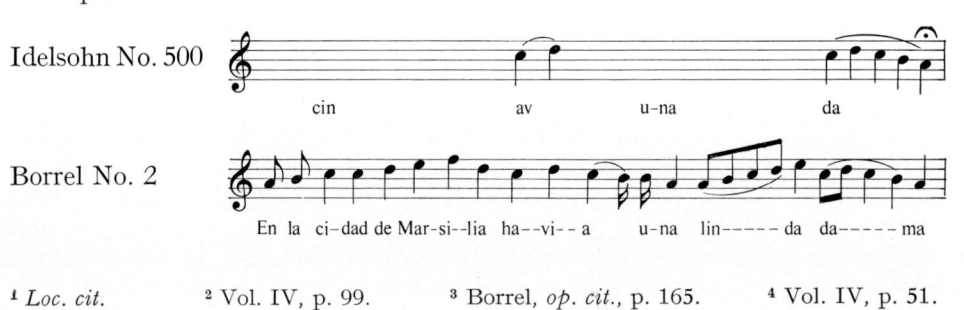

Idelsohn No. 500

cin   av   u-na   da

Borrel No. 2

En la ci-dad de Mar-si--lia ha--vi- - a   u-na lin- - - - -da da- - - - -ma

[1] *Loc. cit.*   [2] Vol. IV, p. 99.   [3] Borrel, *op. cit.*, p. 165.   [4] Vol. IV, p. 51.

se to-ca-va-y s'a-fei-ta---va y se a--sen--ta-va a la ven----ta--------na.

Por a--hi do de nu

Po-ra-hi pa-so un mu-cha-ci-co ves--ti--do de ga------ la De hav-lar me da-

yo na

va ga-na la di---jo Sel---vi yo con mi ga-la---na me quie---ro ir.

[Translation: In the city of Marseilles, there was a beautiful lady. She arranged her hair and adorned herself and sat at the window. A young fellow passed by all dressed in finery, "I feel like talking." Selvi answered, "I have my own girl and I want to go with her."]

With regard to the above examples, both may be considered as being in the *parlando-rubato* style, which is indicated by their manner of transcription. The first, a quatrain strophe based on the melodic stanza structure ABCD, has an ambitus of a major 7th and can be said to be in the Dorian mode with the lowered seventh degree functioning as a *subfinalis*. The chromatic alterations occurring on the notes *e* and *b-flat*[1] were the clues which made Idelsohn consider the modal aspects of the melody in terms of maqamat.

The second example, which Borrel called the Gregorian Hypodorian, is, in reality, the Aeolian mode and can be felt with much assurance in sight reading the melodic line. However, the formal structure of this ballad is that of the couplet, indicated as AB, with the range of a minor 7th. Here, Borrel notated four strophes; still, one should not be fooled by the seemingly rather different melodic pattern of the last strophe since a closer scrutiny will reveal it as a further variant of the first melodic strophe. Furthermore, one may consider this as one of the first examples of a Judeo-Spanish ballad for which several strophes were notated, enabling us to see how each verse underwent variation in the process of singing.

ALBERTO HEMSI (1898-   )

One of the most publicized endeavors in the field of Sephardic folklore and music has been the *Coplas sefardíes*,[1] published by Alberto Hemsi while he was serving as director of Édition Orientale de Musique in Alexandria.[2] Hemsi, long considered an outstanding spokesman for Sephardic culture, was born in Kasaba, Anatolia, and was raised on the Island of Rhodes in a thoroughly Eastern Mediterranean ambience. At the age of twelve, he went to Izmir for the purpose of studying composition with Shem Tov Shikayar and cantorial music with the well-known חזן, Rabbi Yitzḥak Algaze.[3] Both men were impressed with Hemsi's talent and, within three years, the young man was sent to Milan where he continued his musical education at the Royal Conservatory of Music. When the First World War broke out, his studies were interrupted and he returned to Izmir to work as a musician and educator. In his early twenties, Hemsi became intensely active in composition, which later earned him prizes in Rome, Warsaw, Cairo, Paris and New York, and gained him membership in the Italian Association of Composers and Publishers in 1924.[4]

Upon his return to Izmir, Hemsi felt called upon to gather and preserve the living oral tradition of the Sephardim. From 1923 to 1927, Hemsi devoted himself to collecting Sephardic, Turkish and Greek materials in the various centers of Turkey, Greece, and the islands of the Dodecanese, particularly Rhodes.[5] Thus, before the publication of the first fascicle of *Coplas sefardíes*,

---

[1] *Coplas scfardíes* (*Chansons judéo-espagnoles*). Alexandria: Édition Orientale de Musique, 1932-1938. The actual printing was done by Imprimerie de Musique G. & P. Mignani, Florence.

[2] In 1956, Hemsi left Egypt, where for thirty years he had been employed as the musical director of the Grand Temple de la Communauté Israélite. Since then, he has resided in France and has held such positions as music director at the "Bérith Šalom" Sephardic Synagogue of Paris and instructor of music at a Seminary for Rabbis.

[3] Information concerning Algaze can be found in José M. Estrugo, *Los sefardíes* (La Habana, 1958), p. 126, and Isaac Levy, "Rabbi Yitzhak Chlomo Algazi," *Le Judaïsme Séphardi*, No. 23 (December, 1961), 1007.

[4] These biographical notes were taken from Isaac R. Molho, *Tesoro de los judíos sefardíes*, II (Jerusalem, 5719/1959), 111-113.

[5] Communicated by Hemsi, Nov. 8, 1966. He continued to make sporadic trips to Rhodes until 1938.

Hemsi had already made his mark as a composer and had also published several articles on the music of the Sephardic Jews.[1]

Coplas sefardíes consists of a series of five installments, designated by opus numbers, which were issued separately from 1932 to 1938. Each fascicle contains six songs originating in a particular Sephardic community. The first and second parts, Op. 7 (1932) and Op. 8 (1933) spring from the tradition of Rhodes, Op. 13 (1934) and Op. 18 (1935) from Salonika, and Op. 22 (1938) from Izmir.[2]

The highly romanticized preface supplied by José Subirá was reprinted in each fascicle of the series. Commencing with the third installment, Subirá enlarged the preface with a few additional paragraphs of praise for Hemsi's work by Spanish and French critics. Hemsi also contributed historical insights into the communities represented and made comments upon the musical items as well.

The entire collection was presented under the generic title *coplas*, which is a popular designation for many of the Sephardic folksongs found in Eastern Mediterranean countries. Of the thirty melodies in this collection, half are *romances*.[3] On the one hand, Subirá alluded to Menéndez Pidal's work con-

---

[1] Hemsi published a series of articles in the journal *Il Messagero di Rodi* under the title "Rhodas a través de su aspecto folklórico musical." These articles dealt primarily with Sephardic, Turkish, and Greek culture in the city of Rhodes.

While director of Édition Orientale de Musique, Hemsi wrote a pamphlet entitled *El Oriente a través de la Música*, [n.d.], which dealt with the impact of Westernization upon the people of the Near East, and here the called attention to the musical art of these people as it related to the æsthetic requirements of contemporary life. He also discussed "its usefulness as an element of oriental culture on one hand and as a link in the development of the relations between East and West on the other." See Subirá's preface in *Coplas sefardíes*, no page given. Also, under Hemsi's directorship, a twenty-page booklet was published on *La Musique de la Torah* (Alexandria, 1929). In this work Hemsi transcribed in modern notation several passages from the Torah which were normally written with the liturgical accents. A synopsis of this latter work can be found in *Le Monde Musical*, XL (Paris, July 31, 1929), 243-244.

[2] When Hemsi brought out Op. 22, he stated on p. xiii that "this book of songs . . . brings to light . . . a whole series of songs, hitherto unknown to the Jewish, Spanish and general intellectual worlds alike. The music in particular has never before been collected or published."

Opus 22-2, *Una matica de ruda* (= *Una ramica de ruda*), MP 107, was already alluded to as the earliest Judeo-Spanish ballad melody published. Manrique de Lara undoubtedly collected a number of themes which Hemsi published. One such ballad, Opus 22-1, *Don Bueso y su hermana*, MP 49, was collected by Manrique de Lara in Istanbul. See note 52 *supra*. The ballad, *Aquel rey de Francia*, MP 68, from Hemsi's Op. 13, No. 4 was previously collected by Borrel in Salonika and subsequently published. A copy of Borrel's ballad can be found in Idelsohn, *op. cit*.

[3] Following Hemsi's order of musical settings, the *romances* among them can be identified as: *Vos labraré yo un pendón*, MP 120 (Rhodes, I, Op. 7-1); *Landarico*, MP 82 (Rhodes,

cerning the Judeo-Spanish *Romancero*,[1] but Hemsi, on the other, made no reference to the renowned Spanish scholar, nor did he attempt to identify the ballads in conjunction with the *Catálogo*. Hemsi chose not to publish the bare melodies as he gathered them, but instead introduced each melody with an elaborate piano accompaniment. Subirá defended this procedure:

> No se contentó Hemsi con presentar el documento en plena desnudez, sino que, por el contrario, lo realza con acompañamientos pianísticos donde se esquivaron ciertos artificios que podrían desdibujar las fisonomías de los originales autóctonos o, por lo menos, atenuar sus relieves. Quiso, en suma, que el documento melódico se destacase con máxima nitidez sobre un fondo armónico adecuado. Ahora bien, si la opurtunidad lo impone, recuerda rasgueos de laud o de guitarra; y en ocasiones oportunas, incluso constituye ese complemento un fondo instrumental descriptivo, cuya misión no es la de entenebrecer o diluir, sino la de realzar o reforzar.[2]

In spite of this rather presumptuous manner of presentation, Hemsi emerged as a hero of sorts, not only because he retrieved a dying tradition, but also because he made these personal treasures known to audiences through his arrangements, which were suited for performance in salons and concert halls throughout Europe. From the author's note to Op. 8, dated 23rd March 1933, one can readily imagine the great popularity which the first installment enjoyed. It is easy to see how Hemsi, still very much the composer, was encouraged to continue the following fascicles in the same manner. After his second installment, Hemsi wrote harmonizations for more than one strophe and emphasized the accompaniment by increasing its variety. Concerning this procedure, Subirá again commented that this "contribuye a acrecentar el interés ante las viejas canciones sefardíes que aún se cantan por Oriente, con nostalgias de este Occidente tan añorado . . ."[3]

VIII, Op. 8-2); *Delgadina*, MP 99 (Rhodes, IX, Op. 8-3); *Princesa y el segador*, MP 108 (Salonika, XIII, Op. 13-1); *Grandes bodas en Francia*, MP 95 (Salonika, XIV, Op. 13-2, which Hemsi subtitled (Mexidéra = *Canción de cuna*); *El sueño profético*, MP 68, hexasyllabic (Salonika, XVI, Op. 13-4); *La adúltera (á-a)*, MP 80 (Salonika, XVII, Op. 13-5); *Conde Alarcos*, MP 68 + *La infanta deshonrada*, MP 106 (Salonika, XIX, Op. 18-1 with the subtitle *Canción de veladas de paridas*); *La galana y su caballo*, which is a much more explicit title than the customary *Romance para bodas*, MP 136 (Salonika, XX, Op. 18-2 with the subtitle *Canción de noches de almusáma*); *Celinos y la adúltera*, not included in the *Catálogo* (Salonika, XXII, Op. 18-4); *La novia sorteada*, not included in the *Catálogo* (Salonika, XXII, Op. 18-5); *Don Bueso y su hermana*, MP 49, hexasyllabic (Izmir, XXV, Op. 22-1); *Una ramica de ruda*, MP 107 (Izmir, XXVI, Op. 22-2); *Vuelta del hijo maldecido*, MP 124 (Izmir, XXVII, Op. 22-3); and, *La bella en misa*, MP 133 (Izmir, XXIX, Op. 22-5).

Two of Hemsi's ballad melodies, those for *Delgadina* and *Landarico*, can be found in a recent publication entitled *Cuatro canciones sefardíes* by Roberto Plá (Madrid, 1965). Plá set guitar accompaniments to these melodies but neglected to give credit to Hemsi as the source of these tunes.

[1] Preface, n.p.
[2] *Ibid.*
[3] *Ibid.*

Hemsi claims to have enlisted "the assistance of a great number of people of all ages and of the most diverse social conditions, in order to take down the largest possible number of musical and literary versions," but his elaborate endeavor at harmonizing these *coplas* for voice and piano leaves us without any indication of the spontaneous manner in which the ballads and other songs were rendered before he reconstructed his own theoretical prototypes. Although he made promising statements concerning the methods employed, the specific knowledge of these methods, together with the materials processed by Hemsi have been completely denied the musicologist and folklorist, both of whom could profit immensely from the labors of so capable a specialist working with materials so painstakingly gathered in his own "backyard." In Hemsi's own words:

> El material así recogido presentaba varias variantes sin ilación, con frecuencia incomprensibles y casi siempre con alteraciones en su métrica, compás y modalidad. En consecuencia, he debido comparar ante todo varias versiones literarias y musicales de un mismo poema, y eliminar o sustituir enseguida fragmentos de una de esas versiones por otros que parecían acomodarse a la tradición. Tal procedimiento, aunque lento y a veces complicado, me ha permitido reconstruir en las formas actuales una primera serie de melodías para canto y piano.[1]

Considerable interest in Hemsi's methods had already been aroused in a number of scholars, among whom were Eduardo Martínez Torner and José M. Estrugo, who, after having seen the first three installments of *Coplas sefardíes*, established contact with Hemsi. We are fortunate to have published fragments of a letter dated 1st June 1934, which is a reply by Estrugo to a letter written by Hemsi, the total content of which was not made known.[2] Estrugo sought the able assistance of Torner in outlining for Hemsi some practical procedures, undoubtedly those followed by the Folklore Division of the Centro de Estudios Históricos in Madrid:[3]

1. Record the greatest possible number of versions of *romances* and [other] Sephardic songs without harmonizing them. Include with each item the name, age, locale, region, etc. for each singer.
2. Of these materials, together with those already collected [by the folklorists] in Madrid, only those items of artistic and historical value will be picked for the study of the musical and poetical tradition of Spain. It is also hoped that some of the cultural and artistic organizations of Madrid would assist in the publication of a volume of these materials.

---

[1] Author's note to Opus 7, dated 15th May 1932. Hemsi probably meant textual versions rather than literary, since he does not cite any literary sources nor analogs for the materials in his collection.
[2] E. Martínez Torner, *Temas folklóricos: Música y poesía* (Madrid, 1935), pp. 55-57.
[3] Cf. Moshe Attias' classification in *Romancero sefaradí* (Jerusalem, 1956), pp. 272-77.

Furthermore, Estrugo believed that the Sephardic items could be classified into four groups:

1. *Romances* and other songs which issued from the era preceding the expulsion. [These, he felt, were in the greatest majority.]
2. The songs which were brought to the scattered Sephardic communities by *Marranos* after the expulsion and which survived up to the end of the seventeenth century.
3. Liturgical and semi-liturgical hymns composed by Sephardic rabbis in Spain and in the Near East which were sung during the holidays and the Sabbath in both Spanish and Hebrew. [These were the collections of *piyyutim* and *pizmonim*, respectively.]
4. Modern folkore, dating from the last hundred years, reflecting diverse Hispanic and non-Hispanic influences.

To what further extent Estrugo pursued a taxonomy for Sephardic folklore is not fully known. We can only infer from these early indications that the Centro de Estudios Históricos in Madrid had indeed considered the Sephardic branch of Hispanic culture as a vital area of investigation. Undoubtedly there was at this time a particular need for Sephardic scholars who could lay the foundation for a systematic study of Sephardic cultural history. Hemsi should have been the most able candidate for this task. Just as Hemsi would have profited considerably from working closely with scholars who were thoroughly versed in modern methodology, they in turn would have gained much from Hemsi's invaluable experience in the field, so necessary for a qualitative appraisal of the materials collected. Lamentably such a collaborative effort did not become a reality.

Because of the Civil War, which raged throughout Spain from 1936 through 1939, the work of the Centro de Estudios Históricos came to a halt.[1] Hemsi's work was suspended after the printing of his 1938 installment of the *Coplas sefardíes* because of the Second World War, which in a few years brought a nightmarish catastrophe to the Sephardim of the Balkan Peninsula and indeed to Hemsi's family in particular.

---

[1] The Centro de Estudios Históricos was known as the Junta para Amplicación de Estudios e Investigaciones Cientificas which formed part of the Ministerio de Instrucción Pública y Bellas Artes. The latter organization created the Archivo de la Palabra which contained among its vast holdings gramophone recordings of various Sephardic songs. From Jesús Bal y Gay we gather the particulars concerning the scope of activity of the above organizations. It is worth noting that Bal y Gay wrote his article in 1939, the year in which we have indicated that the work of the Junta came to an end. See Jesús Bal y Gay, "Espagne" in *Folklore Musical* (Paris, 1939), pp. 64-84.

The work of the Centro de Estudios Históricos probably came to its end when Eduardo M. Torner left Spain in 1939 after the Civil War to live in London, where he remained until his death in February, 1955.

Not much is known of Hemsi's activities during the War. However, from José Subirá we learn that Hemsi renewed correspondence with him near the close of 1949.[1] From this letter, we get an idea of Hemsi's creative output, as well as his personal outlook in the postwar years. Hemsi had prepared another two installments of the *Coplas sefardíes*,[2] among whose titles seven can be identified as *romances*.[3]

Since his arrival in Paris in 1965, Hemsi has continued to enrich his output of documents relating to Sephardic music and folklore.[4] Since much of his work still remains in manuscript form, we eagerly await the day when his valuable collection will be published under the auspices of interested organizations as a tribute to his unyielding and meritorious efforts.

We may draw the following observations from the vocal lines of Hemsi's ballads published in *Coplas sefardíes*:

1. All the ballad tunes are notated in vocal style and in the treble clef.

2. All key signatures keep the melodies within the confines of the staff. Two melodies modulate, as indicated by change of key signatures (*Delgadina* and *Una ramica de ruda*).

3. Hemsi's use of rather elaborate time signatures may be linked to popular Balkan rhythms. Nonetheless, beginning with the simple time signatures, we find that three melodies employ 2/4, three 3/8, and two 6/8. In the 2/4 category, *La galana y su caballo* was included, since only its first measure was given in

---

[1] "Romances y refranes sefardíes," *Estudios dedicados a Menéndez Pidal*, V (Madrid, 1954), pp. 322-23.
[2] *Ibid.*, p. 323.
[3] Subirá did not give the opus numbers for these installments nor the localities where the items were collected. He merely lists them as the sixth and seventh series, respectively.

From the sixth series: item XXXI may be identified as *Mujer guerrera*, MP 121; XXXIII as *Hero y Leandro*, MP 41; and XXXV as *Vuelta del marido* (é), MP 59. From the seventh series: item XXXVII as *El conde Olinos*, MP 55, and XLII, *La sentencia del bajá*, not listed in the *Catálogo*. Hemsi recently (1969?) published the sixth and seventh series as Op. 34 and Op. 41, respectively. Also, he has issued gramaphone recordings of all his *Coplas sefardíes*, which will comprise ten albums.

However, from *Kol-Sepharad*, II, No. 4 (January, 1959), 62, we learn that these additional installments represent the ballad tradition of Izmir.

[4] Among Hemsi's unpublished works are: fascicles 6 through 9 of *Coplas sefardíes* (*Chansons judéo-espagnoles*) which represent an additional twenty-four accompanied melodies; *Cancionero sefardí*, consisting of 230 poems and 110 melodies; *Mahzor sefaradí*, containing 200 liturgical melodies; *Refranes sefardíes; Investigaciones folclóricas* which discusses Sephardic practices, customs, and anecdotes; and *Sepharade*, a volume in French containing a hundred Spanish poems with their melodies plus a number of articles concerning the history of the Sephardim, observations on the Judeo-Spanish language, proverbs. supersititions, France and the Sephardim, etc.

3/4. Of the more complex signatures, those which remained constant throughout are 6/4 $\left[\frac{2+2+2}{4}\right]$ for *El parto en lejas tierras;* 5/4 $\left[\frac{2+3}{4}\right]$ for *La adúltera* (á-a); 16/8 $\left[\frac{7+9}{8}\right]$ for *Delgadina;* and the epitrite 7/8 $\left[\frac{2+2+3}{8}\right]$ for *Vuelta del hijo maldecido.* Those signatures which appear inconsistent were employed for *El conde Olinos, La bella en misa,* and *La novia sorteada.*

4. Tempo indications are given in Italian.

5. A number of varied strophic patterns can be found among the Hemsi ballads. Five melodies may be considered as couplets, $\frac{AB}{ab}$ for *Grandes bodas en Francia* and *Vuelta del hijo maldecido,* and the tripartite $\frac{ABC}{abb}$, in which the repetition of the second hemistich employs a new melodic section (*Princesa y el segador, Celinos y la adúltera,* and *La novia sorteada*). Quatrains can be found in five ballads: two have the form ABCD (*Don Bueso y su hermana* and *Vos labraré yo un pendón*): two AA'BC (*El parto en lejas tierras* and *Delgadina*), and one AABB (*Landarico*). One ballad, *La bella en misa,* is a quatrain plus a refrain ABCD*E*.

Quite unusual structures can be found for the following ballads: $\frac{AABCC'}{abcdd}$ (*Una ramica de ruda*); $\frac{ABCDBC}{abbbcd}$ (*La adúltera (é)*), $\frac{ABCDAD}{abcrrr}$ (*La galana y su caballo*); and a most peculiar structure

A^{v+w} B^{x+y+z} $A'^{v'+w'}$ $B'^{x'+w''}$ B^{x+y+z} $A'^{v''+y+z}$ shown in the following example:
a   b   b   c   d   d

Example 11: *Conde Alarcos + La infanta deshonrada*

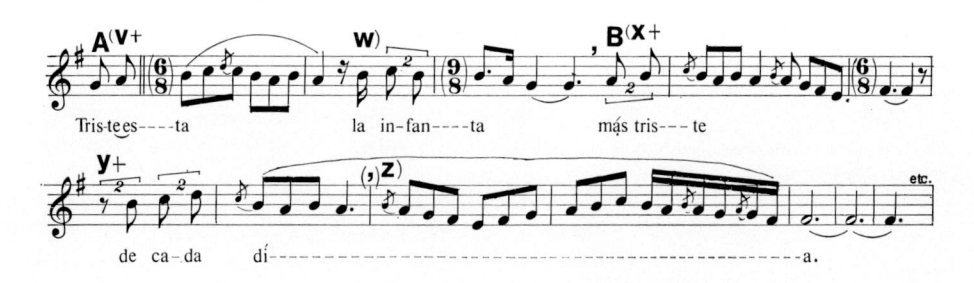

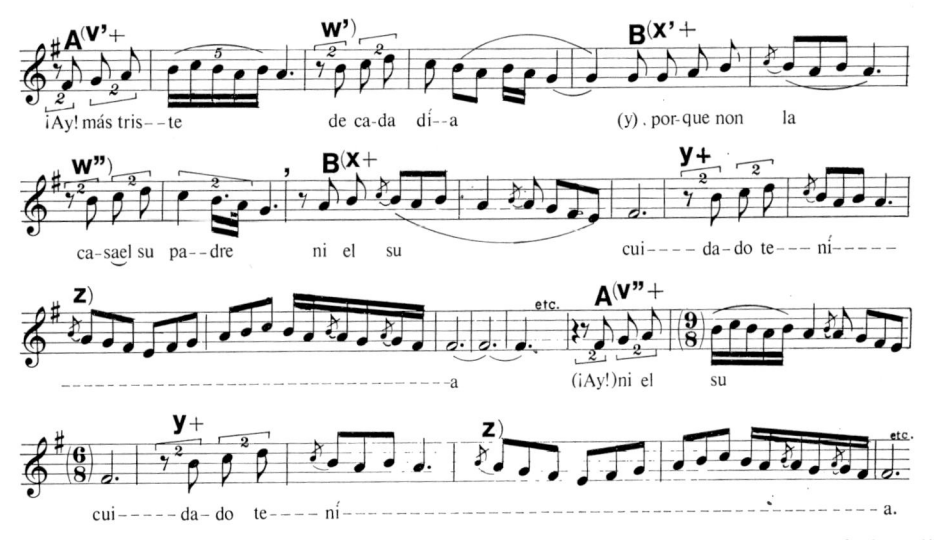

[Translation: The princess is sad and becomes sadder each day because her father did not marry her off nor did he even bother about her.]

6. Hemsi's melodies have a wide modal distribution. We find examples in the Hypodorian (*El partos en lejas tierras*), Phrygian (*Grandes bodas en Francia*), Mixolydian (*Vos labraré yo en pendón* and *La galana y su caballo*) and Aeolian mode (*La adúltera[é]* and *Landarico*). Those melodies in the minor are *Conde Alarcos + La infanta deshonrada, Una ramica de ruda, Princesa y el segador*, and *Vuelta del hijo maldecido*. There appears to be a modulation from C♯ minor to F minor in *Delgadina*. Two ballads are in the major mode (*La bella en misa* and *La novia sorteada*), and the two remaining ballads appear to be in mixed modes: *Celinos y la adúltera* in a mixed major-minor, and *Don Bueso y su hermana* in a mixed Aeolian-major.

Chromatic alterations can be found particularly in the minor melodies for the raising of the leading tone and for the mixed modes. The plagal form can be found for five of the ballad tunes. Nine ballads end on the *finalis*, three on the 3rd (*La bella en misa, Celinos y la adúltera*, and *La novia sorteada*), two on the fifth degree (*Una ramica de ruda* and *Princesa y el segador*), and *Conde Alarcos + La infanta deshonrada* ends on the second degree.

7. In ambitus, two melodies exceed the octave (*La bella en misa*, a major 12th, and *Princesa y el segador*, a major 9th). Eight melodies have the range of an octave, while a major 7th can be found for *Delgadina*, a minor 7th for *La adúltera* (é), *Conde Alarcos + La infanta deshonrada*, and a major 6th for *Grandes bodas en Francia*.

8. The diatonic quality of Hemsi's ballads is extraordinary. Although the interval of the 3rd can be found in all but two examples (*El parto en lejas*

tierras and *Conde Alarcos + La infanta deshonrada*), they are used rather sparingly. Nine melodies employ 4ths, four 5ths, one a minor 6th (*La novia sorteada*), and one a minor 7th (*La galana y su caballo*). The interval of the augmented 2nd can be found in the ballads *Delgadina, Una ramica de ruda,* and *Princesa y el segador*. An interesting case can be made for *Grandes bodas en Francia* which ends [musical notation]. Hemsi appended a note to explain this phenomenon: "Nota leggermente abbandonata in falsetto." The melody actually ends on the *finalis* b^1, whereas the ascent to *f*-sharp' is characteristic of such endings as found in the vocal practices of the Near East.[1]

9. Reïterated rhythmic patterns play an important rôle in four ballads (*El partos en lejas tierras, Landarico, Delgadina,* and *Una ramica de ruda*).

10. Hemsi took special care to underlay his texts with regard to his printed texts observing both spelling and punctuation as well as the correct division of syllables. He elided his syllables accurately but did not indicate these elisions with the customary slur. Interjections such as ¡Ay! are found in *Conde Alarcos + La infanta deshonrada* and *La bella en misa*, while refrains occur in the ballads *La bella en misa* and *La galana y su caballo*.

The agreement of the hemistich with the melodic phrase is consistent in the majority of examples. However, the splitting up of the hemistichs into two or more musical phrases appears in the ballads *Grandes bodas en Francia, Conde Alarcos + La infanta deshonrada* (shown above), *Princesa y el segador, Vuelta del hijo maldecido, La bella en misa, La galana y su caballo, Celinos y la adúltera,* and *La novia sorteada*.

Two ballads repeat textual hemistichs in successive strophes, a practice already commented upon by Manrique de Lara. *El parto en lejas tierras*, whose melodic stanza structure is AA'BC, has a textual rendering for four and a half strophes of abcd, cdef, efgh, hijk, jk. The example *Conde Alarcos + La infanta deshonrada* (shown above) has as its textual setting ab, bc, cd, etc.

11. Hemsi wrote out all the ornaments. The most florid, or highly embellished examples, can be seen in *Grandes bodas en Francia, Conde Alarcos + La infanta deshonrada, Vuelta del hijo maldecido,* and *La bella en misa*.

Among the standard ornaments, Hemsi was particularly fond of the grace note and grace-note pairs, plus triplet figures and the four- and five-note groupings. In *La bella en misa* the trill is employed. As is typical of many ballads in the Eastern tradition, the ornaments fall predominantly on the ultimate and penultimate syllable of the corresponding melody sections.

---

[1] Such characteristic endings can be seen in the transcription of the Jerusalem ballad, *Arbolero*: variant 3. See particularly verses 3, 5, 6, 8, 12, 14, and 15.

12. The ballads are devoid of notational errors.

13. How faithful Hemsi remained in notating the melodies of the Eastern tradition is a point which will be brought out in the ensuing chapter of this study. While Hemsi did not make specific comments regarding the performance of these ballads, we may criticize his æsthetic license in molding these traditional melodies for their acceptance and performance as European art songs.

Hemsi did, however, write out more than one strophe for each ballad, whereby in two cases, *Don Bueso y su hermana* and *La bella en misa*, the stanzaic variations are given much in the manner in which they may have been sung to Hemsi when he collected the tunes. Melodies which appear to have been adapted for performance are *El partos en lejas tierras, Landarico, Delgadina,* and *Vuelta del hijo maldecido*. Here Hemsi either notates a half of a strophe or appends a musical tag upon which to end the performance. This is strictly a European contrivance and was far from the normal practice of the tradition itself. Furthermore, Hemsi's use of phrasing and dynamics is completely out of context and without any foundation whatsoever.

14. We know that Hemsi has a goodly number of other *romance* melodies which have not as yet been published. Whether or not they are all cast in the same manner as those criticized above remains to be seen. We may surmise that Hemsi's personal archives contain a wide variety of musical materials from the Eastern tradition and that when published, they will aid in recreating that abundant and vigorous tradition as Hemsi must have known it. Although Hemsi offers no evidence in his *Coplas sefardíes* concerning the manner and circumstances under which his materials were collected, we see that Hemsi at least endeavored to carry out his investigation along more scientific lines.[1]

---

[1] An interesting review of the first four fascicles of *Coplas sefardíes* was published by Plácido de Montolíu in *Hispanic Review*, VI (1938), 166-168. Isaac Jack Lévy enlisted the aid of Professor Albert T. Luper, of the Faculty of Music at the State University of Iowa, for professional comments concerning the 2nd and 3rd fascicles of Hemsi's *Coplas sefardíes*. In Luper's opinion, Hemsi's arrangements were "tastefully and imaginatively done and should prove to be most effective in public performance." Luper added:
> From the strictly scientific (ethno-musicological) viewpoint, it should be noted that these arrangements represent to some degree a compromise with Western scales and rhythms and modern harmonies, for it cannot be doubted that the originals contained more Oriental melodic inflections and little or no accompaniment, which, in any case, would be of a different character from that provided by Hemsi... It is likely that the melodies themselves are fair approximations of the original oral versions, as nearly correct as it is possible to notate them in the "straight jacket" of normal traditional Western notation and tuning...

Cf. I. J. Lévy's *Sephardic Ballads and Songs in the United States* (State University of Iowa, 1959) [Unpublished Master's thesis], p. 16.

Tri sefardske romanse

harmonisovao: B.Jungić

Quien madre no tiene...

Quien madre no tie - ne mucho la de:

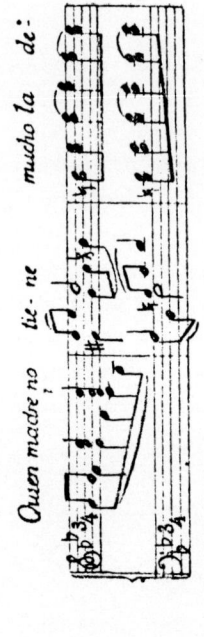

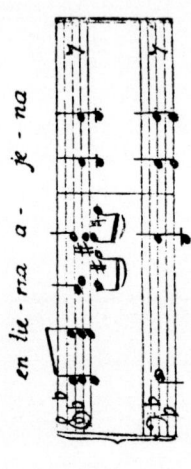

se - a yo que la te - ní - a

en tie - rra a - je - na

• Izvedno god. 1932 na koncertu Jevr(ejskog) društva "Lira" u Sarajevu

ГОДИШЊАК

ИЗДАЈУ

ЈЕВРЕЈСКО КУЛТУРНО-ПРОСВЕТНО ДРУШТВО
"Ла Беневоленсиа" у Сарајеву

и

ДОБРОТВОРНО ДРУШТВО
"Потпора" у Београду

1933 - 5694
ШТАМПАРИЈА МЕНАХЕМ ПАПО
САРАЈЕВО

Arboleda

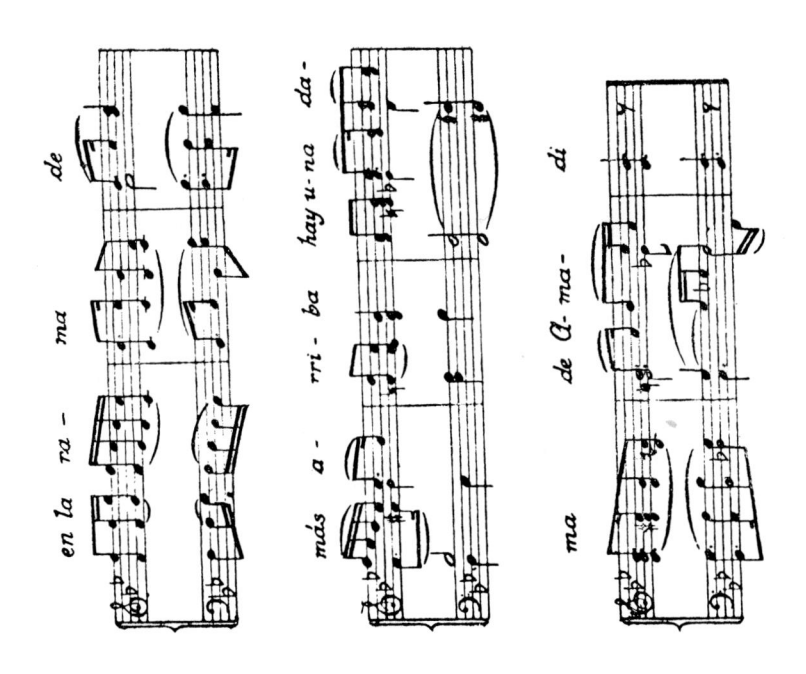

B. JUNGIĆ

The melodies of "Tri sefardske romanse ['Three Sephardic *Romances*'],'' printed on the pages following a scholarly article of Kalmi Baruch which appeared in Sarajevo in 1933, have managed somehow to remain unmentioned wherever Baruch's article was cited.[1] The title is misleading, as only the first two items are *romances* (*El sueño profetico* and *Arbolero*) while the last piece is a popular Sephardic song.[2] The harmonizations made by Miss B. Jungić were performed in 1932 at a concert in Sarajevo by the singing society "Lira."[3]

Actually, there is no connection between these tunes and the texts of Kalmi Baruch. All were written in keyboard notation with their texts placed above the uppermost voice, the melody line of the soprano clef.

Thus taking the melodic lines of the two ballads, we find the following characteristics:

1. Key signatures: although both melodies employ two flats, the first melody is in Aeolian (G minor, without a raised seventh degree) while the second melody is in major (B-flat Major but in plagal form). The *f*-natural indicated by Miss Jungić is not necessary.

2. Time signature: the first is in 3/4 throughout, while the second, written as $\frac{3\text{-}2}{4}$, does not conform to alternate measures of 3/4 and 2/4, but rather to irregular patterns $\left(\frac{3\ 2\ 2\ 2\ 2\ 3\ 2\ 2\ 2\ 2\ 2\ 2\ 2\ 2\ 3\ 2\ 2\ 2}{4}\right)$.

3. Tempo indications are not given.

---

[1] *Godišnjak* ['*Yearbook*'] published by the Jewish charitable organizations La Benevolencia and Potpora (Sarajevo-Belgrade, 1933), pp. 289-292. Kalmi Baru[c]h's article, "Spanske romance bosanskih Jevreja ['Spanish *romances* of the Jews of Bosnia']," *ibid.*, pp. 272-88, precedes these melodies. I owe thanks to the Rev. Eliezar Abinun, *Hazzan* of the Bevis Marks Synagogue of London, for pointing out the existence of these melodies during our meeting in London, 9th July 1962. Furthermore, it was explained that Miss Jungić was at that time a young music student from Sarajevo. Counter pages 78-79.

A reproduction of the three Jungić melodies can be found in *Judeo-Spanish Ballads from Bosnia*, edited by Samuel G. Armistead and Joseph H. Silverman with the collaboration of Biljana Šljivić-Šimšić. Philadelphia: University of Pennsylvania Press, 1971. End of Section B.

[2] The ballad texts can be identified as: *El sueño profético*, MP 68, related to MP 129 [Cf. J. M. de Cossio and T. Maza Solano, *Romancero popular de la Montaña* (Santander, 1933-34), Vol. I, Nos. 156-157] (Jungić, p. 289); and *Arbolero* or *Vuelta del marido* (*i*), MP 58 (Jungić, pp. 290-291). The third harmonized melody is the popular non-*romance* song, *En la mar hay una torre* (Jungić, p. 292).

[3] *Ibid.*, p. 289.

4. Texts are fully punctuated and syllables accurately divided. The first employs a musical strophe consisting of four hemistichs, whereas the second utilizes a musical strophe of eight hemistichs.

5. Ornaments are written out for both melodies.

6. Range: The first melody encompasses an octave while the second, a major 9th.

7. The formal structure of the first melody is ABB; A comprises the first two hemistichs, B a repetition of the following two hemistichs. The second melody, described as ABA′B, is actually a distich or couplet for which Miss Jungić notated the first two strophes. The section beginning A′ alters the melody of A only in its first measure.

While Miss Jungić's contribution of two ballad melodies may be considered slight, we must, nevertheless, praise her for her sincere efforts in preserving both tunes which were undoubtedly popular among the Sephardim residing in Sarajevo. In fact, it may be said that until the appearance of Vol. III of the *Romancero tradicional* (Madrid, 1969), in which there are ballad melodies collected by Manrique de Lara in Sarajevo (circa May to June, 1911), Jungić's melodies represented the only published musical sources from that tradition.

EDUARDO MARTÍNEZ TORNER (1888-1955)

When Eduardo Martínez Torner commented upon "El cancionero sefardí" in 1935,[1] he opened his brief essay with the following remarks:

> El alma de un pueblo manifiéstase en sus monumentos y en sus costumbres. Cada uno de aquéllos que se derrumba y cada una de éstas que desaparece, dejan un vacío eterno en la historia del espíritu humano. Una simple canción popular cualquiera, por insignificante que nos parezca, es el recuerdo vivo de otras usadas en la antigüedad o acaso la misma en cuerpo y alma que en los primeros siglos medievales alegraba estos pueblos que hoy alegra.[2]

Torner then described how the mediæval *Romancero* had developed in all the geographical areas where Spanish was spoken, not only in the Americas but also in the Near East and North Africa where the exiled generations of the Spanish Jews had settled. He quoted the famous song of ridicule addressed to the expelled Jews, taken from Francisco Salinas' *De música libri septem* (Salamanca, 1577),[3] concerning which, he remarks: "¡Cuánto dolor llevaría a su ánimo el eco de aquella cancioncilla con que el pueblo les despedía!"[4]

---

[1] *Temas folklóricos: Música y poesía* (Madrid, 1935), pp. 49-58.
[2] *Ibid.*, p. 51.
[3] P. 312.
[4] *Temas folklóricos*, p. 52.

Example 12:

E a ju---dí--os, a   en-far-de--- lar,   que man-dan los   rey- es que   pa- séis la   mar.

[Translation: Go on Jews, pack up, for the Monarchs have ordered you to cross the seas.]

Torner included many interesting statistics and facts concerning the Sephardim of the Mediterranean basin based upon José M. Estrugo's *El retorno a Sefarad cien años después de la Inquisición* (Madrid, 1933). With regard to the musical studies of the *Romancero*, he mentioned only the work carried out by Manrique de Lara and Alberto Hemsi. He also reproduced a ballad melody, *La jactancia del conde Vélez*, collected by the former in Alcazarquivir.[1]

Torner's serious interest in the *Romancero* began in 1916 when:

> En diciembre de ese año ingresa en el Centro de Estudios Históricos de Madrid entre cuyo plantel de sabios investigadores perfílase su gran personalidad como figura central de la Sección de Folklore. Es enviado por la referida Institución para realizar intensa labor de estudio y recopilación de la música popular a través de las provincias españolas. Las Castillas, León, Extremadura, Andalucía... El Instituto de Estudios Gallegos encárgale de recoger el folklore de sus cuatro provincias. Comienza también como labor especial en colaboración con su insigne maestro en filología, D. Ramón Menéndez Pidal, el estudio y clasificación del Romancero Popular de España por encargo expreso de la Junta de Ampliación de Estudios de Madrid.[2]

Since then Torner's literary output in musicology and folklore has proven to be a substantial contribution to Hispanic culture.[3] However, his familiarity

---

[1] *Ibid.*, p. 54. This ballad is not listed in the *Catálogo*. There exists an error in the notation of this melody with respect to that given for the same item in *Romancero Hispánico*, I, p. 399. For measure 3 Torner shows:

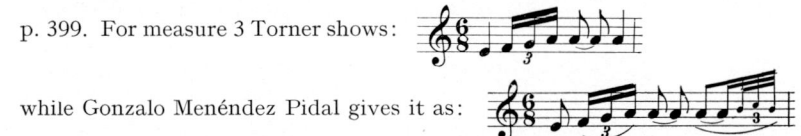

while Gonzalo Menéndez Pidal gives it as:

In the latter case, it was probably edited in order to accomodate the space alloted to it.

[2] Ángel Muñiz Toca, *Vida y obra de Eduardo M. Torner: Musicólogo, folklorista y compositor* (Oviedo, 1961), p. 17.

[3] Torner's earlier contributions concerning the *Romancero* can be found in such publications as: *Indicaciones prácticas para la notación musical de los romances* (Madrid: Centro de Estudios Históricos, 1923), subsequently reprinted with some revision as "Indicaciones prácticas sobre la notación musical de los romances," *Revista de Filología Española*, X (1923), 389-384 and as "Indicación práctica," *Temas folklóricos* (Madrid, 1935), pp. 115-125); "Ensayo de clasificación de las melodías de romance," *Homenaje ofrecido a Menéndez Pidal*, II(Madrid, 1925), pp. 391-402; and "La canción tradicional española," in F. Carreras y Candi, *Folklore y Costumbres de España,* II (Barcelona, 1931), pp. 7-166. A brief yet interesting biography of Torner with an almost complete survey of his publications can be found in D. Ángel Muñiz Toca, *op. cit.*

with Sephardic balladry was mainly second-hand, particularly through his handling of the Manrique de Lara manuscript notations which, unfortunately, he did not study closely. After the appearance of his essay, "El cancionero sefardí," Torner published another Judeo-Spanish ballad melody, *El rey envidioso de su sobrino*, in his article, "La rítmica en la música tradicional española."[1]

His reason for including this "curious" example was to corroborate the existence of 5/8 meter as a widely diffused Hispanic phenomenon, for which he claimed historical antecedents could be found in the *Cancionero musical de Palacio* (No. 125 of the Barbieri edition) and in the *vihuelista* collection of Salinas, *De musica libri septem* (notably the fourth book from which Pedrell made transcriptions included in his *Lírica nacionalizada*).[2] While 5/8 in the Spanish tradition is most popularly rendered as $\frac{3+2}{8}$, the melody for *El rey envidioso de su sobrino*, which was collected from a Sephardic woman of Tetuán, is unique in its contrary manifestation of $\frac{2+3}{8}$.[3] I cite the melody as printed:

Example 13: *El rey envidioso de su sobrino*

[Translation: Güeso is walking through all Sevilla with a golden sword of great value in his hand.]

Torner regarded the melody "de carácter antiguo" most probably after having ascribed its modality to the eighth Gregorian mode, *Hypomixolydian*. However, in the paragraph preceding this example, we learn that it was recorded on a gramophone record for the Archives of the Centro de Estudios Históricos. This statement is important in that it substantiates the inclusion of Sephardic items among the numerous Peninsular ballads preserved on discs at the Center. However, we are still without any indication of the dates and geographical origin of these recordings.

---

[1] The article was first published in the journal *Música* (Barcelona, Jan., 1938). However, I cite here a reprinting of the original work which can be found in *Nuestra música*, III, No. 9 (México D.F., Jan., 1948), Suplemento No. 3, p. 67.

[2] *Ibid.*, pp. 67-68.

[3] Hemsi also notated one of his ballads with the metric designation $\frac{5}{4}\left[\left(\frac{2+3}{4}\right)\right]$. See Example 31.

PAUL BÉNICHOU (1908-)

Paul Bénichou's remarkable and excellently edited collection of the Moroccan Sephardic ballads (1944) contains twenty-one melodies.[1] Bénichou makes no direct statements concerning the manner in which the melodies were obtained; they are grouped together at the end of the study under the heading "Melodías tradicionales," and are preceded by a paragraph of detailed acknowledgments:

> Algunas de ellas las aprendí en Orán y las transcribió mi amigo el señor Léon Algazi, de Paris; ... Las demás transcripciones se hicieron en Buenos Aires, sobre las melodías cantadas por las señoras Coriat y Lévy: algunas se deben a la señora Jane Bathori; las demás, y la revisión del conjunto, al señor Daniel Devoto; a ambos les agradezco su amistosa ayuda y su paciencia en la notación de esta difícil música tradicional.[2]

Bénichou did not indicate the names of the transcribers for each notation, so regretfully he left us without this valuable documentation.[3] We may conclude from Bénichou's remarks that Devoto made the final copies printed in this study since a close investigation of the melodic notations will reveal that they were made by one hand. However, we are fortunate to learn from

---

[1] "Romances judeo-españoles de Marruecos," *Revista de Filología Hispánica*, VI (1944), 36-76, 105-38, 255-79, and 313-381. This study was also brought out as a separate volume with the same title (Buenos Aires, 1946). Of the twenty-one melodies (pp. 374-381), only twenty accompany ballad texts. In 1968, this study was revised and up-dated, carrying the title *Romancero judeo-español de Marruecos* (Madrid: Editorial Castalia).

The ballads containing melodies are identified as: *La infantina*, MP 114 (Bénichou, I, p. 374); *De la linda Melisenda*, MP 28 (Bénichou, II, p. 374); *La infanta deshonrada*, MP 106 (Bénichou, III, p. 375); *Gerineldo*, MP 101 (Bénichou, IV, p. 375); *La malcasada del pastor*, hexasyllabic, MP 72 (Bénichou, VI, p. 375); *La mujer engañada*, hexasyllabic, MP 74 (Bénichou, VII, p. 376); *¿Por qué no cantáis la bella?*, MP 57 (Bénichou, X, p. 376); *Mujer guerrera*, MP 121 (Bénichou, XI, p. 376); *Hermanas reina y cautiva*, MP 48 (Bénichou, XIII, p. 377); *Don Bueso y su hermana*, MP 49 (Bénichou, XIV, p. 377); *Vuelta del marido (é)*, MP 59 (Bénichou, XV, p. 377); *La boda estorbada*, MP 60 (Bénichou, XVI, p. 378); *El cautivo del renegado*, MP 51 (Bénichou, XVII, p. 378); *Diego León*, MP 63 (Bénichou, XX, p. 378); *Bernardo del Carpio*, MP 1 (Bénichou, XXI, p. 379); *Don Sancho y doña Urraca*, MP 4 (Bénichou, XXIII, p. 379); *Virgilios*, MP 46 (Bénichou, XXV, p. 379); *El conde Olinos*, MP 55 (Bénichou, XXVIII, p. 380); *El rey envidioso a su sobrino*, hexasyllabic, MP 123 (Bénichou, L, p. 380); and *El caballo robado*, hexasyllabic, MP 121 bis (Bénichou, LX, p. 381). Bénichou, LVIII, p. 380, is a religious song. In the 1968 edition, Bénichou included an extra melody (p. 298), *Siempre lo oyi yo dezir*, which is identified as as *Vos labraré yo un pendón*, MP 120. Constantin Braïloïu quoted a few measures from two of Bénichou's ballad melodies (Nos. II and XXI) in his "Sur une mélodie russe," *Musique Russe*, II (Paris, 1953), pp. 343 and 345, respectively.

[2] Bénichou, *ibid.*, p. 374.

[3] Bénichou gave Devoto further acknowledgement for his valuable bibliographical assistance (p. 43). No further mention was made of Jane Bathori other than that cited by Bénichou.

Prof. Daniel Devoto the extent to which each of the afore-mentioned transcribers participated in this endeavor.[1]

A collection of twenty *romances* preserved in manuscript form by Bénichou's

---

[1] From a recent communication by Prof. Daniel Devoto, dated 14th July 1969:
"... La transcripción de los romances recogidos por Bénichou se hizo hace un cuarto de siglo, y nunca creí que fuera tan importante delimitar la tarea de cada uno de los transcriptores. Planteado, esto, le digo exactamente todo lo que recuerdo:
El núcleo inicial, los ocho romances del homenaje a Martinenche, fueron transcritos por Algazi; los restantes se grabaron en Buenos Aires y la transcripción se hizo — por lo que a nosotros respecta — sobre los discos, aunque estuvimos presentes durante la grabación y allí comenzamos a notar las melodías. (Digo "nosotros", porque mi amiga la cantante Dora Berdichevsky colaboró muy eficazmente en la tarea). La señorita Coriat, que cantaba las melodías, era una persona de bastante edad, y muchas veces era imposible decidir sobre justeza de sonido, ornamentos y "chevrotements", hasta el punto que fue absolutamente imposible realizar la transcripción de muchos romances, más "cantilados" que cantados, y con tales diferencias de copla a copla que evidentemente la informante estaba improvisando una melopea y no trasmitiendo una melodía tradicional clara. En cuanto a los romances en que personalmente colaboré, según un recuerdo que puedo garantizar, son (en el orden de la edición Castalia): *El conde de Sandaria* [*Bernardo del Carpio*], *El rey Fernando* [*Don Sancho y doña Urraca*], *Gerineldo*, *Vergico* [*Virgilios*], *A caçar va el caballero* [*La infantina*], *El conde Niño* [*Conde Olinos*], *Paseábase Bueso* [*El rey envidioso de su sobrino*], *En ca del buen rey* [*El caballo robado*], *En el nombre dilo tú*. Es decir, en general, los que tienen una melodía menos regular y necesitan mayor número de cambios de compás (quizás influyó en ello el "estilo" de la Srta. Coriat, pero Bénichou, que conocía las tonadas, elegía en las varias coplas grabadas, los versos más fieles de cada una de ellas para componer una versión más fidedigna, ya que la informante — por deficiencias vocales entre otras razones, rara vez cantó de manera uniforme todo un romance). *Belisera* [*Melisenda insomne*], *?Qué se pensaba la reina?* [*La infanta deshonrada*], *Siempre lo oyí yo dezir* [*Vos labraré yo un pendón*. N.B. This melody was not included among the original melodies in Benichou's article of 1944], *Canto de un galán* [*?Por qué no cantáis la bella?*], *Grandes bodas hay en Francia* [*La boda estorbada*], me parecen no notados por nosotros (Dora Berdichevsky de Arias y yo). *La reina Xerifa mora* [*Hermanas reina y cautiva*]me suena a notado por D. Berdichevsky, y *Escuchís señor soldado* [*Vuelta del marido (é)*], por nuestra maestra, Jane Bathori. *El sevillano* [*La mujer engañada*], *Mi padre era de Francia* [*La malcasada del pastor*], *Pregonadas son las guerras* [*Mujer guerrera*], y *En la ciudad de Toledo* [*Diego León*] me parecen transcritas o retocadas por mí, sin que pueda asegurarlo; casi seguro estoy de haber transcrito yo *Al salir i yo a un rebasque* [*El cautivo del renegado*]; y absolutamente seguro de que Bathori notó *Mora bella* [*Don Bueso y su hermana*] — recuerdo perfectamente que Bénichou me la cantó para verificarla, y que la transcripción era absolutamente perfecta, con el acento en el primer tiempo y no en anacrusa. Por lo demás, todas las melodías pasaron por mi mano, para verificación y control, de modo que quizás en las oranesas se haya deslizado algún cambio y de ahí proceda miidea de que — por lo menos parcialmente — las noté yo (creo que Bénichou fue, para Algazi como para nosotros, el informante de esas melodías, y su oído musical es muy notable). Además, como última verificación, Dora Berdichevsky las cantó en público acompañada por mí, y recuerdo que la Srta. Coriat y su familia, que estaban en el auditorio, cantaban también muy audiblemente lo mismo que nosotros (esto se lo agrego en razón de las "observaciones" de Larrea Palacín a las

aunt, Mrs. R. Sefarti of Orán, formed the basis of the collection.[1] Mrs. Sefarti had carefully copied down the texts of thirteen ballads as her mother sang them, and collected the remaining seven texts from close friends. Eight of these had already appeared in print, though with some inaccuracies, as explained by Bénichou.[2] In hopes of editing these texts, which his aunt had transmitted to him earlier, Bénichou undertook, in March of 1942, a trip to Orán where he could revise the collection under her guidance.[3]

Bénichou's original intention to publish these newly revised ballads was further delayed by a prodigious discovery. Upon his return to Buenos Aires, Bénichou had the good fortune to meet Jacobo Coriat, President of the Community of Moroccan Sephardim who were residing in that city.[4] Through the efforts of Jacobo's wife and her two sisters, Bénichou not only obtained more correct versions of his aunt's répertoire but was able to add a host of additional Moroccan ballads of an older and rarer vintage.

The notations of the twenty traditional melodies in Bénichou's study reveal the following traits:

1. All were notated in the treble clef and written in vocal notation.

2. The key signatures utilized confine all melodies within the staff.

3. Of the time signatures employed, triple meter is indicated in the majority of examples with a preference shown for 3/4 and 3/8. Manrique de Lara, on the other hand, had a personal preference for 6/8 in his transcriptions of Moroccan ballads. There is a bit more sophistication in the transcriptions of Bénichou's study by their use of mixed time signatures which were employed for two-thirds of the melodies. This peculiarity probably arose out of a consideration for the textual accent.

4. There are no tempo indications whatsoever.

---

que tuve que contestar en el *Bulletin Hispanique*, LXIII: 249-250, 1961). Lo que sí sé es que todas las melodías las recopié yo y las di luego a un copista que trabajaba para nosotros (versiones de la *RFH*; las de Castalia han sido hechas sin que yo tomara parte en ellas). Esto es todo cuanto recuerdo . . ."

[1] *Ibid.*, p. 38. The Sephardic community of Orán consisted primarily of Moroccan Jews, especially those of Tetuán, who emigrated there in the last decade of the nineteenth century.

[2] *Ibid.*, p. 40. Cf. Romain Thomas, "Huit romances judéo-espagnoles," *Hommage à Ernest Martinenche* (Paris, 1940), pp. 282-292. Thomas taught Bénichou Spanish at the Lyceum Janson de Suilly in Paris.

[3] Bénichou, *op. cit.*, p. 40.

[4] *Loc. cit.* Bénichou explained that the Moroccan colony in Argentina numbered a few hundred families that migrated there during the fifty years preceding his publication.

5. All but one of the examples are in quatrain form. The exception, *Mujer guerrera*, is a ballad composed of five melody sections, $ABCD^{x+y} E^{z+y}$, where the last melody section carries the textual repetition of the last hemistich:

Example 14: *Mujer guerrera*

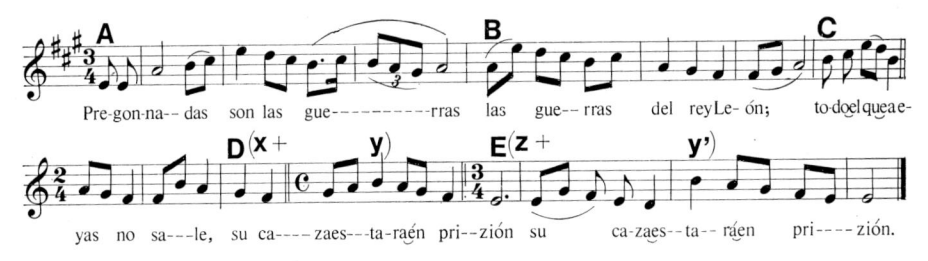

[Musical notation with sections labeled A, B, C, $D^{(x+y)}$, $E^{(z+y')}$ and lyrics:
Pre-gon-na-- das son las gue-------rras las gue-- rras del rey Le- ón; to-do el que a e-
yas no sa---le, su ca----zaes---ta-raén pri--zión su ca-zaes--ta-- raén pri----zión.]

[Translation: The wars of the King of León have been proclaimed and anyone who does not go forth (to serve) will forfeit his home.]

Musically speaking, the phrase pattern ABCD is employed for seventeen ballads, AA'BC for two ballads (*Gerineldo* and *La infantina*) and ABCDE as shown above.

6. Modal structure: fifteen examples are in the major mode, two in Mixolydian (*El cautivo del renegado* and *El caballo robado*), one in Lydian (*El conde Olinos*), one in Aeolian (*Diego León*), and the remaining example, *El rey envidioso de su sobrino*, in a mixed major-minor tonality. While fifteen of the examples end on the *finalis*, four end on the fifth degree and one on the second degree (*Diego León*). Six ballads are plagal in character.

7. Of the twenty examples, five exceed the octave in range. Four have an ambitus of a major 9th, one a minor 9th. In the octave category are twelve ballads, and the three remaining examples have an ambitus of a minor 7th.

8. The melodies are basically diatonic, and the interval of the 3rd can be found in all the examples. Thirteen melodies employ the 4th, six employ the 5th, one melody contains a 6th (*Mujer guerrera*), and two have leaps of an octave (*Hermanas reina y cautiva* and *Vuelta del marido[é]*).

9. The ballads which appear to have reïterated rhythmic patterns as a unifying element linking melodic sections are *Don Bueso y su hermana*, *¿Por qué no cantáis la bella?*, *Mujer guerrera*, and *El rey envidioso de su sobrino*. The underlying rhythm for *Vuelta del marido*(é), like that of Bustelo's example, is a basic martial pattern.

10. The texts which were placed under the ballad melodies comprise the first four hemistichs of the printed texts; yet without strict adherence to the

punctuation and capitalization of the printed ballads. The transcriber [Devoto?] chose to capitalize the first word of each hemistich. As Bénichou indicated, the ballads I through XX collected in Orán were given in their entirety. The variants of these ballads, which he collected in Buenos Aires, were given only in their variant form in order to avoid textual duplication. The ballad melodies from XXI on, which represent those gathered in Buenos Aires, were given in their complete textual rendering.[1] However, the texts which were set to the melodies I through XX, represent both the Orán and Buenos Aires versions for eight melodies, the Orán text for *Hermanas reina y cautiva, Don Bueso y su hermana, El cautivo del renegado*, and *La boda estorbada*, and the Buenos Aires text for *La infantina*, being the first melody given.

Although the elisions have been indicated with the slur mark, accents were not marked distinctly and were even omitted in the majority of cases. Sixteen texts are octosyllabic, the remainder hexasyllabic. Apostrophes are used in many instances to indicate the cæsura. The *fermata* sign employed for two examples shows, in one case, *La infanta deshonrada*, the holds of the last notes of each melodic phrase, and in the other case, *Gerineldo*, an expressive hold. The *rit.* [ritardando] found in *Bernardo del Carpio* is also for expressive purposes.

11. There is slight to medium use of ornamentation, with the bulk of the melismata falling on the penultimate syllable of each musical phrase. Of the embellishments employed, the following were taken from the European tradition:
   a. Glissando ( ): *La malcasada del pastor, Gerineldo, La infanta deshonrada*, and *La infantina*.
   b. Mordents ( ), possibly to indicate tremolos: *Bernardo del Carpio, El conde Olinos*, and *La infantina*.
   c. Grace notes ( ) were written in lightly.
   d. Turn : ( ) *Virgilios*
   e. Various ligature patterns were found in several examples: in *Bernardo del Carpio*; in *Virgilios*; in *Hermanas reina y cautiva*; and in *El conde Olinos*.

12. Notational errors could not be found.

13. Other than the excessive use of mixed time signatures, the melodies have much in common with those collected by Manrique de Lara and Bustelo in North Africa.

---

[1] *Ibid.*, p. 41.

14. No mention was made concerning their performance, although Devoto who transcribed some of them, described this aspect in a later publication.[1] Again, only the first melodic strophe was transcribed. If the expression marks, as cited above, were employed for several of the ballads, were they to continue as such in successive strophes?

Bénichou took care to cite analogs with the *Catálogo* along with six other Judeo-Spanish collections, none of which contained music.[2] He also provided cross-references for those ballads linked with the Peninsular tradition utilizing such sources as Durán, Wolf, and Menéndez y Pelayo.

Bénichou deserves great praise for including the twenty ballad melodies from the Moroccan tradition and, above all, for his perceptiveness in seeking out musically qualified individuals (Algazi, Bathori, and Devoto) to preserve in notated form the melodies which would have otherwise passed into oblivion.

JOSÉ ANTONIO DE DONOSTIA (1886-1956)

The *Canciones sefardíes para canto y piano* of Padre José Antonio de S[an] S[ebastián] are an appropriate companion to the Salonikan texts of Hemsi's *Coplas sefardíes* (Op. 13 and 18). There seems to be some confusion concerning the place and date of this publication. Menéndez Pidal cites them as Tolosa, [1945],[3] while Larrea Palacín gives them as Barcelona, 1948.[4] The final copy was probably put together by the printers, Laborde and Labayen, in Tolosa,[5] while the musical plates for the five accompanied songs were prepared by A. Boïleau Bernasconi in Barcelona as indicated (*Canciones*, p. 19). The songs were harmonized between 1938 and 1941 (*Canciones*, p. 7). The introduction to this edition was dated 15-XII-1943 in the city of Lecároz (*Canciones*, p. 8). It is most likely that the printing was postponed until after the close of the Second World War (1945).

Larrea Palacín alludes to the *Canciones* as written by Padre José Antonio Donostia.[6] Gilbert Chase clarifies this ononmastic problem: Donostia is the Basque name for San Sebastián.[7] Padre Donostia is well known not only for

---

[1] "Poésie et musique dans l'oeuvre des vihuélistes," in *Annales Musicologiques*, IV (1956), 91ff.
[2] Bénichou, *loc. cit.*
[3] *Romancero Hispánico*, II, p. 216.
[4] At the conclusion of his article, "La saeta," in *Anuario musical*, IV (1949), 135.
[5] The work in question is also listed as item No. 680 of the *Catálogo de la Exposición Bibliográfica Sefardí Mundial* (Madrid, 1959), p. 119. Here, Laborde and Labayen were given as the printers but without indicating the date of publication.
[6] Larrea, *loc. cit.*
[7] *The Music of Spain* (New York, 1941), p. 311, n. 10. See 2nd edition (New York, 1959), p. 333, n. 10 [for Chapter XI]. Donostia's family name is José Gonzálo Sulaica. He

the *Canciones sefardíes* but for contributions in the field of Spanish folk music, particularly that of the Basque region.[1]

The melodies contained in this edition were collected orally from Sephardic women in Salonika during the First World War by R. P. Bordachar.[2] Although Bordachar did not take any steps to publish his collection, he made some of his materials available to Lucian L. Bernheim[3] and to Padre Donostia.

Before evaluating the inherent characteristics of the ballad transcriptions contained in *Canciones sefardíes*, we must make mention of the fact that, although Bordachar collected these melodies, there appear to be some very obvious stylistic differences between the melodies given in the introduction and those with elaborate accompaniments added by Padre Donostia.[4] One should be on guard in scrutinizing the accompanied melodies as they seem to have been edited for concert use. A glance at Donostia's accompaniments leaves no doubt about their purpose, being actual arrangements in the broader sense.

Five ballad themes can be identified among the items in the work attributed to Donostia.[5] One of these themes, corresponding to *Julián el falso hortelano*, is provided with two different melodies. Furthermore, of the six melodies

entered the order of the Capuchins in 1902, which is an independent order of the Franciscans. Cf. *Diccionario de la música «Labor»* I (Barcelona, 1954), p. 751.

[1] Donostia, also a distinguished composer, studied composition in Paris with E. Cools. Donostia's works reflect the French impressionist style and include such compositions as: *Le Trois Miracles de Sainte Cecile, le Noël de Grecio, Tríptico franciscano, Poema de la Pasión*, and *Missa pro defunctis*. His accompaniment of folksongs, particularly those of the Basque region have been widely acclaimed. For a substantial listing of his musicological bibliography see *Diccionario de la música «Labor»* (Barcelona 1954), I, p. 752.

[2] Padre Bordachar was identified as the Rector of the Colegio de Bétharran, France, Basse Pyrénées (p. 1).

[3] According to Donostia (p. 6), L. Bernheim's contribution "Chansons populaires judéo-espagnoles," which was to have appeared in *Pages d'Art* (Geneva, August, 1920), may have been damaged by a fire at the printers. Although it is not known whether this publication exists, we know that Bernheim published *Cinq chansons populaires judéo-espagnoles du XVIe siècle (Smyrne)* (Zagreb: Ed. Omanut, 1939), which contains piano accompaniments. The song titles are given as: *En la mar, A la una, Las estreas, Arvoles Joran*, and *Los bilbilikos*. These are not *romances* but popular songs, as the title of the collection indicates.

[4] However, Donostia's statement that "los textos literario y musical que acabamos de transcribir son los que el P. Bordachar nos comunicó. Los damos tal como él las transcribió . . ." still appears questionable.

[5] *La choza del desesperado*, MP 140 (No. 4, pp. 4, 15-18); *Julián el falso hortelano*, a ballad not listed in the *Catálogo* (No. 6, p. 4, first and second versions); *La adúltera*, MP 80 (No. 7, p. 4); *El sueño profético*, hexasyllabic, MP 68 (No. 8, pp. 4-5); and *Andarleto*, MP 82 (No. 10, p. 5).

Levanteis, vos (No. 1, pp. 7-8) is contaminated by a verse from *El conde Olinos* (the third textual strophe, p. 3) which was placed under the melody. In spite of this contamination, we may consider this melody as a ballad tune.

printed, one was provided with an accompaniment by Donostia, while the remainder are (hopefully) copies of Bordachar's original MSS. The ballad melodies in question may be further characterized as follows:

1. All appear in the treble clef and are notated in vocal style.

2. Only two ballad tunes carry a key signature: *Landarico* has two flats, while the example employed by Donostia, *La choza del desesperado*, has five flats.

3. Of the time signatures, 6/8 can be found for *La choza del desesperado*, 3/4 for *El parto en lejas tierras* and *Julián el falso hortelano* (first version), 3/8 for *Landarico*, and 2/4 for *La adúltera (á-a)* and for the second version of *Julián* . . .

4. Other than the designation "Andante expressivo: ritmado con exactitud," for *La choza del desesperado*, the ballads bear no tempo markings.

5. Two ballads are definitely distichs, *La adúltera (á-a)* and *Landarico*, both designated as $\frac{AB}{ab}$. The quatrain strophe is apparent in both versions of the ballad *Julián el falso hortelano*, although each may be described in a different way. The second version employs the pattern ABCD, while the first version, because of similarities of the cadential patterns found in the melody sections, may be depicted as $A^{x+y} \ A'^{x+z} \ B^{w+y} \ A'^{x+y'}$, shown below:

Example 15: *Julián el falso hortelano* (second version)

An-dan-do po-res-tas ma-res na-vi--guí con la for--tu--- na; ca- i en tie-rra-sa-- je-nas don-de me no co-no-cí-an.

[Translation: Voyaging upon these seas, I sailed before the storm; I fell upon foreign lands where I was not known.]

Other ambiguities with regard to structure can be found for *El parto en lejas tierras*: the hemistichs, composed of hexasyllables, appear to conform to a musical phrase structure which calls for their amalgamation into paired hemistichs, or dodecasyllabic lines. Thus, we have a distich AB composed of twelve syllables per melody section:

Example 16: *El parto en lejas tierras*

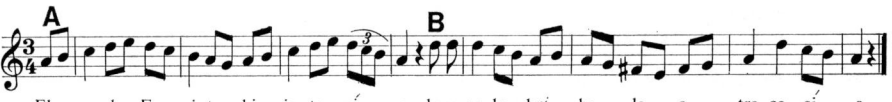

El rey de Fran-cia tres hi---jas te--ní----a la u-na la--brá---ba la o-----tra co--si----a.

[Translation: The king of France had three daughters; one was weaving, the other sewing . . .]

It is most likely that Donostia's elaborate setting for *La choza del desesperado* was intended to be sung as a quatrain. The clue is in the second strophe, where the text underlay, composed of verses 3-4, indicate the textual basis of a quatrain strophe given as $\frac{ABCDC'EB}{g\,h\,i\,j\,i\,j\,j}$, whereas for the first strophe Donostia underlays the text as $\frac{ABCDC'EE}{a\,b\,c\,d\,e\,f\,f}$. Musically speaking, this may be considered as an extended quatrain form, with two of the three extended melody sections based upon musical phrases of the basic quatrain structure. Whether or not this was taken literally from Bordachar's MS notation is not known. However, it is most peculiar that the MS ballad tunes which Donostia set to accompaniment were not included among the tunes printed in the introduction. Therefore, one can only surmise that Donostia may have altered the melodies given him by Bordachar in spite of their omission.

6. As to modal structure, two melodies are in the Dorian mode (*El parto en lejas tierras* and *Landarico*), three are in the Phrygian mode (*La adúltera* [*á-a*] and both versions of *Julián el falso hortelano*), it can be argued that the second version of the latter ballad is a mixture of the Phrygian and Aeolian modes, because of the spasmodic interchanges of *f*-sharp and *f*-natural. Again, Donostia's modal setting of *La choza del desesperado* vacillates between a major and an Aeolian modality resulting from chromatic alterations, particularly the preponderant interchange of the major and minor 3rd. Only *La choza del desesperado* exhibits plagal characteristics.

7. One example exceeds the octave in range (*Julián el falso hortelano* [second version]), being a major 9th. Two melodies have an ambitus of an octave (*El parto en lejas tierras* and *La choza del deseperado*), one a major 6th (*Landarico*), one a minor 6th (*Julián el falso hortelano* [first version]), and *La adúltera* (*á-a*) a perfect 5th.

8. The interval of the 3rd can be found in all but one example (*El parto en lejas tierras*). Four melodies contain 4ths, while one has the leap of a 5th (*Landarico*). Minor 7ths are to be found in *La choza del desesperado* and *Julián el falso hortelano* (second version).

9. For reïterated rhythmic patterns, see particularly *El parto en lejas tierras*, *La choza del desesperado*, and both versions of *Julián* . . .

10. The text underlay given for the melodic stanzas agrees for all examples, though with minute disagreements in punctuation, misspelling, and improper division of syllables. Syllabic treatment is most apparent for *Landarico* and *Julián* (first version). The remaining ballads may be described as neumatic in treatment.

11. Ornamentation, as employed in these ballads, is very slight except for those melismata which occur mainly on the penultimate syllable as seen in *La adúltera* (á-a) and *Julián* (second version). Triplet figures are employed in *El parto en lejas tierras* and *Julián* (second version), while the trill designation can be found in *La choza del desesperado*.

12. The *f*-natural shown in the second melody section of *Julián* (first version) is not necessary.

13. It is interesting to note that Bordachar took care to append melodic variants which undoubtedly occurred in successive strophes. These can be found for *La adúltera* (á-a) and *Julián* (first version). The sole instance of a cæsura indication, marked by an apostrophe, between the first and second melody sections, can be found in this latter ballad.

14. Donostia commented upon each of Bordachar's texts and even went to some length to "complete" these texts from other known sources such as Danon, Gil, Galante, Hemsi, etc. He also attempted to identify some of the texts with those of the *Catálogo*. It is surprising that Donostia did not comment upon the musical worth of these *romances*, nor give some clue as to the scope of Bordachar's collecting in Salonika, and perhaps in other centers of the Balkans.[1]

MICHAEL MOLHO (1891-1964)

Michael Molho's *Usos y costumbres de los sefardíes de Salónica* was published in Madrid in 1950.[2] The original French manuscript, intended for publication in 1940, was never printed because of unforeseen conditions caused by the Second World War. In a paragraph dated 1st October 1944, which was appended to the original introduction, Molho explained how German troops had entered Salonika on 6th February 1943, subsequently causing the deportation of some 50,000 Jews from that city. Within months this great Jewish metropolis of Macedonia was completely destroyed. Molho, accompanied by his wife and children, managed to escape to the village of Keramídi, north of Péleion, in Thessaly.[3] However, the book was finally published in 1950 in a Spanish translation of the French MS by F. Pérez Castro.

Molho was a rabbi in Salonika for many years and from his youth had been

---

[1] However, S. de Ansejo made some interesting observations in a review of Donostia's *Canciones sefardíes*. See *Sefarad*, VIII (1948), 228-30.

[2] Published by the Instituto Arias Montano (Madrid-Barcelona, 1950). This organization is primarily an Institute for Hebrew Studies and forms a branch of the Consejo Superior de Investigaciones Científicas (Madrid).

[3] *Ibid.*, pp. 12-13.

an enthusiastic student of Sephardic folklore.[1] In scanning Molho's book, one immediately comes to agree with his sense of organization, using the wedding festival in all its elaborate stages as his point of departure for developing the events and customs of the life cycle of Salonikan Jewry. A number of pertinent song and ballad texts are interwoven into the chapters. The melodies for a number of these texts are included in one of the appendices entitled "Melodías sefardíes," among which are three elegiac ballads or *endechas*.[2]

While no mention was made of the transcriber for these melodies, we shall, nevertheless, proceed to comment upon the notations made for the three elegiac ballads:

1. The tunes were notated in treble clef and in instrumental style.
2. Key signatures were employed to keep the melody within the confines of the staff.
3. Of the time signatures, two employ duple time and one triple time.
4. Tempo indications were given in Italian, Andante for *La muerte del príncipe Don Juan* and Lento for the others.
5. The three ballad melodies are in quatrain form, ABCD; however, the text for *Los siete hermanos* is sung as a distich with the refrain "Y ¡guay!, ¡qué dolor!" corresponding to the third melody section, followed by a repetition of the first hemistich for the last melody section. This latter example, sung as $\frac{ABCD}{abra}$, is given here:

---

[1] Molho's interests in folklore as well as history and literature can be seen in a chronology of such important works as: *Histoire des Israélites de Castoria* (Salonika, 1938); "Cinq Élégies en judéo-espagnol," *Bulletin Hispanique*, XVII (1940), 231-35; *Le Me'am Loez, encyclopédie populaire du séphardisme* (Salonika, 1945); *In memoriam: Hommage aux victimes juives des nazis en Grèce* (Salonika, 1948); "Tres romances de tema bíblico y dos canciones de cuna," *Comentario* (Buenos Aires, 1957), 60-70; "Consideraciones sobre folklore sefaradí," *Davar*, No. 76 (Buenos Aires, 1958-1959), 61-71; and *Literatura Sefardita de Oriente* (Madrid-Barcelona, 1960). The ballads contained in the latter work are discussed by S. G. Armistead and J. H. Silverman in "A New Collection of Judeo-Spanish Ballads," *Journal of the Folklore Institute*, III, No. 2 (Bloomington, 1966), 133-153.

[2] The three *endechas* can be identified as: *La muerte del príncipe Don Juan*, MP 15 ("Malato está el hijo del rey," p. 330); *Los siete hermanos y el pozo airón* (p. 330) and *Los siete hijos de Haná* (p. 328) neither of which are listed in the *Catálogo*. See S. G. Armistead and J. H. Silverman, "A New Sephardic *Romancero* from Salonika," *Romance Philology*, XVI (1962), 66-67.

Endechas can be heard during the week preceding *Tiša b'Ab* (the ninth day of the Hebrew month Av, which commemorates the destruction of the Temple) and during the period of family mourning. In the latter case, *endechas* are sung by hired wailing women who come to the home of the bereaved. For an interesting account of the *endecha*, see Manuel Alvar, *Endechas judeo-españolas* (Granada, 1953). A reëdited and augmented edition together with four notations of traditional *endecha* melodies was published by the Instituto Arias Montano (Madrid, 1969). (Publicaciones de Estudios Sefardíes, Serie II: Literatura, Número 2.)

Example 17: *Los siete hermanos y el pozo airón*

[Musical notation with lyrics:]
Ya se van los sie-teer-ma----------nos ya se van pa--ra A-ra-gón Y iguay! yique! do lor! Ya se van pa----ra A---ra----gón.

[Translation: Now the seven brothers depart, now they depart for Aragón and oh, what sorrow! Along the road, they find no water and oh, what sorrow!]

6. As to modal structure: *Los siete hermanos* is in major and *Los siete hijos de Haná* is a mixture of Dorian and Aeolian. *La muerte del príncipe Don Juan*, based upon the traditional hexachord, is given here:

Example 18: *La muerte del príncipe Don Juan*

[Musical notation with lyrics:]
Ma--la toes tael fi--jo del rey, ma-la to que no sal---va--------va, Sie-te do----to-----res lo mi-ran, los mi--jo------res de Gre--na-------da.

[Translation: The King's son is ill, so ill that he cannot be cured. Seven physicians examine him, the best in all Granada. Seven go up and seven come down and none does anything for him; and still the physician with the woolly beard did not arrive.]

7. Only one melody, *Los siete hijos de Haná*, exceeds the octave, i.e., a major 9th. *Los siete hermanos* has the range of an octave, and *La muerte del príncipe Don Juan*, a major 6th as shown in Example 18.

8. All three melodies are exceedingly diatonic in character. 3rds can be found in *Los siete hermanos* and *La muerte del príncipe Don Juan*, a 4th in *La muerte del príncipe Don Juan*, and 5ths in *Los siete hijos de Hana* and *Los siete hermanos* . . .

9. The discrepancies existing between the printed texts and the text underlays are far too numerous to explain.[1] I have, therefore, copied out the three me-

---

[1] The corresponding texts for the ballad melodies can be found on the following pages of *Usos y costumbres*: for *Los siete hijos de Haná*, pp. 270-71; *Los siete hermanos*, p. 265; and *La muerte del Príncipe don Juan*, MP 15, p. 269.

lodies (Examples 17 and 18 above, and Example 19 below) in order to correct the textual and notational errors in them. It should be noticed that two textual strophes have been placed under each musical stanza.

10. Ornamentation is quite heavy particularly on the ultimate and penultimate syllables. The ornamental figurations of *Los siete hijos de Haná* are given here:

Example 19: *Los siete hijos de Haná*

Sie-te fi-jos tie-ne Han------ na, [i]Hanna la bue-na giù----di------a. Los man-dó a lla---mar el rey, a to--do sie----tee-nun di------a.

[Translation: Hanna, the good Jewess, has seven sons. The King ordered that they be called, all seven of them in one day. "Come here, son of Hanna, the good Jewess, I will give you my crown. You may sit upon my throne."]

While the direct sources of these melodies remain a mystery, we must content ourselves with the knowledge that they spring from the Salonikan tradition. If other musical notations should be found among Molho's unpublished manuscripts, they will indeed be cherished with equal veneration.[1]

RAYMOND R. MACCURDY AND DANIEL D. STANLEY

The first attempt by a team of American scholars to transcribe Sephardic *romances* from gramophone recordings resulted in the article "Judaeo-Spanish Ballads from Atlanta, Georgia," which appeared in December, 1951.[2] The texts and notes of the study were edited by Raymond R. MacCurdy; the musical

---

[1] Federico Pérez Castro, long time friend of Molho, paid homage to him in "In Memoriam: Michael Molho," *Sefarad*, XXIV (1964), 464-65, and reprinted in *Le Judaïsme Séphardi*, No. 30 (July, 1965), 1312-13.

[2] Cf. *Southern Folklore Quarterly*, XV, No. 4 (December, 1951), 221-38.

Mair José Benardete was probably the first to collect ballad texts among Sephardim in the United States, as indicated by his Master's thesis, *Los romances judeo-españoles en Nueva York* (Columbia University, 1923). Mrs. Emma Adatto Schlesinger likewise collected Sephardic *romances* in Seattle (1934-1936), some of which were included in her Master's thesis, *Study of the Linguistic Characteristics of the Seattle Sefardi Folklore* (University of Washington, 1935). Cf. also Susan Bassan [Warner], *Judeo-Spanish Folk Poetry*. (M. A. Thesis, Columbia University, New York, 1947), and David Romey, *A Study of Spanish Tradition in Isolation as Found in the Romances, Refranes, and Storied*

transcriptions are by Daniel D. Stanley.[1] Atlanta has a large Sephardic community. Estimates regarding the size of its Sephardic population at the time of the publication are difficult to establish, varying from one hundred to two hundred or more families. Immigrants from the Island of Rhodes appear to be in the majority.[2] Mrs. Catina Cohen, a native of Rhodes who had been living in Atlanta since shortly after the First World War, sang the ballads, which were recorded on gramophone discs and provided the basis for this study. MacCurdy further explains that Mrs. Cohen was approximately fifty years old at the time of the recording and that she had learned the ballads during her childhood.[3] Six ballad texts with five musical examples are comprised in the article.[4] There are two additional popular Sephardic lyric songs with their melodies. The ballad of *Don Bueso y su hermana*,[5] represented by a fragment of twenty-three hexasyllabic lines, is not accompanied by its tune.

Daniel D. Stanley's musical transcriptions may be characterized as follows:

1. All five ballad melodies are notated in treble clef and in instrumental style.

2. Key signatures were chosen which would confine the melodies to the staff; however, because of the wide range of *El villano vil*, a major 13th, the melody extended below the first leger line. For example in *Arbolero*, it would have been more practical to employ a key signature of four flats rather than three, as d-flat occurs throughout the rendering.

3. The time signature 6/8 was given to four examples. The ballad *El villano vil* alternates between 6/8 and 4/8 in an irregular manner, appearing quite awkward, if not altogether unconvincing. On the other hand, the example

---

Folklore of the Seattle Sephardic Community. (M. A. Thesis, University of Washington, Seattle, 1950).

Concerning early recorded items, it is interesting to note that in 1932 Franz Boaz and George Herzog made four discs of Ladino folksongs from a Moroccan informant (female) residing in New York City. This was done under the auspices of the Archives of Primitive Music of the Department of Anthropology at Columbia University. There is a MS account which describes these recordings in detail (See Alfred Šendrey, *Bibliography of Jewish Music*, item No. 9941, p. 337). The Columbia Archives, founded by George Herzog in 1936, were moved to the University of Indiana in 1948 where the four discs in question are presently located.

[1] *Ibid.*, p. 222, n. 3, expresses appreciation to Mrs. C. Emmons who copied out the musical transcriptions appearing in the study.
[2] *Ibid.*, p. 221.
[3] *Ibid.*, p. 222.
[4] The ballads having melodies can be identified as: *Arbolero*, MP 58 (Text A, p. 223); *Mujer guerrera*, MP 121 (Text B, p. 225); *El villano vil*, MP 139 (Text D, p. 230); a contamination of *La malcasada del pastor*, MP 72, with *Hero y Leandro*, MP 41 (Text E, p. 232); and *Landarico*, MP 82 (Text F, p. 234).
[5] MP 49, text only (Text H, p. 237).

Landarico appears quite comfortable in 6/8. The remaining melodies should have been designated as *parlando-rubato*.

4. Stanley's omission of tempo indications is extremely unfortunate, since they could have been more easily and more accurately obtained from the gramophone records.

5. Two melodies definitely have quatrain strophes, ABCD (*La malcasada del pastor* + *Hero y Leandro* and *Mujer guerrera*). *Arbolero,* having the appearance of a quatrain, is in essence a distich. The example of *Mujer guerrera* is actually ABCDE, the appended melody section E being designated "hum." It is also interesting to note that section E comprises melodically a descending Phrygian scale and derives its material from previous melody sections:

Example 20: *Mujer guerrera*

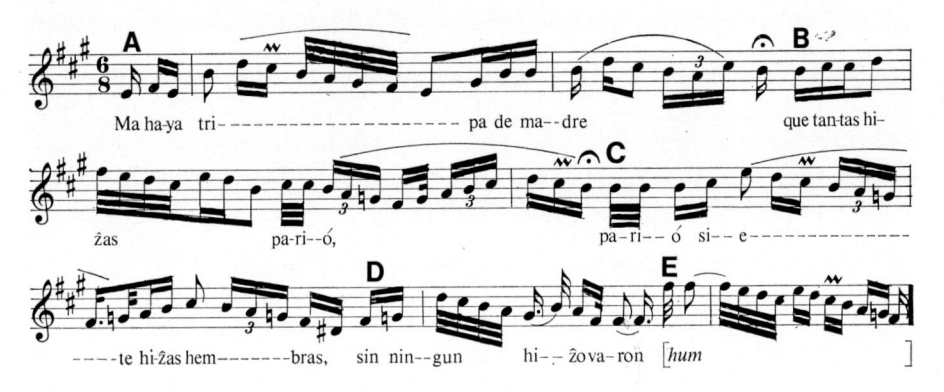

[Musical notation with lyrics:
Ma ha-ya tri- - - - - - - - - - - - - - - - pa de ma- -dre que tan-tas hi-
žas pa-ri- -ó, pa-ri- -ó si- - e- - - - - - - -
- - - -te hi-žas hem- - - - - -bras, sin nin- -gun hi- - žo va- ron [hum]]

[Translation: Cursed be the womb of a mother who gave birth to so many children; she gave birth to seven daughters and to not a single son.]

The ballad *Landarico,* although traditionally rendered as a quatrain strophe, undoubtedly posed problems for Stanley. Had Mrs. Cohen sung the opening few stanzas with the usual repetition of each hemistich, he probably would have obtained a more accurate version of the ballad. Thus, taking her rendition into account, we arrive at the formal structure $\frac{AABA'BC}{a\ a\ b\ c\ d\ d}$. This derivative structure may be considered as a composite of two full strophes:

Example 21: *Landarico*

[Musical notation with lyrics:
El rey que mu- -cho ma-dru- - - -ga, el rey que mu- - -cho ma-dru- - - -ga, on- -]

[musical notation]

de la rei-----na se i------ba el rey qui-zo bur-lar co-ne------lla,el
la--di-co al a-pri-ta-----ba, el la--di--co laa---pri-ta-----ba.

[Translation: The king who arises early went to the queen's quarters. The king wished to jest «with her» and pinched her waist.]

In this instance, we may look to the text for a clue. The repetition of the first hemistich is linked to the melody section A and its repetition. The second hemistich is the textual underlay for melody section B. However, since the hemistich is not repeated textually, it is difficult to ascertain whether B or A would follow to round out the strophe. With the appearance of the third hemistich, Mrs. Cohen naturally repeated melody section A, because this third hemistich was, in reality, the first hemistich of the new strophe. However, she did not repeat the third hemistich but moved on to the next hemistich, thus bypassing the reiteration of the first melody section and proceeding immediately to B. Again, one would expect the informant to reiterate her last textual hemistich with melody section B; and this she did, though in a haphazard manner. She began the last melody section with the opening notes of A, then, having caught herself, she immediately jumped to the latter half of melody section B, now in a different pitch sequence ending on the subdominant.

Another variant of *Landarico* also collected in Atlanta by Isaac Jack Lévy provides us with an excellent example of the ballad's transmission in the Rhodes tradition:[1]

Example 22: *Landarico*

[musical notation]

El rey que mun----cho ma-dru------ga. On--de la rei-----na
se i--------va, on--de la rei---na se i--------va.

[Translation: The king who arises early went to the queen's quarters.]

---

[1] *Sephardic Ballads and Songs in the United States*, p. 262. The melody of Lévy's text No. 90, which was sung by Mrs. Marie Beton (a resident of Atlanta, formerly from Rhodes), was notated from tape by Garret Laning.

The elaborate form encountered in the example *El villano vil* stands quite apart from the usual formal structures, and also incorporates a refrain. We may describe this *romance* melody as: $\frac{A\ B^{w+x}\ A\ B^{w+x}\ C\ D^{y+x\,b'}\ E^{z+x''}}{a\ b\quad c\ d\quad e\ r\qquad r}$

Example 23: *El villano vil*

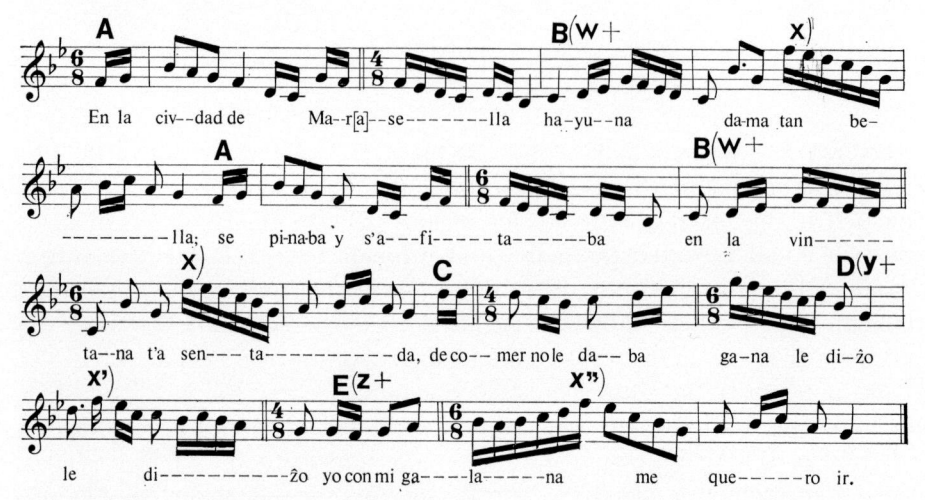

[Musical notation with labeled sections A, B(w+, x), A, B(w+, x), C, D(y+, x'), E(z+, x''), with lyrics:
"En la civ--dad de Ma--r[a]--se------lla ha-yu--na da-ma tan be---lla; se pi-na-ba y s'a---fi----ta------ba en la vin------ta--na t'a sen----ta--------da, de co--mer no le da--ba ga-na le di-žo le di--------žo yo con mi ga----la-----na me que-----ro ir."]

[Translation: In the city of Marseilles, there is a beautiful lady. She combs her hair and adorns herself and seats herself at the window. She did not wish to eat «sic?» He said, "I have my own girl and I want to go with her."]

Here we have no alternative but to resort to subscripts since no clear-cut melody divisions are apparent between the first pair of textual distichs. In fact, this may be a good example of a sixteen syllable line with an additional melody section carrying a fifth, assonating, hemistich before moving on to the rather elaborate refrain. The inclusion of this fifth hemistich is most peculiar indeed. However, a glance at the printed text following the notated example will confirm that this manner of performance is consistent at least for the second strophe. To my knowledge there is no other case in Sephardic balladry, nor in the numerous melodies encountered from the Peninsular tradition, where such a structure exists. Even the refrain *le dižo* (read *dišo*), *le dižo: Ŷo con mi galana*, employs melodic derivatives from previous melody sections. Perhaps a simpler designation, $\frac{AB^{x+y}\ AB^{x+y}\ CDE^{z+y}}{ab\qquad cd\qquad e\,r\,r}$ could also be considered.

6. A modal analysis of Stanley's melodies taken at their face value may be considered as follows: *Arbolero* is Dorian; *Mujer guerrera* is a mixture of Mixolydian and Phrygian; *El villano vil*, Aeolian; *La malcasada del pastor* + *Hero y Leandro* and *Landarico,* Aeolian with Phrygian cadential features.

7. All five ballad melodies exceed the octave in ambitus. *El villano vil*, with a range of a major 13th, may be distinguished as the sole Sephardic *romance* possessing such a wide ambitus. The ranges found for the remaining examples are: a minor 10th for *Mujer guerrera*, and a major 9th for the others.

8. The interval of the 3rd can be found in all the *romance* melodies, 4ths in *Landarico*, and 5ths in four examples. Leaps of a minor 6th are employed in *Arbolero* and a of minor 7th in *La malcasada del pastor* + *Hero y Leandro* and *El villano vil*. In the latter tune, the leaps of a minor 7th are indeed astounding as seen in Example 23 above in the fourth measure, and again [sic!] in the ninth measure. An octave leap occurs in *Mujer guerrera* (shown above), where it conveniently separates the designated "hum section" from the previous melodic phrase.

9. Reïterated rhythmic patterns are inherent in *Landarico* and *El villano vil*.

10. There are a goodly number of discrepancies between the textual underlays and the printed texts, particularly with regard to phonetic renderings of the text and punctuation.[1] The syllables are divided properly and the elisions are indicated with the usual slur.

11. Stanley transcribed all the ornamental figures; however, in one example, *Mujer guerrera*, he made use of the diacritical sign ∼ without explaining whether this indicated the customary turn or a tremolo. Ornamentation varies from slight to heavy (*Mujer guerrera*), while the remaining melodies can be considered firmly as neumatically treated. The bulk of ornamental figures appear to fall on the ultimate and penultimate syllables; however, Mrs. Cohen's rendition in many instances exhibits a number of inconsistencies which would make a most interesting subject of study, when compared with other variants of the same ballad.

12. Although one cannot find any notational errors, except for weak impressions which at times make it difficult to discern the dotted-note values, Stanley must be criticized for his strict adherence to the instrumental style of notation. Had he taken care to separate the note groupings belonging to a particular syllable, he might have reconsidered his original appraisal of the time signature indications. The manner in which a ballad, or any song for that matter, is transcribed should be considered a basic step, remarkably intuitive if you will, toward an objective and accurate analysis.

13. Stanley and MacCurdy offered no remarks concerning Mrs. Cohen's performance nor did they speculate about the ballad tunes themselves. However, Stanley's use of the *fermata* in two examples, *Arbolero* and *Mujer guerrera*, on the final tones of certain melody sections may be construed as a case for *parlando-rubato*, particularly where their occurrence is irregular.

---

[1] Reasons for some of these discrepancies are pointed out by the authors, *op. cit.*, p. 222.

14. It is commendable that, in their effort to collect and preserve the ballads included in their study, MacCurdy and Stanley not only gave the name and age of the informant together with the locale where she learned the ballads at an early age, but accurately classified all items with the aid of Menéndez Pidal's *Catálogo*.

ARCADIO DE LARREA PALACÍN

The town of Tetuán, located approximately fifty-six kilometers southeast of Tangier, figured prominently in all the early Moroccan collections (Manrique de Lara, Bustelo, and Bénichou). Concerning Tetuán and the *Romancero*, Larrea Palacín states:

> ... conserva con mayor pureza que el Tánger actual sus ancestrales usos y, si acaso no pueda compararse con la de Alcazarquivir en este aspecto, su mayor densidad de población ofrece la ventaja de más crecido número de variantes.[1]

Many of the *romances* preserved among the Sephardim of Morocco unquestionably antedate the expulsion from Spain and Portugal. However, certain Moroccan communities were almost continuously occupied by the Spaniards, and the cultural contact between the Sephardim and the Peninsular tradition was probably never completely broken. Thus, Bénichou cautions us to be on our guard against believing that the Moroccan tradition is purely archaic.[2]

The printing of *Romances de Tetuán* in 1952 was hailed as one of the milestones of traditional Sephardic balladry.[3] Arcadio de Larrea Palacín, who collected, edited, and notated the 270 texts and 285 melodies of this gigantic work,[4] offers some preliminary remarks in his introduction concerning the particulars leading up to this study. The decision to embark upon this en-

---

[1] "Romances hispánicos del medievo," *Mundo Hispánico*, V, No. 49 (1952), p. 54.

[2] Bénichou, "Le «Romancero» castillan chez les juifs espagnols," *Évidences*, No. 17 (Paris, 1951), p. 22.

[3] Published by the Instituto de Estudios Africanos in two volumes (Madrid, 1952). The organization in question is a branch of Consejo Superior de Investigaciones Científicas. A third companion volume, *Canciones rituales hispano-judíos*, was issued by the same Instituto in 1954. Larrea Palacín alluded to a fourth volume which was never published. See *Romances de Tetuán*, II, p. 5.

[4] The total number of *romances* in this work is actually 136, with 265 variant texts and 282 melodies.

In Larrea Palacín's short article, "Romances hispánicos del medievo," *Mundo Hispánico*, V, No. 49 (1952), 51-54, there are six ballad melodies which are duplicates of those contained in Vol. I of *Romances de Tetuán*. The ballad melodies can be identified as: ¿*Por qué no cantáis la bella?*, MP 57 (p. 51 = I, p. 190); *Hermanas reina y cautiva*, MP 48 (p. 52 = I, p. 148); *Don Bueso y su hermana*, MP 49 (p. 52 = I, p. 158); *La malcasada del pastor*, MP 72 (p. 53· = I, p. 251); *Destierro del Cid*, MP 5 (p. 53 = I, p. 48); and *Nacimiento de Montesinos*, MP 25 (p. 53 = I, p. 107).

deavor dates from the time Larrea Palacín was invited by the Instituto Español de Musicología to collaborate in the preparation of a projected monumental anthology, the *Cancionero Musical Popular Español*. It was unaminously agreed upon by the participants in this collaborative endeavor that an intensive study of the Spanish folksong would be incomplete without some knowledge of the *villancicos* of the sixteenth and eighteenth centuries, preserved in remote cathedrals and collegiate churches, and the Sephardic songs circulating in oral tradition since the fifteenth century.[1] Larrea Palacín was convinced by this decision, especially since he had recently completed a study on the *saeta* in which he speculated about its possible Hebraic antecedents.[2] In late October, 1950, he undertook an expedition to Spanish Morocco for the purpose of collecting melodies and texts from the Sephardic répertoire.

The original goal of the mission was flexible, in that it could either deal with one or with several Sephardic communities. Actual fieldwork was subsequently restricted to the community of Tetuán. There were undoubtedly two reasons for this choice. The first, judging from Larrea Palacín's own words, was that the number of items collected among the five family circles encountered in Tetuán far exceeded earlier expectations, thus arresting any urge to continue on to other centers, as previously planned.[3] Secondly, earlier collections made in Tetuán undoubtedly proved invaluable to Larrea for comparative purposes.[4]

While we are informed that the oral texts were taken down in shorthand, the manner in which the melodies were obtained remains somewhat of a mystery.[5] The names of the informants do not accompany their respective

---

[1] *Mundo Hispánico*, I, p. 7.
[2] "La saeta," *Anuario Musical*, IV (1949), 105-135.
[3] *Romances de Tetuán*, I, p. 10. The five family circles represent approximately twenty-four persons, four of whom were men.
[4] Larrea Palacín cited Bustelo's *romances* from the 3rd edition (1929) of Ortega's *Los hebreos en Marruecos*. José Subirá made him aware of some of the early Manrique de Lara MS transcriptions. Still, it was not until the appearance of the second volume of *Romances de Tetuán* that Larrea Palacín became aware of the melodies in Paul Bénichou's outstanding contribution "Romances judeo-españoles de Marruecos." At the same time, he called attention to the MacCurdy and Stanley melodies in "Judæo-Spanish Ballads from Atlanta, Georgia." See the addenda to Larrea, Vol. II, pp. 5-7. These latter contributions, together with Hemsi's *Coplas sefardíes*, cited in the first volume, are merely mentioned by Larrea without any discussion of their musical content. It is strange indeed that in his article on the *saeta*, Larrea Palacín referred to Donostia's *Canciones sefardíes* in his short bibliography, but failed to mention it here as a source of musical materials.
[5] I have learned from one reliable source, an informant from Tetuán, that Larrea Palacín notated some of his tunes at the Conservatory of Music in Tetuán, making use of a piano while the singer dictated ballad melodies.

contributions. Certainly one would have expected a mission of such importance, under the joint sponsorhip of the Instituto de Estudios Africanos and the Instituto Español de Musicología, to have provided the investigator with the necessary equipment for recording such precious materials. Had such equipment been made available, perhaps trips to adjacent communities could also have been realized.

If the mission was, as Larrea claimed, intended to stress musicological features, then one must take his methods severely to task. However, to do so would require not only an exhaustive reëditing of the two volumes (i.e., correcting innumerable notational errors, as well as errors in the textual underlay), but also a complete revision of the analytical tables of Larrea's appendix entitled "Ensayo de análisis musical de los romances judíos." Such a task lies completely beyond the scope of the present study. A thorough appraisal of Larrea Palacín's transcriptions and analysis would constitute a separate study of monographic proportions. My own experience with the Moroccan tradition has, in fact, provided me with the necessary data for a thorough critical review of Larrea's "musicological" endeavor, though such an undertaking must, for now, be postponed.[1]

Larrea organized his collection according to the *Catálogo*, with additional cross references to Rodolfo Gil's chaotic and unreliable *Romancero judeoespañol* (Madrid, 1911) and the Bustelo ballads in Ortega's *Los hebreos en Marruecos*, 3rd edition (Madrid, 1929).[2] After each ballad text, Larrea has appended the number of its analog in the *Catálogo*, together with a special IDEA numerical designation, undoubtedly signifying that Larrea's collected items were on file at the Archives of the Instituto de Estudios Africanos in Madrid. Furthermore, Larrea differentiated those texts which were collected orally from those which were copied from manuscripts, also noting, where applicable, whether the ballads had been sung or recited.

A year before Larrea Palacín engaged in fieldwork in Tetuán, Professor Manuel Alvar of the University of Granada had gone to Morocco (Summer, 1949), for the purpose of collecting ballad texts among the Sephardim. By early 1951, Alvar had visited the communities of Tetuán, Melilla, Larache, and Tangier. He planned a systematic investigation of the tradition, though

---

[1] Daniel Devoto has already called attention to some of the shortcomings of Larrea Palacín's two volumes in a "Nota adicional sobre las melodías de los «Romances de Tetuán»," *Bulletin Hispanique*, LXIII (1961), 249-250. For a textual criticism, see Paul Bénichou's "Nouvelles explorations du romancero judéo-espagnol marocain," which precedes Devoto's "Nota..." in the same journal, 217-248. See also Vicente Mendoza's review in *Tribuna Israelita*, No. 107 (Oct., 1953), 23-24. For further information on Alvar and subsequent field work in North Africa, see Bénichou's *Romancero judeoespañol de Marruecos* (Madrid, 1968), pp. 307-359.

[2] See the synoptic table in *Romances de Tetuán*, I, pp. 13-22.

it is not known how he gathered his materials nor whether he also collected and notated melodies.[1] Already in 1951, Bénichou had remarked that, in Morocco, *romances* were hardly known by people under sixty years of age; however, in Tetuán there were some people who still knew many ballads. Bénichou voiced a plea for a systematic collection of this tradition while the opportunity was still present.[2]

JOAQUÍN RODRIGO (1902-   )

In 1954, "Dos canciones sefardíes armonizadas" by Joaquín Rodrigo, one of the most renowned composers of modern Spain, was published in the journal *Sefarad*.[3] Ramón Menéndez Pidal entrusted Manrique de Lara's ballad collection to Rodrigo, who chose from it two melodies for *a cappella* settings. The first ballad, *Malato está el hijo del rey* (= *La muerte del Príncipe Don Juan*), was written for six voices (two sopranos, mezzo-soprano, alto, tenor, and bass) while the second, *El rey que mucho madruga* (= *Landarico*), was for four voices (soprano, alto, tenor, and bass).[4] Inasmuch as the vocal stylizations of Manrique de Lara's melodies exhibit Rodrigo's masterly hand at contrapuntal writing, one is immediately struck by the markedly different character displayed by Rodrigo's settings of *romance* melodies in contrast to the thirty-six *romances* in the *Cancionero musical de Palacio* where they are shown as homophonic settings. It would have been extremely useful if Rodrigo had reproduced the manuscript melodies he utilized for these compositions. Nonetheless we may infer that Rodrigo's interest in the Sephardic melodies was indeed a boon toward stimulating future research into Sephardic culture.

---

[1] Bénichou, "Nouvelles explorations du romancero judéo-espagnol morocain," *Bulletin Hispanique*, LXIII (July-Dec., 1961), 230-231.

In the bibliography of Manuel Alvar, *Poesía tradicional de los judíos españoles* (México D.F., 1966), we read: "Alvar, *Romancero*. Colección de textos que he ido recogiendo en Marruecos de julio de 1949 a enero de 1959. Todos estos materiales están inéditos; mis textos editados aparecen con referencia bibliográfica completa" (p. 249).

[2] "Le «romancero» castillan . . .," p. 249.

[3] *Sefarad*, XIV (1954), 353-62. Both arrangements were also published under the title *Dos canciones sefardíes del siglo XV para coro mixto* (Madrid, 1954).

On page 121 of the *Catálogo de la Exposición Bibliográfica Sefardí Mundial*, item No. 693, there is mentioned another ballad that was arranged by Rodrigo: *Triste estaba el Rey David* (Para coro mixto a Capella, Madrid, 1952). This arrangement was reprinted in Izaak A. Langnas and Barton Sholod, eds., *Studies in Honor of M. J. Benardete: Essays in Hispanic and Sephardic Culture* (New York, 1965), pp. 389-398. The melody was taken from a Sephardic source; the text represents *David llora a Absalón*, MP 38. For sixteenth-century Peninsular versions, see Querol Gavaldá, "Importance historique et national du romance," *Musique et Poésie* (Paris, 1954), pp. 318-19.

[4] The ballads are *La muerte del príncipe Don Juan*, MP 15 (pp. 355-358) and *Landarico*, MP 82 (pp. 359-362).

ISRAEL J. KATZ

Further fieldwork on Sephardic ballads in America, some five and a half years after MacCurdy and Stanley's initial contribution, was undertaken by two professors of Spanish at UCLA, Drs. Samuel G. Armistead and Joseph H. Silverman. Both were primarily interested in recording the folk-literary traditions of the primarily Eastern Mediterranean Sephardic community of Los Angeles. The success of their early endeavors in the summer of 1957 prompted them to embark upon further collecting trips in San Francisco, Seattle, and New York. All their recorded items, gathered on tape — ballads, folktales, proverbs, lyrical songs, etc. — have been carefully edited, classified, and catalogued. The tapes themselves were properly indexed and stored under optimum archive conditions.[1]

I began to collaborate with Armistead and Silverman in the spring of 1959. Since that time, my field research in Israel (1959-1961)[2] and our joint field trip to the Sephardic communities of Morocco in the summer of 1962[3] have proven to be most successful.[4]

HENRIETTA YURCHENCO

In her report to the American Philosophical Society in 1958, Prof. Henrietta Yurchenco outlined the progress of a project entitled "The Music of the Jews in Morocco."[5] Two years had elapsed since her recording expedition to Tangier and Tetuán, where among other items, she had collected a number of *romances*.[6] Although Prof. Yurchenco did not publish any of her transcriptions, she discussed briefly the salient musical features of the ballads and other secular musical materials, as well as *piyyutim*.[7] The *piyyutim* were obtained from an informant

---

[1] At the first international symposium of the newly founded Institute of Sephardic Studies, held in Madrid (June 1964), Profs. Armistead and Silverman presented a joint communication entitled "Para un gran Romancero sefardí: I. El Romancero judeo-español en los Estados Unidos; II. Sobre la historia del proyecto." Actas del Primes Simposio de Estudios Sefardíes (Madrid, 1970), pp. 287-294. See Iacob M. Hassán, "El Simposio de Estudios Sefardíes," *Sefarad*, XXIV (1964), 23-24.
[2] Concerning the initial field work in Israel, see "Toward a Musicological Study of the Judeo-Spanish *Romancero*," *Western Folklore*, XXI (Berkeley, 1962), 83-91.
[3] Information about the Moroccan field trip can be found in the *Bulletin of the International Folk Music Council*, No. XXIII (April, 1963), p. 15.
[4] For a discussion of our collaborative endeavors, see "A Judeo-Spanish *Romancero*," *Ethnomusicology*, XII (January, 1968), 72-85.
[5] *The American Philosophical Society Year Book* 1958 (Philadelphia, 1959), pp. 518-20.
[6] A summary of this field trip, written by Prof. Yurchenco, can be found in "Taping History in Morocco," *The American Record Guide*, XXIV, No. 4 (Dec., 1957), 130-132, 175.
[7] *The American Philosophical Society Year Book 1958*, p. 520.

106

who placed at her disposal several valuable collections of liturgical poems, many of which were undoubtedly sung to *romancero* melodies. Prof. Yurchenco collected about one hundred and fifty songs, including forty-four *piyyutim*.[1] Her field work is to be considered an important step in the study of Moroccan balladry, especially since she was able to tape record a number of singers who had previously informed for Larrea Palacín in 1950. It is greatly to be desired that she carry forward her projected study on the folk-poetry and music of the Moroccan Jews.[2]

LÉON ALGAZI (1890-   )

When the First International Congress of Jewish Music got underway in Paris, 4th-13th November, 1957, Sephardic music was well represented.[3] Léon Algazi, who organized the Congress, invited internationally renowned musicologists, Jews and non-Jews alike, whose contributions to the field of *musica hebraica* were indeed diverse. Among the spokesmen representing Sephardic music were Alberto Hemsi, who spoke on "The [Sacred] Traditions of the Eastern Sephardim", and the Rev. Roland Mossé, of Paris, who spoke on "The [Sacred] Traditions of the Western Sephardim." Paul Bénichou and Alberto Hemsi collaborated on "Judaeo-Spanish (Ladino) Songs," while Dr. Leo Levi presented a paper on "The Italian [Sephardic] Tradition," Msgr. Higini Anglès, Director of the Instituto de Musicología in Barcelona, spoke about "Jewish Music in Medieval Spain", and Eric Werner presented a paper on "The State of Research in Jewish Music." In an atmosphere of prestigious scholarship, such presentations were indicative of the scope and breadth of research into new and untapped areas of Jewish musical traditions, both secular and sacred.

Surveying recent developments in methodology, Curt Sachs opened the conference with a paper on "The Method of Ethnomusicology in the Field of Jewish Music." One of the Congress' aims was most promising:

> To set up a programme, according to strict critical methods, for the establishment and publication of a *Corpus* [Corpus Musicæ Hebraicæ], as complete as possible, of authentic Jewish musical traditions: Ashkenazi, Sephardi, etc., both religious (syna-

---

[1] From personal correspondence with Prof. Yurchenco, dated February 26, 1967.

[2] *The American Philosophical Society Year Book 1958*. p. 520.

[3] The Congress was given under the auspices of the Cultural Department of the World Jewish Congress with the joint participation of members from I.S.J.M. (International Society of Jewish Music).

Concerning the Congress, see *Música*, XII (1958), 55-56; Higinio Anglés, "El I Congreso Internacional de Música Judía," *Sefarad*, XVIII (1958), 211-213; and Alberto Hemsi, "Le Premier Congrès Internacional de Musique Juive à Paris, quelque réflexions," *Le Judaïsme Séphardi*, No. 16 (March, 1958), 733.

gogal and private) and popular (Yiddish, Judeo-Spanish, Judeo-Arabic, etc.) songs as well as art music in keeping with these traditions. Both the choice and the method of notation of the melodies to be included in the *Corpus* are to be decided by the Congress. In addition, objective and scientific criteria will be established to verify the authenticity of a given musical tradition.[1]

Leo Levi, the Israeli musicologist and authority on the Sephardic music of Italy, was one of the severest critics of the Congress.[2] In an article published in the Israeli journal גשר, Levi bluntly dubbed the Congress a failure and added that the resolutions adopted in Paris would remain "on paper only" because Paris, not Jerusalem, was chosen as the headquarters for the Society of Jewish Music.[3]

The fact of the matter is that nothing really did come of the projected aims of the Paris Congress. Nor did the guidelines of the First Congress of Oriental and Sephardic Music held in Jerusalem, 26th-27th April 1959, have any lasting impact on the future of research in these areas.[4] Even Gerson-Kiwi's article, "Musicology in Israel," which appeared in 1958, could do no more than mention a handful of names (Algazi, Hemsi, and Bénichou) as active collectors of Sephardic music.[5] It is also revealing that neither of the Congress reports nor Gerson-Kiwi mention work being undertaken on the Sephardic *Romancero*.

However, in 1958 the World Sephardi Federation initiated the first of a series of anthologies containing Sephardic liturgical chants and secular songs.[6] Obadiah Camhy, the Federation's Secretary General and Cultural Director, wrote the introductory notes for the first volume and the subsequent publications. The Federation's objectives were to "conserver les trésors spirituels, culturels et artistiques de la grande famille juive séphardie," in view of the

---

[1] From the fifth unnumbered page of the program guide given to the participants of the Congress. The titles of the papers presented were taken from this guide.

[2] See particularly his article. "על היחס בין מוסיקה וחברה אצל הספרדים ובני עדות המזרח" ['On the Relation of Music and Society among the Sephardim and the Jews of the Orient']" שבט זעם [*Ševet v-'Am*], V (Jerusalem, 1960), 89-96.

[3] "מוסיקה יהודית ומדינת ישראל" ['Jewish Music and the State of Israel']," גשר [*Gešer*], III (Jerusalem, Oct. 1959), 98-106.

[4] This Congress was organized by Leo Levi and Joseph ben Israel, the latter, a Jewish musician from Iraq who is currently a staff member of the Oriental Jewish Music Section of Radio Station Kol Israel. The Congress was sponsored by the World Sephardi Federation and the World Jewish Congress. For this occasion, Leo Levi delivered a paper on "Musique dans les communautés séfardies." Other topics of interest can be found in Léon Algazi's "Premier congrès de musique orientale et séfardie," *Kol-Sepharad*, II, No. 8 (June, 1959), 117-18.

[5] *Acta Musicologica*, XXX (1958), 24. A revised version of this article appeared under the same title, but in Hebrew, "המוסיקלוגיה בישראל" in גשר [*Gešer*], III (Jerusalem, Oct., 1959), 107-115. Having participated in the Paris Conference, Gerson-Kiwi became aware of the activities of these men.

[6] *Chants séphardis, recueillis et notés par Léon Algazi*. London: World Sephardi Federation, [1959].

fact that "certains de ces trésors courent le danger de disparaître sans laisser de trace."[1]

Perhaps the reputation which Léon Algazi had already established both as a composer and choir master prompted Obadiah Camhy to enlist his aid in preparing the first handsomely printed edition in the series: *Chants séphardis*.[2] Algazi, born in Bucharest in 1890, had always enjoyed an active and fruitful life in the pursuit of music. His musical career had already shown promise when, in the year 1906, as a lad of sixteen, he travelled to Jerusalem to visit his great uncle, a rabbi in one of the Sephardic synagogues of that holy city. During his ten-month stay, Algazi, at the request of his great uncle, attended the *Lämel-schule*, a normal school for teachers.[3] It was at this school that A. Z. Idelsohn was employed as a professor of music. Idelsohn's confidence in Algazi's musical maturity lead to the latter's appointment as director of the boys' choir when the school gathered for services, with Idelsohn himself acting as precentor. Algazi recalled proudly this early encounter with the musical giant and added that Idelsohn confided in him the dream of the extraordinary project yet before him.[4]

With such an impressive start, it is no wonder that Algazi chose to follow music as a career. Just when Algazi took up residence in Paris is not known; however, his appointment as Musical Director at the Synagogue de la rue de la Victoire and his later appointment as Professor of Music at the Séminaire Israélite earned for him a place of eminence as an authority on Sephardic music in France, if not in all Western Europe.[5] Later years found him associated quite prominently with Radiodiffusion-Television Française in Paris.

---

[1] *Ibid.*, p.v. Joaquín Rodrigo and Victoria Camhi [Camhy] took Obadiah Cahmy's words as the starting point for their review of *Chants séphardis* in *Sefarad*, XVIII (1958), 366-69.
[2] Algazi studied composition with André Gédalge, Raoul Laparra, and Charles Koechlin. A rather complete list of his compositions can be found at the end of his article "La Musique religieuse israélite en France," *La Revue musicale*, No. 222 (1953-54), 165-166.
[3] The *Lämel-schule* was founded by Elise von Herz-Lämel in Jerusalem in 1856 in memory of her father. This idea was suggested to her by the poet Ludwig August Frankl. In 1911, it came under the jurisdiction of the Hilfsverein der deutschen Juden as its Jerusalem boys' school. Cf. Henrietta Szold, *Recent Jewish Progress in Palestine* (Philadelphia, 1915), pp. 28, 124-25.
[4] Léon Algazi, "Chants traditionnels et populaires juifs," *Évidences*, No. 16 (Paris, Jan., 1951), 13-14.
[5] Some of Algazi's endeavors in the field of Jewish Music, including those cited above, were published under such titles as: "Musique Biblique," *L'Univers Israélite*, XLII (Paris, July 13, 1923), 395-396; "Les Juifs dans la musique française," *Cahiers Juifs*, II, No. 4 (Paris, 1933), 55-64; "Musique juive de Russie," *Évidences*, No. 33 (Paris, 1953), 24-30, which is an extract from his contribution in *Musique Russe*, 2 vols., Presses Universitaires de France (Paris, 1953); "Le Drame liturgique," *Évidences*, No. 44 (Paris, 1954), 37-40; and "Le Folklore Séphardi," *Le Judaïsme Séphardi*, No. 10 (March, 1956), 421-424.

For *Chants séphardis*, Algazi had drawn his materials from the personal collection of notations taken down from Eastern Mediterranean informants residing in Paris.[1] It is interesting to note that additional items were taken from recordings which Algazi had made in collaboration with the eminent ethnomusicologist Constantin Braïloïu (1893-1958). Together they made twenty recordings under the auspices of the University of Paris, utilizing the studios and equipment of the Musée de la Parole et du Geste.[2] Although Algazi, in his introduction, mentioned the names of the informants as well as the geographical areas represented, he failed to correlate this information with each of his notations.

Of the thirty-two popular Judeo-Spanish songs he published, four are *romances* and one is a religious narrative song (*Nacimiento y vocación de Abraham*).[3] Many of these melodies were completely new, while others, according to Algazi's preliminary remarks (p. xiv), were made known earlier by such men as A. Z. Idelsohn, W. Simoni,[4] and L. Bernheim,[5] although deviating somewhat from Algazi's notations. Algazi had already arranged four of these

---

[1] *Chants séphardis*, p. xiv.

[2] These discs contain both sacred and secular items which were recorded from two *hazzanim* the Rev. M. Angel, from Paris, and the Rev. M. Kalifa, from Algiers. See "Chants traditionnels et populaires juifs," *Évidences*, No. 16 (Paris, 1951), p. 15.

Unesco's International Archives of Popular Music issued a 10" (= 25 cm) 78 rpm disc of six Judeo-Spanish songs, five of which were included in *Chants séphardis*. Cited as record number 9 A1 61/62, side one contains *Alta, alta va la luna*, *Partos trocados* (Algazi, No. 47), and *Ya salió de la mar la galana* (Algazi, No. 50); side two contains *La rosa enflorece* (it resembles the melody for Algazi, No. 68), *A la una nací yo* (Algazi, No. 61), and *Un cavritico*, a Passover song (Algazi, No. 27, the third melody given). Notice that the order of items on the second side differs from that listed in the *International Catalogue of Recorded Folk Music* (London, 1954), p. 129.

It is not known whether Algazi engaged Braïloïu's collaboration for the Unesco recordings. Side one was sung by Sephardic women, and side two by Sephardic men; all the informants are from Salonika. Algazi's transcriptions leave much to be desired. An interesting comparison can be made for the recorded example *Partos trocados* (= *Hermanas reina y cautiva*) with that which I notated in "Toward a Musicological Study of the Judeo-Spanish *Romancero*," *Western Folklore*, XXI (1962), 80.

[3] The *romances* can be identified as: *Nacimiento y vocación de Abraham*, hexasyllabic, MP 30 (Algazi, No. 45); *Hermanas reina y cautiva*, MP 48 (Algazi, No. 47), also found in the Unesco recording; *Melisenda insomne*, MP 28 (Algazi, Nos. 52 and 53, the first example given as a couplet, the latter as a quatrain); *La adúltera (á-a)*, MP 80 (Algazi, No. 62); and *Arbolero* or *Vuelta del marido (í)*, MP 58 (Algazi, No. 65).

[4] Wolf Simoni, *Cuatro canticas sefardies: chants populaires* (Paris, [c. 1937]). Simoni set elaborate piano accompaniments to the four melodies in this collection. Two of these items are traditional ballads and can be identified as MP 41, *Hero y Leandro* (pp. 5-7), and MP 74, *La mujer engañada* (pp. 8-10). The popular religious song *Abraham avinu*, listed in the *Catálogo* as number 30, is also included (pp. 11-12).

[5] See page 90, note 3.

melodies for voice and piano accompaniment.[1] However, it is not known which items included in *Chants séphardis* were taken down "by ear" and which from the recordings.

A careful took at Algazi's notations may be useful:

1. The treble clef and vocal notation are employed for all the examples.

2. With regard to key signatures, Algazi indicates only those accidentals which are valid throughout the entire piece. For example, he utilizes the key signature [♯] for both versions of *Melisenda insomne*, since both melodies do not move to the upper *f*-sharp[1]. A peculiar case is to be found in *Nacimiento y vocación de Abraham*, whose key signature [♭] does not include the chromatic altering of the lower *e*-natural. Here, Algazi inserts the "flat" sign above the note when it is to be lowered. This designation appears seven times, especially after the note *f*-sharp which precedes it; however, only in two instances is the note left unmarked, namely in measures 7, 11, and 15 of *Nacimiento y vocación de Abraham*, where the melody is given as [music example]. It seems rather strange that Algazi, in keeping with his concept of key signatures, did not choose to indicate this flat and mark the unaltered *e* with a natural sign for those measures shown above. It is unlikely that Algazi's "flat" indication meant a lowering of less than a semi-tone as he would have clearly stated his intentions. [♯]

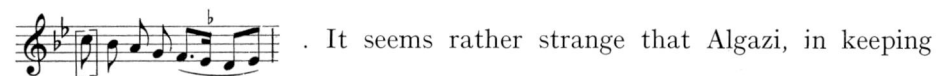

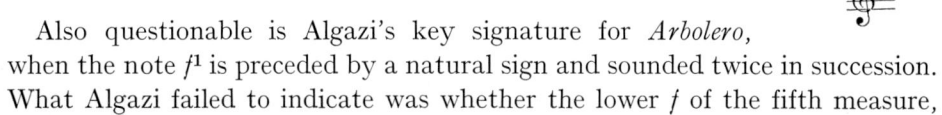

Also questionable is Algazi's key signature for *Arbolero*, when the note *f*[1] is preceded by a natural sign and sounded twice in succession. What Algazi failed to indicate was whether the lower *f* of the fifth measure, [music example] was to be raised or left natural. On the latter probability, I have identified the tune's modality as the Mixolydian (see No. 5 below). Furthermore, if *f*-sharp[1] holds true for the lower tone, then we have an augmented 2nd-interval.

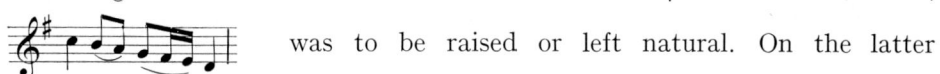

3. One example, *Arbolero*, is in common time, while *Nacimiento y vocación de Abraham* employs common time for the ballad and 3/4 interchanged with

---

[1] Algazi states (*Chants séphardis*, p. xiv) that the transcriptions of these arrangements differ somewhat from those of his collection. Among the four settings are versions of *Melisenda insomne* and *Vuelta del marido* (*i*), which were published without date by Éditions Salabert of Paris.

4/4 in the refrain section. The remaining examples, undoubtedly in the *parlando-rubato* style, are marked with dotted bar-lines which most probably designate the accented syllable as Algazi felt it, or he may have used it, as in *Melisenda insomne* (the second version) and *La adúltera* (á-a), to mark out the important phrase units. The technique of using dotted bar lines for *parlando-rubato* renditions is useful only when its consistent employment characterizes a particular aspect of performance, be it accentuation, phrasing, or even depicting the various melody sections. In these examples, and the rest of *Chants séphardis* for that matter, it is not clear what Algazi intended to suggest by his use of this technique.

4. We must applaud Algazi for his careful consideration of tempo markings, undoubtedly obtained with the aid of a metronome. Only in one other previous instance do we find metronomically derived tempo indications for Sephardic ballad melodies, and that is in Larrea Palacín's collection *Romances de Tetuán*. Algazi used both the quarter and eighth note as the generating *tactus*, the former, in four examples, ranging from approximately M.M. = 54 to 84, and the latter in two examples, *Hermanas reina y cautiva* and *La adúltera* (á-a), with M.M. = 182 and 144, respectively.

5. All but one example are quatrains; the exception is the melody, *Melisenda insomne* (first version), a tripartite form with the scheme $\begin{smallmatrix} A^{u+v} & B^{w+x} & C^{y+z} \\ a & b & b \end{smallmatrix}$, of which the second hemistich is repeated. Also noticeable is the division of the hemistich to accommodate two musical phrases.

Other than the basic quatrain designation ABCD for *Melisenda insomne* (second version), the other examples are somewhat more elaborate. *Arbolero* employs the scheme $\begin{smallmatrix} A^{x+x'} & BCD \\ a & bcd \end{smallmatrix}$, which in the first hemistich is divided into two musical phrases. The remaining examples contain refrains which are indicated as follows: $\begin{smallmatrix} ABA'CDEFB' & GG'F'B'GG'F'B' \\ a\,b\,c\;d\,e\,f\,g\,h & (\text{refrain}) \end{smallmatrix}$ for *Nacimiento y vocación de Abraham*, shown below:

Example 24: *Nacimiento y vocación de Abraham*

Av-ram a-vi---nu, pa-dre que-ri------do pa-dre ben-di---cho luz de Is--ra-el

Av-ram a-vi---nu, pa-dre que-ri-------do, pa-dre ben-di---cho luz de Is-ra-el.

[Translation: When King Nimrod went out into the fields, he looked at the heavens and at all the stars, He saw a holy light among the Jews, for Abraham, our Father, was to be born. Our father Abraham, beloved father, blessed father, light of Israel.]

The ballads *Hermanas reina y cautiva* and *La adúltera* (á-a) both subscribe to the scheme $\frac{ABCDE}{a\ b\ c\ d\ r}$, with the melody section *E* carrying the refrain burden.

6. The modal structures of the six musical examples are clearly identified as: Phrygian (*Melisenda insomne* [second version]); Mixolydian (*Hermanas reina y cautiva* and *Arbolero*); minor (*Nacimiento y vocación de Abraham* and *Melisenda insomne*, first version); and major (*La adúltera* [á-a]). Both melodies in minor end on the lower 5th and are plagal in character, whereas the remaining tunes end on the *finalis*.

7. Four ballads have an ambitus of an octave, one a major 9th (*Nacimiento y vocación de Abraham*), and one a minor 10th (*Arbolero*).

8. While all the melodies are characteristically diatonic in movement, they each contain a few intervals of the 3rd. Four examples utilize 4ths, one employs the 5th (*Hermanas reina y cautiva*), and one a major 6th. A minor 7th can be found in *Arbolero*, and the leap of an octave in *Nacimiento y vocación de Abraham*. The interval of the augmented 2nd can be found in *Melisenda insomne* (first version) *d*-sharp to *c*.

9. An interesting example of reïterated patterns, rhythmically speaking, can be found in *Nacimiento y vocación de Abraham*, shown above. Notice particularly the patterns which are duplicated in the refrain as well, and the motif ♪. ♪ ♪ , found repeated throughout the melody.

10. The printed texts which follow the notated strophes are continuations of the text underlay. The idea appears to be a good one, and was probably proposed for economic reasons. However, one must not lose sight of the purposes for which folksong collections and anthologies are issued. Apart from the important matter of preservation, these collections serve as valuable sources for scholars, whose work necessitates the analysis of texts as well as music. The ideal to strive for would be a complete phonetic rendering of all

texts collected. The text underlay of the musically notated strophes, whichever they may be, should be in full agreement with the printed texts, with elisions, punctuation, etc., included.

Algazi divided syllables accurately but failed to indicate the elisions with the slur or any other designation. The interjection ¡ah! can be found at the beginning of the last melody phrase in *Melisenda insomne* (first version). As for the text-tune relationship, the settings vary from strict syllabic settings (*Hermanas reina y cautiva* and *La adúltera* [*á-a*]) to highly melismatic renderings (*Melisenda insomne* [both versions] and *Arbolero*).

11. Those examples which are highly embellished have their ornaments written out, with the commonly employed grace note and grace-note pairs. Also found are triplets and groupings of five, six, and seven notes. The melismata fall generally on the ultimate or penultimate syllables of the various melodic phrases.

12. Algazi's transcriptions have been carefully edited.

13. In only one instance is a second notated strophe given (*Hermanas reina y cautiva*) which varies considerably from the first.

14. In the introduction, Algazi made general comments about the music contained in *Chants séphardis*; however, he did not correlate his ballads with the *Catálogo* nor did he cite any other analogs. Furthermore, he failed to distinguish between the ballads recorded on discs and those taken down "by ear."

ISAAC LEVY (1919-   )

Isaac Levy's *Chants judéo-espagnols*,[1] printed in the same handsome format as its predecessors, was completely non-liturgical in content. Levy, born in

---

[1] *Chants judéo-espagnols, recueillis et notés par Isaac Levy*. Introduction by O. Camhy, London: World Sephardi Federation, [1959].

The coïncidental appearance of two contributions to the field of Sephardic balladry by two men bearing the same name must be clarified. In February 1959, there appeared a Master's thesis entitled *Sephardic Ballads and Songs in the United States: New Variants and Additions* (The State University of Iowa). The author of this thesis, Isaac Jack Lévy, collected the ballads with the aid of a tape recorder from Sephardic informants in private residences and in old age homes in Brooklyn, New York, and Atlanta, Georgia.

Although Isaac Jack Lévy included musical examples in his appendix, they were mainly copied from previous collections, such as Hemsi and Vicente Mendoza. However, two examples, *La serena de la mar* (p. 253) notated without text underlay by Harry Kruger of Atalanta and *El rey que mucho madruga* [= *Landarico*, MP 82] (p. 262) notated by Laning were new. An additional ballad melody, that for *Vuelta del hijo maledecido*, MP 124, was collected by Lévy and notated by Roger M. Arnett and published in the *Romancero tradicional*, Vol. III (Madrid, 1969), p. 131.

the town of Magnésia, near Izmir, Turkey, had lived in Palestine from the year 1922, when his parents emigrated there.[1] His musical education was primarily in the Western tradition with concentration upon the study of voice at the conservatories in Jerusalem and Tel Aviv. His career as a concert artist, and his skill in composing and arranging vocal music, earned him in 1955 the directorship of the Judeo-Spanish Section of the Israel Broadcasting Station, Kol Israel. Mr. Levy's enviable position as a prime spokesman for Sephardic culture has for long been a bone of contention among the more traditionally minded Sephardic leaders who have criticized him for his stylized renditions of traditional music. In fact, Mr. Levy's views on Sephardic music in general have been severely criticized by Israeli musicologists.

The materials in this volume in general represent the same geographical regions as Algazi's collection. Although he claims to have collected his melodies from informants from these regions, Levy, like Algazi, failed to include such inportant information as their names, the locales represented, and approximate dates when the items were collected. Of the ninety-seven *canciones populares* bearing Levy's notation, eighteen can be identified as *romances*.[2] However, it is questionable whether some of these texts are truly representative of the Eastern Mediterranean tradition.[3]

The twenty-four ballad melodies notated by Levy may be described as follows:

1. The melodies are notated in vocal style and utilize the treble clef.

2. The key signatures were chosen to keep the majority of these examples within the staff; however, two melodies go below middle c (*La venganza de la*

---

[1] *Chants judéo-espagnols*, p. vii.
[2] Levy's ballad melodies, taken in their numerical order with the incorporation of subsequent versions and variants, can be identified as: *La malcasada del pastor*, hexasyllabic, MP 72 (Levy, No. 1); *Silvana*, MP 98 (Levy, No. 2); *Vuelta del hijo maldecido*, MP 124 (Levy, No. 3); *Hero y Leandro*, MP 41 (Levy, 4 and 5); *Landarico*, MP 82 (Levy, Nos. 6 and 14); *Arbolero* or *Vuelta del marido* (í), MP 58 (Levy, Nos. 7 and 8); *La choza del desesperado*, MP 140 (Levy, No. 9); *Don Bueso y su hermana*, hexasyllabic, MP 49 (Levy, No. 10); *Melisenda insomne*, MP 28, which after six verses continues with the text of MP 140 (Levy, No. 12); *Rachel lastimosa*, MP 79 (Levy, No. 13); *Vuelta del marido* (é), MP 59 (Levy, No. 15); *La mujer de Juan Lorenzo*, MP 12 (Levy, No. 16); *Amantes perseguidos* or *El conde Olinos*, MP 55 (Levy, No. 18); *La mujer engañada*, MP 74 (Levy, No. 19); *La adúltera (á-a)*, MP 80 (Levy, Nos. 25, 27, and 85); *Una ramica de ruda*, MP 107 (Levy, No. 32); *Venganza de la novia rechazada*, not in the *Catálogo* (Levy, No. 62); and a contamination of *Celinos y la adúltera* plus *Vos labraré yo un pendón*, MP 120 (Levy, No. 67).
[3] Armistead and Silverman investigated this aspect of Levy's collection in their review published in *Nueva Revista de Filología Hispánica*, XIV (1960), 345-349. Max Wholberg's brief review casts doubt upon the origin of a few of Levy's melodies. Cf. "The Music of the Sephardim," *Le Judaïsme Séphardi*, Nouvelle Serie, No. 25 (December, 1962), 1058.

novia rechazada and *Vos labraré yo un pendón*), and one melody extends to a^{11} above the staff (*Rachel Lastimosa*). Levy seems to favor the flat signatures, used in twelve examples, more than the sharp signatures, found in four examples. One key signature is given as [musical notation] for *Melisenda insomne*.

3. Fifteen examples are notated in duple time: fourteen in 2/4, and one in 4/4. Four examples are in triple time: three in 3/4, and one in 3/8. The remaining five ballad melodies carry mixed time signatures: 2/4 interchanged with 3/4 (*Landarico*), 3/4 interchanged with 2/4 (*El conde Olinos* [first version]); 3/4 2/4 3/4 (*Hero y Leandro* [first version]) the 2/4 is only employed for one measure]; C 3/4 2/4 3/4 2/4 (*Arbolero* [second version]); and 2/4 3/4 4/4 2/4 4/4 2/4 (*Melisenda insomne*).

4. Levy used the conventional Italian tempo designations.

5. With regard to the formal structure, the distich and quatrain are to be found much varied. Basic distich schemata such as $\frac{AB}{ab}$ and $\frac{AABB'}{aabb}$ can be found in *Silvana* and *Landarico*, respectively. More elaborate distich schemata occur in such tripartite structures as $\frac{ABC}{aab}$ with the consistent repetition of the first hemistich to a new melody section (*Melisenda insomne*), and $\frac{ABC}{abb}$ with the consistent repetition of the second hemistich to a new melody section (*La adúltera* [á-a] [first version]). The second version of *Hero y Leandro* employs the scheme $\frac{ABCDCD}{arabab'}$, in which the second melody section carries the refrain ¡*Blancas de roz, Ay, ramas de flor!*, which is repeated for all strophes. A unique setting of a ballad distich can be found in the example, *La choza del desesperado*, shown below, whose scheme is given as $\frac{A^{x+z}\ B\ C^{y+z}\ D\ E^{(z)}\ D}{a^{4+}\ 4\ b^{4+}\ 4\ i\ b^{4}}$ with the melismatic interjection ¡*Amán*! consistently employed.

Example 25: *La choza del desesperado*

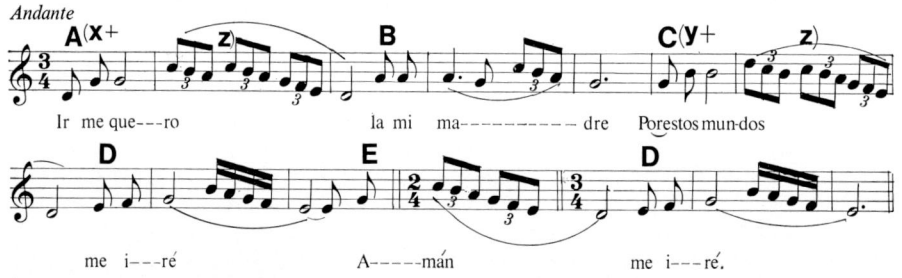

[Musical notation with lyrics:]
Ir me que---ro / la mi ma---------dre / Porestos mun-dos
me i---ré / A-----mán / me i---ré.

[Translation: Mother, I wish to go. I will go out into the world. Have mercy on me, I will go.]

Eight examples adhere to the quatrain strophe ABCD. The scheme ABAC is employed for *Vuelta del hijo maldecido* and *La venganza de la novia rechazada*, while $\frac{A^{x+x'}BCD}{a\ \ \ bcd}$ and $\frac{A^{x+y}BCD}{a\ \ \ bcd}$ are used for the first and second versions, respectively, of *Arbolero*. In both schemata, the first hemistich is divided into two melody sections. The remaining three examples may be depicted as $\frac{ABCDCD}{abcdcd}$, although similar to the melody section structure of *Hero y Leandro*, outlined above, they carry four textual hemistichs (*Hero y Leandro* [second version], *Una ramica de ruda*, and *Vos labraré yo un pendón*).

6. As regards modal structure, the Phrygian mode can be found in *Una ramica de ruda* and *La choza del desesperado*, the Mixolydian in *La adúltera (á-a)* (second version), and the Aeolian in *La adúltera (á-a)* (first version). Ten melodies subscribe to the major mode, seven to the minor mode. Major-minor combinations can be found for the ballad melodies *Hero y Leandro* (second version) and *Don Bueso y su hermana*. *Landarico* modulates from C Major to G Major. While fourteen melodies end on the *finalis*, seven conclude on the lower 5th, one on the lower 6th (*Silvana*), one on the upper 3rd (*Hero y Leandro* [first version]), and one on the second degree (*La adúltera [á-a]*, [second version]). Eight melodies are in the plagal form.

7. As for ambitus, nine examples have the range of an octave, and seven a minor 7th. Eight melodies exceed the octave: *La venganza de la novia rechazada* has the range of a major 11th; *Hero y Leandro* (first version), a major 10th; *La mujer de Juan Lorenzo* and *Rachel Lastimosa*, a minor 10th; *La adúltera* (á-a) (third version), and *Vuelta del hijo maldecido*, a major 9th; and *Landarico* and *Vos labraré yo un pendón*, a minor 9th.

8. Every ballad melody contains at least one or more 3rds, while twenty-one examples have 4ths. Only eleven examples have 5ths, two have the interval of a minor 6th (*La adúltera [á-a]* [first version], and *Una ramica de ruda*), and three melodies have leaps of an octave (*Hero y Leandro* [second version], *La mujer engañada*, and *La venganza de la novia rechazada*). The latter example also contains the augmented-2nd interval.

9. Reïterated rhythmic patterns appear in *La malcasada del pastor* and in those melodies whose melody sections are repeated. In *Una ramica de ruda*, the reïteration occurs for the melody sections B and D, and the martial rhythmic pattern, so characteristic for *Vuelta del marido (é)*, is also stated.

10. Though also published by the World Sephardi Federation, Levy's texts, unlike Algazi's *Chants séphardis,* were printed in their entirety under the notated melodies, together with a parallel translation in French. Levy, however,

was not careful in matching his textual underlay with the printed texts in regard to punctuation and hyphenation, and in two instances there is an omission of a word or even an entire hemistich. For the ballad *La mujer engañada,* he omits the world *el* from the second hemistich of the printed text. In *La mujer engañada,* he omits the third hemistich of the refrain "*Dúrmite mi alma,*" plus the interjection ¡*Ay!* from the following hemistich.

It is curious that the texts for *Landarico* (second version) and *Vuelta del hijo maldecido* are printed as distichs when their melodic and textual structures conform to the quatrain strophe. In at least twenty of the examples, inaccuracies can be found in Levy's division of the syllables. In those examples where elisions occur, they are not indicated as such. Perhaps the capitalization of the first word of each hemistich for every ballad text has been carried over from *Chants séphardis.* All but two of the ballads have octosyllabic lines, the exceptions being *Don Bueso y su hermana* and *La malcasada del pastor,* which are hexasyllabic.

11. The degree of ornamentation varies from slight to quite elaborate, particularly on the ultimate and penultimate syllables of each melody section. Levy employs the grace note in four examples and the triplet figure in four other instances. The bulk of Levy's melodies are diatonic in nature, ranging from syllabic treatment (*Vuelta del marido*[é], *La malcasada del pastor, La adúltera* [á-a] [second version], and *Una ramica de ruda*) to highly melismatic treatment (*Melisenda insomne, La mujer engañada, Landarico* [second version], *Silvana,* and *La choza del desesperado*).

12. The errors which occur in Levy's notations arise from the problem of inaccurate textual underlay. In only two instances can these errors be rectified:

a. In *La venganza* . . . [musical notation] should read [musical notation]
  tae------scu--   --ta   escu--

b. In *La mujer engañada,* [musical notation] and [musical notation] should read [musical notation]
  --seha-ga   chaa-le
and [musical notation] respectively.

Moreover, it is difficult to correct such printed anomalies as:

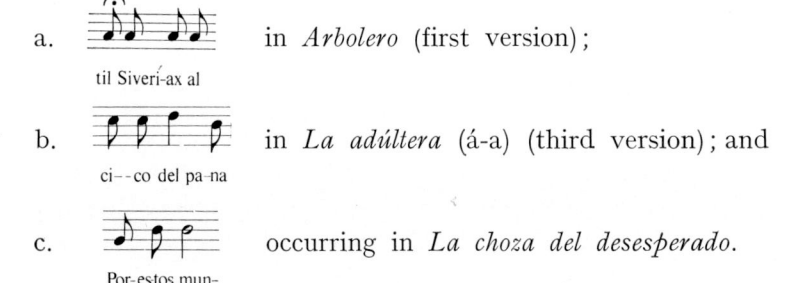

a. [musical notation] in *Arbolero* (first version);
til Siverí-ax al

b. [musical notation] in *La adúltera* (á-a) (third version); and
ci--co del pa-na

c. [musical notation] occurring in *La choza del desesperado.*
Por-estos mun-

13. A second strophe was notated for *Arbolero* (first version) which only deviates slightly in its repetition from the first two measures of the opening melody section.

14. Like Algazi, Levy commented upon the music in a general manner and did not make any attempt to cite other ballad tunes or textual analogs. However, one idiosyncrasy deserves mention. In a little more than half the ballads, Levy indicates with the mark √ the cæsuræ occurring between the various melody sections. In one instance (*Arbolero* [second version]) he adds the *fermata* sign over the last sung syllable of the second and third melody section in both strophes. Why Levy resorted to this practice is not clear. Are we to understand that these designations hold true throughout the rendering?

Since the publication of *Chants judéo-espagnols*, Levy's talents as a performer and lecturer have been much sought after in Israel and abroad.[1] In the summer of 1960, he was awarded a scholarship by the World Sephardi Federation to attend the Third International Course on the Information and Interpretation of Spanish Music at Santiago de Compostela, where his vocal renditions and talks on the Sephardic *Romancero* received much acclaim.

Utilizing the materials he compiled from his experiences as a *ḥazzan*, Levy has recently published four volumes of his projected five-volume *Antología de Liturgia Judeo-española* (Jerusalem, 1965-   ), as a further measure for preserving the heritage of his beloved Sephardim.[2] There exist other valuable anthologies as well as a number of critical works dealing with varied aspects of Sephardic music.[3]

Dr. Leo Levi has contributed much to the study of Sephardic music, mainly

---

[1] One such concert given at El Club las Haras, Buenos Aires, was described in "El arte de Yitsjah Levy," *Kol-Sepharad*, II, No. 10 (Oct., 1959), 158-59.

[2] A review of the first volume was written by María Teresa Rubiato in *Sefarad*, XXVI (1966), 238-41.

[3] Among the anthologies are included: A. Z. Idelsohn's Vols. IV and V of the *Hebräisch-orientalische Melodienschatz* which contain citations of earlier collections (See note 71 supra); *Liturgie séphardie*, based upon the liturgical renderings of the Revs. Eliezar Abinun and Joseph Papo with the musical transcriptions of Franz Reizenstein (London, 1959); and M. J. Benharoche-Baralia, *Chants hebraïques traditionnels en usage dans la communauté séphardie de Bayonne* (Biarritz-Paris, 1961). See also A. Larrea Palacín's *Canciones rituales hispano-judías*, Vol. III, *Cancionero judío del Norte de Marruecos* (Madrid, 1954).

Cf. also Hanoch Avenary, "The Sephardic Intonation of the Bible, Amsterdam 1699", *Le Judaïsme Séphardi*, No. 21 (Oct., 1960), 911-13; Abraham Lopez Cardozo, "The Music of the Sephardim," *The World of the Sephardim* (New York, 1960), pp. 37-71; Theodor Fuchs, "Prilog muzici sefardskih židova u Turskoj," with a resumé in German "Zur Musik der spaniolischen Juden in der Türkei," *Omanuth*, I (Agram [= Zagreb], 1936-1937), 157-164; Alberto Hemsi, "המוסיקה העממית של הספרדים" ['The Popular

from Italian sources; however, he may have gathered *romances* from among the Italian Sephardim. On the other hand, the noted Israeli authority on Hassidic music, Me'ir Simeon Geshuri [listed in French publications as Gueschouri], did contribute some articles on the Sephardic *Romancero*.[1] Dr. Edith Gerson-Kiwi, the eminent Israeli musicologist who has been engaged in the systematic study of Jewish music since 1936, has published numerous articles based upon her extensive field recordings of non-European Jewish informants, the Sephardim included.

EDITH GERSON-KIWI (1908-   )

At one of the sessions of the Fourteenth Annual Conference of the International Folk Music Society (Québec, 28th August-3rd September 1961), a paper entitled "Musical sources of the Judaeo-Hispanic *romance*" was read by Dr. Gerson-Kiwi.[2] The paper, which was subsequently published in 1964 with some revisions and additions,[3] suggested that "possible sources of the

Music of the Sephardim']," [מזרח זמערב] *Mizraḥ u-Ma'arav*, II, No. 6 (Jerusalem, 1929), 414-418 (In Hebrew), and "Cancionero sefardí," *Sefarad*, XIX (1959), 378-384; Nikolay Kaufman's summary of "Jewish and Gentile Folk Song in the Balkans and its Relation to the Liturgical Music of the Sephardic Jews in Bulgaria," *Journal of the International Folk Music Council*, XVI (1964), 63; H. Keller, "The Music of British Jews," *The Jewish Quarterly*, III (London, 1956), 21-23; Isaac Elijah Navon, המוסיקה בין יהודי המזרח ['The Music Among the Jews of the Near East']," *Hallel*, I, No. 3 (Jerusalem, 1930), 55-57 (In Hebrew); and Walter Wünsch, "Der Jude im Balkanslavischen Volkstum und Volksliede," *Die Musik*, XXX (Stuttgart-Berlin, June, 1938), 595-598.

Photocopies of the catalog holdings of Sephardic and oriental music which existed at the Jacob Michael's Jewish Music Library, 120 Wall Street, New York City, were also exhibited at the Exposición Bibliográfica Sefardí Mundial (Madrid, 1959). Cf. the *Catálogo de la Exposición* . . ., p. 140, item No. 825. In the early spring of 1967, the complete collection of Jewish Music was moved from Wall Street to the Jewish Music Research Centre at the Hebrew University, Jerusalem. The Research Centre was established in 1964 with Israel Adler as its director. The present director is Amnon Shiloaḥ.

[1] Geshuri is a staff member of the Israeli Institute for Religious Music which was established in 1958. He is also editor of the Institute's journal, *Yedi'ot*, which has appeared yearly since 1959. In *Yedi'ot*, II (Jerusalem, 1960), 125-131, there appears an impressive bibliography [in Hebrew] of Geshuri's writings on Jewish music of the Near East. Of the twenty-six items listed for Sephardic music, two deal primarily with the *Romancero*: "(«שלש אחיות» הרומנצים של יהודי ספרד (עם המנגינה של ['The Romances of the Spanish Jews (with the Melody of «Tres hermanicas»)']" כל־נוע [*Kol-no'ah*], II (Tel Aviv, 1932) and "הרומנצות הספרדיות ומנגינותיהן ['Sephardic *Romances* and their Melodies']," הציוני הכללי [*Ha-tzioni ha-clalli*] (Jeruzalem, 1933). The *romances* which Geshuri contributed to the journal *Le Judaïsme Séphardi* were texts only.

[2] *Journal of the International Folk Music Council*, XIV (1962), p. 158. Only a brief summary of her paper is presented here.

[3] "On the Musical Sources of the Judaeo-Hispanic *Romance*," *The Musical Quarterly*, L (Jan., 1964), 31-43.

music for the *romance* melodies [were] indigenous Hispanic tunes [to which were] added those of Asiatic origin which apparently merged with the former and resulted in the present-day style of the *romance*, as now practiced by the Oriental Sephardic Jews."[1] Gerson-Kiwi then outlined what she considered to be important influences upon the Sephardic *romance*: those of the French heritage, namely the *chanson de geste*; the parallel epic forms of the Eastern Mediterranean; traditional *canciones* and *cantigas* of the Iberian peninsula; and lastly, synagogal music together with Islamic ornamental vocal style.

Two ballad melodies are found among the examples in the article.[2] These examples, undoubtedly recorded by Gerson-Kiwi, offer no references concerning the informants nor their place of origin. The transcriptions and analyses are her own. A third ballad melody, collected by Gerson-Kiwi [Phon. G-K 3890/1], is included under the heading "Music of the Spanish-Sephardic Jews" in her article "The Legacy of Jewish Music through the Ages."[3] This *romance*, *Arbolero*, was sung by a Sephardic woman of the Old City of Jerusalem whose family came from Salonika. Gerson-Kiwi's transcriptions will be discussed under the ballad titles where they apply.

The Jerusalem Archive for Oriental Music, of which Gerson-Kiwi is the Director, has vast holdings of sacred and secular music representing a wide geographical spread and is especially rich in recordings from Oriental and Sephardic communities of the Near East.[4] What specific secular items collected

---

[1] *Ibid.*, 32-33.
[2] The ballads can be identified as: *El parto en lejas tierras*, MP 68 (Example 5, p 38) and *Landarico*, MP 82 (Example 8, p. 39).
[3] התפוצות הגולה ['*In the Dispersion*'], V, No. 4 (Jerusalem, Winter 1963), 62. This also appeared with an English translation in *In the Dispersion: Surveys and Monographs on the Jewish World*, No. 3 (Jerusalem, Winter, 1963-1964), 160.
[4] The Jerusalem Archive for Oriental Music was founded in 1935 by the late Dr. Robert Lachmann (1892-1939), considered the true successor to Idelsohn in Palestine. [Cf. the posthumous article by Lachmann "Preserving Oriental Music," *Israel's Messenger*, XXXVII (Shanghai, 20th December 1940), 10.] Lachmann brought with him numerous recordings of Jewish Oriental music from the Phonogramm-archiv in Berlin, among which were a collection of seventy recordings made by Idelsohn. Gerson-Kiwi became interested in Lachmann's endeavor and worked closely with him until his death. The recorded materials gathered at the Archive comprised only the *oral* oriental musical tradition. In 1938, the Jerusalem Archive already contained a substantial amount of recordings from "African Sephardim and non-African Sephardi Jews from the coastal regions of the Eastern Mediterranean e.g. Salonika, Smyrna [Izmir], Aleppo, etc.," [Cf. Gerson-Kiwi's "Jerusalem Archive for Oriental Music," *Musica Hebraica* I-II (Jerusalem, 1938), 41]. When Raphael Patai established the Palestine Institute of Folklore and Ethnology in 1947, the Archive formed part of the Institute, but under Gerson-Kiwi's guidance. In 1950, the Israeli Ministry of Education and Culture established a Music Department which sponsored the work of the Archive, and in 1953 both Patai's Institute and Gerson-Kiwi's Archive were incorporated into the Hebrew University School of Oriental Studies.

from Sephardic sources are stored at these archives is not immediately known, as Gerson-Kiwi has yet to publish a catalog of the Archive's musical treasures.

INSTITUTO DE ESTUDIOS SEFARDÍES, MADRID
(FOUNDED IN 1961)[1]

In 1961, the World Sephardi Federation of London together with the Consejo Superior de Investigaciones Científicas of Madrid co-founded the Instituto de Estudios Sefardíes. The aims of this Institute are: "(1) to foster Sephardic studies in their various aspects, and (2) to maintain a lively relationship with Sephardic individuals and communities in different countries." In addition, the Instituto was to be responsible for the section entitled "Sefardismo" of the journal *Sefarad*, published by the Instituto Arias Montano. It was the intention of the editors, through this section, to keep the scholarly world informed of the work being undertaken at the Instituto de Estudios Sefardíes, along with pertinent book-reviews, notices, and other informative Sephardic items.[2]

Among the varied and significant projects undertaken, special consideration was recently given to the study of Sephardic music, both sacred and secular.[3] Mr. Iacob M. Hassán and Miss María Teresa Rubiato Díaz — now Señora Rubiato de Cubillo — have been particularly active in realizing this endeavor. During the early part of 1966, Mrs. Rubiato de Cubillo was kind enough to distribute to individuals interested in Sephardic music a number of carbon copies of a typewritten report, which outlined the musicological work in progress at the Instituto de Estudios Sefardíes.[4] In this, she itemized the bibliographical materials on hand in the library of the Instituto, together with those available at the Instituto Arias Montano. The musical items contained in these works, comprising a total of more than 350 melodies, have been re-notated on cards and classified according to their particular genre with additional information, where possible, as to informant, his/her age, and place and date of transcription. In addition, numerous taped recordings of synagogal music from North Africa were also received by the Instituto. Manuel Alvar graciously contributed

---

[1] In 1968, the Instituto de Estudios Sefardíes was absorbed by the Instituto Arias Montano. However, it is still actively carrying forward a number of Sephardic research programs.
[2] Cf. Richard D. Barnett and Frederico Pérez Castro, co-directors, "Institute of Sephardic Studies, Madrid," *Kol-Sepharad*, II, Nos. 3-4 (London, 1966), 18. For a complete summary of the Institute's activities the whole article should be consulted, 18-19. An informative article on the World Sephardi Federation can be found in *Kol-Sepharad*, I, No. 6-7 (London, 1965), 16-20.
[3] *Ibid.*, II, 19.
[4] "Memoria informe de los trabajos realizados durante el año 1.965 [sobre] el tema «Musicología sefardí», 9 pp.

copies of *endechas* and wedding songs which he collected in Morocco.[1] Further recordings of Sephardic *canciones* and *romances* made at the Instituto from Sephardic informants have been the subject of recent publications.[2]

In an effort to broaden the scope of its musical investigations, the Instituto has taken the initiative in establishing contact with other organizations and institutions such as the Research Centre for Jewish Music at Jerusalem, the Centre Communautaire de Paris, the Sorbonne, and interested universities in the United States. It has also maintained correspondence with a number of interested scholars. It is to be hoped that the continued participation of these institutions through the initiative of interested individuals will bring together at the Instituto a fund of knowledge concerning newly discovered source materials and on-going fieldwork. The idea of a central archive for Sephardic music has great merit, and its location in Madrid, where so many other important Spanish institutions house musical documents vital to the Sephardic culture nurtured in Spain, seems particularly promising and appropriate.

CONCLUDING NOTE

We have seen that the first melody obtained for a ballad from a Sephardic informant was published in 1897 by Joseph Passy and J. Benaroya. Even ten years later, when Menéndez Pidal made known in his *Catálogo* the extent of the existing Sephardic répertoire by listing over 140 ballad themes, Passy and Benaroya's contribution still remained the sole musical example from this tradition.

Although it was the purpose of Menéndez Pidal's *Catálogo* "to promote and facilitate the search for additional ballads," he made no direct reference to the musical aspects of the Sephardic *Romancero* nor did he call attention to the much needed musical investigation of the Sephardic tradition. Such silence

---

[1] Twenty-eight of the wedding songs have been transcribed and appear in Manuel Alvar's *Cantos de boda judeo-españoles* Madrid: Instituto Arias Montano, 1969. (Publicaciones de Estudios Sefardíes, Serie II: Literatura, Número 1.)

[2] The first informant, Mrs. Obadiah Camhy, was recorded during her recital before the Simposio de Estudios Sefardíes (Madrid, June, 1964). Six items from her répertoire were notated for the study "Transcripción anotada de seis canciones sefardíes," *Actas del I Simposio de Estudios Sefardíes*, Apendice 2, pp. 559-567. The second informant, Dr. Yosef Abraham Sadikario, a Sephardic Jew from Skolpje was born in Monastir, 1919. Mrs. Rubiato de Cubillo transcribed five of the twelve items which he sang and incorporated them in her article "El repertorio musical de un sefardí," *Sefarad*, XXV (1965), 453-463. None of the items are *romances*. However, Mrs. Rubiato de Cubillo mentions (p. 457) that Dr. Sadikario sang a small and as yet unedited fragment of the ballad *Vuelta del hijo maldecido*, MP 124.

on his part must not be construed as ignorance in musical matters, because, in truth, Menéndez Pidal did play a very significant rôle, when a year before the publication of the *Catálogo*, he not only induced the talented Manrique de Lara to pursue the music of the *Romancero*, but also initiated him in actual field work. From that time on, Manrique de Lara notated the melodies of ballads both in Spain and in the widely dispersed Sephardic communities of the Mediterranean region. By the time of his death in 1929, he had amassed a gigantic collection of ballad tunes, a task for which he earned recognition as the first serious student of the Judeo-Spanish ballad melodies. It is not necessary at this point to mention again the collectors who followed. Nonetheless, it is important to note that to date over 200 different narrative themes have been recorded for Sephardic ballads, and that we now possess accompanying musical notations for nearly 130 of them.[1]

---

[1] See Appendix I, where I have indicated in a synoptic table the ballads of the Menéndez Pidal *Catálogo* for which melodies have been collected and notated.

CHAPTER THREE

A MUSICAL STUDY OF BALLAD TUNES FROM THE JERUSALEM REPERTOIRE

The musical antecedents of the Spanish *romance* were probably patterned upon secular and possibly also liturgical forms composed according to similar metrical principles:[1] strophic (stanzaic) form, syllable count, assonant rhyme, accentual verse or, more appropriately, qualitative meter. In its final and popular form, the *romance* has emerged as a sixteen-syllable verse divided by a medial pause into two octosyllabic hemistichs, the former hemistich without rhyme, the latter closed in assonance.[2]

Wherever the *romance* was carried in the Sephardic Diaspora, the same metrical principles were strictly maintained. Nonetheless, the musical evaluation of the Judeo-Spanish ballad répertoire has prompted a number of varied speculations among the early collectors and musicologists. In addition to the surmises of de Sola, Danon, Attias, and Avenary discussed at the beginning of the preceding chapter, it may be useful to scrutinize the statements of music specialists concerning their own field experience in the pursuit of Sephardic ballads.

Manrique de Lara, who studied the Sephardic *Romancero* at firsthand, suggested that a study of the ballad melodies might resolve the much debated question as to whether or not these were the tunes of mediæval *cantares de gesta*.[3] Alberto Hemsi, a composer, folklorist, and expert in the musical cultures

---

[1] Vicente T. Mendoza, in *El romance español y el corrido mexicano: estudio comparativo* (México D.F., 1939), pp. 16, 35, and 43, lists a number of liturgical and secular musical forms which preceded and most probably influenced the musical structure of the *romance*.
[2] These principles are discussed in detail by Menéndez Pidal in *Romancero Hispánico (hispano-portugués, americano y sefardí)* (Madrid, 1953), I, pp. 81-147. See also R. H. Webber, *Formulistic Diction in the Spanish Ballad* (Berkeley and Los Angeles, 1951), pp. 175-278; and, for some background on other genres utilizing these principles, see D. C. Clarke, *A Chronological Sketch of Castilian Versification Together With a List of Its Metric Terms* (Berkeley and Los Angeles, 1952), pp. 279-382.
[3] "Romances españoles en los Balkanes," *Blanco y Negro*, Año 26 (Madrid, 2nd January 1916), No. 1285.

of the Eastern Mediterranean who was applauded by José Subirá as the greatest living authority on Sephardic balladry, stated that:

> Se ha avanzado a menudo la hipótesis de que la música de los judíos españoles no era sino aires turcos aplicados a textos españoles. Ello equivale a desconocer los unos y los otros. Evidentemente, la prolongada vecindad de los dos elementos — vecindad sobre todo muy cordial — ha producido una influencia musical turca que no se podría negar y que es por otra parte fácil de discernir. Pero el fondo de la mayor parte del repertorio sefardí — notoriamente los cantos religiosos y los romances — ha guardado su huella functionalmente ibérica a pesar de esta influencia y de las alteraciones debidas a las tradiciones ex[c]lusivamente orales. Basta pues comparar los estilos y las formas de las dos músicas para destruir esta hipótesis. Si en todo caso hay un cierto parecido, global o particular, éste proviene del empleo de los mismos modos orientales que son desde luego comunes no sólo a estas dos clases de música sino a toda la música popular de los pueblos del Mediterráneo. Pero cuando este parecido es vago y no especificado, puede igualmente inspirar la hipótesis contraria o sea la influencia de las melodías judías de procedencia andaluza sobre el canto oriental y primitivo de los turcos. Contrariamente pues, esta influencia me parece probable, hasta posible en cierto modo, toda vez que es sabido que no fué ésta la única y eventual influencia que los turcos de las grandes ciudades debieron de sufrir a lo largo de los siglos a su contacto con los judíos españoles.[1]

Recently Gerson-Kiwi made the assumption that:

> ... along with the original texts as sung and collected today whether in Jerusalem, Istanbul, Sarajevo, Morocco, or Los Angeles, their tunes may be traced back and eventually identified with the historical minstrel songs of the pre-exilian times, or at least with the general frame of their melodic models.[2]

It is unfortunate that these investigators did not probe deeper into the musical origins of the Judeo-Spanish *Romancero* or attempt to evaluate in a scientific manner the ballad melodies in terms of the environment in which they were collected. Naturally, to the musically minded Hispanist, the thought of musical remnants from Spain's historic past persisting in oral tradition at both extremes of the Mediterranean region is indeed a fascinating possibility.

While we may consider Manrique de Lara to be the first musical giant of Sephardic balladry, we must also remember that his close association with Menéndez Pidal had much to do with his interest in looking to the *cantares de gesta* as a possible musical antecedent of the ballads. Manrique de Lara made the aforementioned statement in 1916, at a time when he was deeply involved in collecting ballads in southern Spain and in Spanish Morocco. It is to be lamented that he left no other documents, published or unpublished, con-

---

[1] Hemsi, *Coplas sefardíes* (*Chansons judéo-espagnoles*) Op. 22 (Alexandria, 1938), p. xiv.
[2] "On the Musical Sources of the Judaeo-Hispanic *Romance*," *The Musical Quarterly*, L (January, 1964), p. 33f.

taining his thoughts about the Sephardic melodies. Even Ramón Menéndez Pidal, who remained his close friend until his death in 1929, had not offered comments concerning Manrique de Lara's work on the musical aspects of Sephardic balladry.

Hemsi, on the other hand, was in a much better position to evaluate the existing tradition. Having been raised in the Eastern Mediterranean area, and having travelled to the important Sephardic centers in that region, he possessed the natural qualifications for approaching the study of ballad melodies in terms of his and their environment. However, Hemsi's brief and somewhat inscrutable hypotheses are completely devoid of the musical analyses necessary for their substantiation. Hemsi's theory suggesting the overwhelming influence of Jewish melodies of Andalusian origin upon the "oriental and primitive [sic!]" music of the Turks especially in the larger cities of Turkey, echoes a popular myth concerning Sephardic balladry's Spanish heritage. Hemsi failed to explain the "fundamentally Iberian character of the Sephardic répertoire," nor did he make clear the use of the term "oriental modes" when he stated that these modes were common to the popular music of all Mediterranean peoples. Even Isaac Levy viewed the Judeo-Spanish melodies, especially the liturigical ones, in Pan-Mediterranean terms, but again no substantiating evidence was provided.[1] Hemsi's keen interest in composition completely overshadowed his pretended scholarly approach. He was intent on harmonizing the melodies he had collected, thus taking them out of their modal context and forcing the irrationally sung intervals into the tempered intervals of the Occident for the purpose of concert performance. Any person who has heard ballads from the areas represented in Hemsi's collection will immediately agree that his melodies have been doctored to suit the composer's honest, but from a scholarly point of view, naïve intentions.

When Miguel Querol investigated Hemsi's *Coplas sefardíes* together with the *romance* melodies contained in several Moroccan collections (Bustelo, Bénichou, and Larrea Palacín), he concluded that:

> Tous les *romances* de ces collections sont certainement traditionnels, les mêmes que ceux du XVIe siècle pour le texte, mais, pour la musique, ma première impression est qu'elle n'est pas plus ancienne que celle des autres chansons folkloriques qui, dans l'ensemble, ne remontent pas au delà du XVIIIe siècle...[2]

Querol must have based his opinion upon ballads from the Moroccan sources, since these are much closer to the Spanish tradition; yet, because of the predominance of ornamentation in Hemsi's melodies, he was inclined to agree

---

[1] *Chants judéo-espagnoles* (London, 1959), p. vi.
[2] "Importance historique et national du romance," *Musique et Poésie au XVIe Siècle* (Paris, 1953), p. 301.

with Hemsi in principle. Taking his cue from the *vihuelistas* who advised singers to add ornaments to their melodies, Querol argued:

> Si donc à certaines mélodies des *romances* traditionnels de la péninsule on ajoute des ornements mélodiques, la parenté matérielle entre les mélodies des *romances* recueillis par Hemsi et ceux que nous ont conservé les documents du XVe siècle paraît plus étroite encore, et nous disons parenté matérielle, parce que la parenté spirituelle se manifeste avec la plus grande clarté.[1]

Gerson-Kiwi, certainly considered among the most competent critics of Near Eastern musical traditions, offered additional suggestions concerning the forbears of the Judeo-Spanish *Romancero*, but only with limited musical substantiation.[2]

The superficiality of the scholarly judgments rendered to date points to the need for a conclusive musical study of the Sephardic *Romancero* and its relationship to the fifteenth-century Peninsular tradition. Two fundamental questions must be posed: (1) What were the original tunes which accompanied the ballad répertoire of the Sephardim at the time of the expulsion? (2) What became of these tunes in the process of oral transmission over the past four centuries? The problem becomes perplexing indeed in the light of Daniel Devoto's (1916-   ) observation that in the extant indigenous ballad tradition of Spain none of the tunes traditionally sung today resembles any of the *tonadas* which appear in the ancient musical collections of the Peninsula.[3]

In the case of the Sephardic branch of Hispanic balladry, very special conditions must be taken into account. The exiled Sephardim did not comprise a single regional nucleus, but represented many regions of Spain each of which possessed its own peculiar ballad tradition. The tunes employed for specific ballad texts undoubtedly differed from region to region. Indeed, the diversity of musical styles on the Peninsula was not only regional, but included variations in musical style nurtured in Christian and in Moslem Spain. The legacy of tunes inherited from both the Christian and Islamic musical traditions undoubtedly had a pronounced effect upon the ballad répertoires which the Jews had carried away from their Iberian homeland.

We possess almost no documentation for the early musical tradition of the Sephardic *Romancero*. We can surmise what its general character must have

---

[1] *Loc. cit.*
[2] See Chapter II, pp. 120-121 *supra*. In her paper, "Der Stand der Mittelmeertraditionen im hohen Mittelalter," delivered before the Ninth International Musicological Society Congress (Salzburg, 1964), Gerson-Kiwi maintained that the extant Sephardic ballad oral tradition constitutes a rare document of "prä-kolumbianischer Musikübung." See *Bericht über den neunten internationalen Kongress Salzburg 1964* (Basel, 1966), p. 130.
[3] "Sobre el estudio folklórico del romancero español. Proposiciones para un método de estudio de la canción tradicional," *Bulletin Hispanique*, LVII (1955), 236.

been in view of the early broadsides (*pliegos sueltos*) and ballad books (*romanceros* and *cancioneros*) printed in Spain during the sixteenth century. The only textual evidence of the Judeo-Spanish *Romancero* during the more than two centuries following the exile of the Sephardim are the ballad *incipits* used as tune indicators in collections of liturigical poetry (*piyyutim*).[1]

The use of *contrafacta* tunes in the liturgical books became a popular practice in both the Eastern and Western Mediterranean communities. The practice itself was established in Spain among the great Hebrew poets of the Golden Age of Hispano-Hebraic poetry, who enriched the liturgy with poems modelled upon existing or newly composed tunes. The *incipits* were primarily employed as memory aids for recalling the tunes. They proved to be overwhelmingly popular for their initial purpose and seem to have evolved into a kind of internationally accepted make-shift notation, confirmed in this function by the lack of proper facilities for printing even skeletal notations, coupled with basic limitations of space and printing costs.[2]

However, in time, the substitution of one tune for another without regard for the "once cherished" tune of the *incipit* must have taken place. In the Sephardim's new environment, indigenous melodies must have replaced many of the old tunes brought from Spain. Substitutions doubtless made allowances for the metrical requirements peculiar to the *romance*, especially in the case of ballad tunes used in the liturgical hymnals. One could surmise that even the cantors, who functioned as the musical representatives of the scattered congregations, were in part responsible for the interchange of melodies as a means of stimulating greater participation in the singing of liturgical hymns by their congregations. Nonetheless, these are but a few instances which

---

[1] Hanoch Avenary, "Études sur le cancionero judéo-espagnol (XVIe et XVIIe siècles), *Sefarad*, XX (1960), 377-394.
  In Spain, the first printing of broadsides dates from the beginning of the sixteenth century. However, the first *cancionero* to include ballads, among other items, was the *Cancionero general de Hernando del Castillo*, printed in 1511. One must take care to distinguish this work from that of the *Cancionero de romances* (also known as the *Cancionero sin año* [*circa* 1549]) (see p. 29 *supra*) which is usually cited as the first *cancionero* to contain ballads only. However, the *Cancionero sin año* is greatly antedated by the *Libro en el cual se contienen cincuenta romances* (*circa* 1525-1530), of which only a fragment is preserved today. See A. Rodríguez-Moñino, *Los pliegos poeticos de la colección del Marqués de Morbecq* (Madrid, 1962), pp. 48-49.

[2] Even W. J. Entwistle's remarks in *European Balladry* (London, 1939), p. 34, appear rather speculative: "To print texts only is a tradition dating back to the ballad collections of the sixteenth century in Spain ... The publisher could rely on his clients to know the traditional tunes, though they might trip over the words; or, alternatively, they might prefer to sing the words to one of the new polyphonic settings which contemporary composers produced in abundance. On either supposition, those who bought the books of words did so because of their fondness for music."

point to the unreliability of the earlier *incipits* as proof of the ancient currency of the present-day inventory of extant "traditional" melodies.

The substitution of tunes has been found to be true in all areas of the Jewish Diaspora, where liturgical and semi-liturgical texts were sung to certain melodies on the Sabbath and to different melodies on the holidays. Such renowned hymns as יגדל [*Yigdal*] and אדון עולם [*Adon olam*] have been accompanied by a multitude of melodies through the ages, many of which have been claimed to be traditional. Recently, in Morocco, I heard several hymns sung to traditional *romance* melodies. Yet who is to argue which genre employed the tune first? The question concerning the original tunes of the Judeo-Spanish ballads, as one can readily see, is indeed extremely complex.

For well over a century after the expulsion, active communication was still maintained with the Iberian Peninsula. During this time, the most popular ballads from the *Romancero* must have circulated throughout the greater Mediterranean area, where they became firmly entrenched within the various Sephardic communities. After this period, contacts with Spain grew more sporadic and the relations among the widely scattered Sephardic settlements may also have slackened. The natural outcome of this situation resulted in the isolation of particular communities, each subjected to the cultural influences of the new environment. Whereas in Spain, the *romance* had achieved an enormous popularity between the late-fifteenth and mid-seventeenth centuries, the propagation of Peninsular *romances* to the Sephardic Diaspora was already on the decline by the late-sixteenth century. But up to this time, the Sephardim had had ample opportunity to amass a vigorous ballad tradition. From 1700 on, the differences in the Eastern Mediterranean and Moroccan répertoires must have become more and more marked.[1]

Certain themes exist in both the Eastern and Western traditions, but the latter, because of geographic proximity, had the advantage of receiving an almost uninterrupted renovative flow of ballads from the Peninsula, while the Eastern tradition fell into even greater isolation.

Among the major Eastern Mediterranean communities, Salonika is perhaps the most important from a balladic point of view, but Istanbul, Izmir, Edirne, Bursa, Larissa, Sofia, Sarajevo, Bucharest, Belgrade, Jerusalem, Damascus, Aleppo, Alexandria, Cairo, and Rhodes were all prominent Sephardic centers. Concerning the diffusion of the Sephardic ballads throughout these areas, Armistead and Silverman wrote:

> The general geographic spread of Judeo-Spanish ballad collections is sparse enough when compared to the number of communities represented in detailed language studies [of Judeo-Spanish]. And when the total number of Eastern Mediterranean communities

---

[1] R. Menéndez Pidal, *Romancero Hispánico* (1953), II, pp. 219-220.

where Judeo-Spanish is known to be or to have been spoken in the 20th Century is contrasted with the number of centers from which even a single ballad text has been reported, the panorama is even more depressing... At this date, after profound social disturbances and the holocaust of the early 40's, such imposing geographic gaps can best be bridged by intensive field work among the immigrant populations of Israel and the United States.[1]

Oddly enough, in the collections of Eastern ballads published to date, Jerusalem's native Sephardic population has been thoroughly neglected.[2] Although, historically, the Sephardic population of Jerusalem became increasingly important after the expulsion, until 1953 only three ballads had been reported from Jerusalem: *El conde Olinos* [MP 55], *Julián el falso hortelano* [not listed in the *Catálogo*], and *Expulsión de los judíos de Portugal* [MP 13]. Of these, only the last may be considered an authentic Jerusalem text; the first two being from the ספר רנונת [*sefer renanot*], which, though printed in Jerusalem, copied Salonikan versions from one of the chapbooks of Yacob Abraham Yoná.[3]

With this fact in mind, and with the understanding that Israel would also

---

[1] "Judeo-Spanish Ballads in a MS by Salomon Israel Cherezli," *Studies in Honor of M. J. Benardete* (New York, 1965), p. 368, n. 7. For extensive bibliographies of these studies see Simon Marcus, השפה הספרדית־יהודית [*'The Judeo-Spanish Language'*] (Jerusalem, 1965) and Henry V. Besso, "Bibliografía sobre el Judeo-español," *Bulletin Hispanique*, LV (1952), 412-422. For the singular contributions of M. L. Wagner, see "Bibliografia di Max Leopold Wagner," *Boletín de Filología*, XV (Lisbon, 1964-1965), 39-124.

[2] It does seem strange indeed that ballad tunes were never published from the Jerusalem tradition, for many collectors had the opportunity to investigate this tradition. Even A. Z. Idelsohn, who resided for many years in that city must have been acquainted with the Sephardic *Romancero*. When Manrique de Lara visited Jerusalem in the early part of this century, he undoubtedly took the opportunity, as was his custom, to notate melodies from local Sephardic informants (see page 35, note 1). In more recent times, we have reason to believe that tape-recorded ballads can be found in the personal archives of such Jerusalem residents as Edith Gerson-Kiwi, Moshe Attias, Simeon Geshuri, Isaac Levy, Leo Levi and Amnon Shiloah. Another important source is the Kol Israel Radio Archives which has a vast amount of materials, both sacred and secular, collected from Sephardic informants.

[3] R. Menéndez Pidal, *Romancero Hispánico* (1953), II, pp. 331 and 336; S. G. Armistead and J. H. Silverman, "Judeo-Spanish Ballads in a MS by Salomon Israel Cherezlí," p. 368, footnote 7. On the identity of the ספר רנונת versions with those of Yoná, see, by the same authors, *The Judeo-Spanish Ballad Chapbooks of Yakob Abraham Yona* (Berkeley & Los Angeles, 1970), Nos. 12 and 21. From the *Catálogo de la Exposición Bibliográfica Sefardí Mundial*, p. 142 (item 847), we learn that it was Manrique de Lara who made known the ספר רנונת to Menéndez Pidal. Here the publication date of ספר רנונת is given incorrectly as 1708; it should read 1909. Other than the mention of Manrique de Lara's visit to Jerusalem in Manual Ortega's *Los hebreos en Marruecos* (1919 ed., p. 234 and subsequent editions, p. 206), the *Catálogo de la Exposición* provides us with additional evidence that Manrique de Lara travelled to Jerusalem.

be an ideal laboratory for collecting ballads and other folkloric materials from Sephardic informants representing a wide variety of diaspora communities, I decided to undertake field research among the Sephardic inhabitants of Jerusalem. While in Israel (1959-1961), I was not only able to collect ballads from a number of communities belonging to both the Eastern and Western Judeo-Spanish traditions, but was also able to discover an extant native ballad tradition among the Jerusalem-born Sephardim or *Sabras*.[1] Concerning Jerusalem as a ballad center Armistead and Silverman surmise that:

> Every Eastern Mediterranean and North African Sephardic community has doubtless made some contribution to the amalgam and, as we should expect, one of the results has been the formation of an eclectic ballad tradition embodying features derived from various branches of the Sephardic *Romancero*.[2]

Musically speaking, the Jerusalem ballad tradition can be more readily explained. In Jerusalem and in other parts of Israel where I had the opportunity to hear and record ballads sung first hand, the musical differences between the Eastern-Mediterranean and the North-African tunes and their renderings were so pronounced that they could easily be considered as two fundamentally different style categories representing an Eastern and Western division of the Mediterranean Sephardim. The former emanated from Turkey, whose centers were Istanbul, Izmir, and Rhodes, while the latter was from Morocco, especially Tangier and Tetuán. However, it was not until I had transcribed a number of ballad melodies from Salonikan informants that I came to realize the possibile existence of a third category, namely Greek.[3]

The ballads sung by the *Sabra* informants are directly related to the Eastern style category. To judge by the number of ballads for which there are an ample

---

[1] For a list of the ballad themes collected in Jerusalem among the *Sabras*, see Appendix III.

Two works in particular proved extremely useful in interrogating Jerusalem informants: Menéndez Pidal's *Catálogo* and Moshe Attias' *Romancero sefaradí*. Professors Armistead and Silverman provided me with an additional list of ballad incipits used for their own field collecting in the United States.

Other valuable field manuals for collecting ballads in the Hispanic tradition are: Julio Vicuña Cifuentes, *Instrucciones para recoger de la tradición oral romances populares* (Santiago, 1905); María Goyri Menéndez Pidal, "Romances que deben buscarse en la tradición oral," *Revista de Archivos Biblioteca y Museos*, X (1906), 374-386; XI (1907), 24-36; and the more recent *Romances tradicionales y canciones narrativas existentes en el folklore español* (*Incipit y temas*) (Barcelona, 1945).

[2] "Judeo-Spanish Ballads in an MS by Salomon Israel Cherezli," *Studies in Honor of M. J. Benardete* (New York, 1965), p. 369.

[3] The style categories were discussed previously in my article "Toward a Musical Study of the Judeo-Spanish *Romancero*," *Western Folklore*, XXI (April, 1962), 83-91. I have offered a more detailed account of their differences in "A Judeo-Spanish *Romancero*," *Ethnomusicology*, XII (January, 1968), 72-85.

amount of variants collected from *Sabra* and other Eastern Mediterranean informants, it became clear that the Jerusalem *Romancero* did not exist as a musically independent tradition, but that it clearly formed part of the Eastern tradition which had nurtured it. Idelsohn's experience with Ladino folksongs led him to believe that "the tunes have an Oriental color and are either adoptions [adaptations?] or imitations of Greek-Turkish melodies."[1] If in fact the Jerusalem ballad répertoire did constitute an amalgam of melodies from the north-eastern Mediterranean centers, then the Jerusalem tunes would be an ideal starting point for a study of the basic stylistic characteristics of Eastern-Sephardic ballad melodies.[2]

With regard to the published Sephardic ballad melodies, no matter how dubious their notations may appear, it has been shown in the previous chapter that in the majority of cases the melodies were notated by competent musicians who attempted to set them down "as they had heard them." These notations constitute a precious tool for evaluating the formal, the melodic-skeletal, and in some cases, the modal aspects of ballads for which similar variants exist in the *Sabra* tradition. We owe a debt of gratitude to those previous generations of musicologists whose efforts have saved these melodies from oblivion.

The major criticisms of previous musical collections of oral traditional materials, the Sephardic ballad melodies included, mainly concern the manner in which the tunes were collected and particularly how the final published version was realized. In most of these collections, melodies are given only in skeletal form with little or no ornamentation. Usually only one melodic stanza is provided, accompanied by textual underlay, thus preventing us from following the ballad melody as it unfolded throughout the ballad's rendition. As to rhythmic organization, many transcribers had few scruples about affixing a time signature to signify a rigid performance throughout. Many melodies lack tempo indications, yet, those which have them, employ the standard Italian designations. Only a small percentage are prefaced by metronome markings. No effort was made to indicate irrational pitches,

---

[1] *Jewish Music in its Historical Development* (New York, 1929), p. 378.
[2] Ramón Menéndez Pidal's geographic method of investigation offers useful guidelines for our study. It was his idea to study the diffusion of important motives and variants for the purpose of defining the mass of motives which forms a particular type or version of a *romance*. See R. Menéndez Pidal, "Sobre geografía folklórica: ensayo de un método," *Revista de Filología Española*, VII (1920), 299-388. In this fundamental study, Menéndez Pidal investigates the diffusion and interrelation of two ballads, *Gerineldo* and *La boda estorbada*, which are listed in the *Catálogo* as MP 101 and MP 60, respectively. This fundamentally important study is reprinted in R. Menéndez Pidal, Diego Catalán, and Alvaro Galmés, *Cómo vive un romance: Dos ensayos sobre tradicionalidad* (Madrid, 1954).

Diego Catalán and Alvaro Galmés likewise base their studies on the geographic method. The former contributed the article "El *motivo* y la *variación* en la transmisión tradicional del romancero," *Bulletin Hispanique*, LXI (1959), 149-182.

which, of course, are more readily perceptible when transcribing melodies from discs or tapes. With or without key signatures, the modal aspects of many melodies remain questionable, and the lack of irrational pitches considerably hinders the analysis of certain tunes embodying non-European modal practices. On the whole, most of the collections are completely devoid of musical analysis and there is hardly any comment about the fundamental matter of performance. Such vital information as the informant's name, age, or sex, as well as place and date of recording, is almost never provided. Such information would have been invaluable to us in tracing more accurately the movement of certain melodies through space and time.[1]

Taking the above mentioned criticisms into consideration, I have attempted to present an accurate musical account of five ballad themes from the Jerusalem *Romancero*, combining evidence drawn from previously published materials with the results of my own field work. In each case, I have followed a pre-established outline which includes pertinent introductory notes together with a prose synopsis of the ballad text before proceeding directly to musical matters.[2] My immediate objective was to seek out from the transcriptions of the *Sabra* ballads [see volume II] those salient features common to each group of variants comprising a ballad theme. With these features clearly stated, it was then possible to compare them with analogs collected from other tape-recorded and published sources [see Appendix II][3] in an attempt to substantiate the predominant influences exerted by other Eastern Mediterranean Sephardic traditions upon the Jerusalem répertoire.

I have transcribed the *Sabra* melodies only, but I have also attempted to explain in detail any marked differences between the Jerusalem ballads and their analogs in other Eastern Judeo-Spanish traditions. In the case of certain ballads, I have made complete transcriptions; for others, I have notated them up to the point where their melodic lines became stabilized. The skeletal notations and note values for each of the variants were derived on the basis of

---

[1] One collection in particular, namely Kurt Schindler's *Folk Music and Poetry of Spain and Portugal* (New York, 1941), has long been cherished by Hispanic musicologists and folklorists as a model for collecting, transcribing, and classifying folksongs. Still, for all its merits, it would not be able to stand on firm ground in view of a good many of the above criticisms. There are numerous regional collections made in Spain by the *Instituto Español de Musicología* founded in 1943 by Higinio Anglés as a branch of the *Consejo Superior de Investigaciones Científicas*. While this institute undertook organized work in the regional collection of folk music, it appears that they have been more concerned with collecting than with analyzing their materials.

[2] The full texts of the Jerusalem ballads and others from my collection will appear in the projected study briefly discussed (page 30, *supra*).

[3] Before the vast corpus of ballad melodies is brought together in any organized form, the search for melodies and their tune analogs will have to start with the texts as the first consideration for their immediate recognition or ordering.

their majority usage in their text-tune relationships. Where certain ornamental figures were stereotyped, I incorporated them in the skeletal form with smaller note heads. In cases of irregular syllable structure, I was forced to choose those notes which would best suit the ballad in its strict adherence to the traditional syllable count. In order to make their modal features more readily discernible, I transcribed the ballads on the basis of the *finalis*, thus avoiding key signatures. The melodies would then be notated in the context of the church modes, the correct context for ballads found in the musical *cancioneros* of fifteenth- and sixteenth-century Spain.

I have intentionally avoided a discussion of intonation, although it plays an important rôle in oral transmission. A definitive study would naturally include an indication of pitches in *Cents*; however, due to the ages of the informants (55-75), I am doubtful about the scientific reliability of such an undertaking. Furthermore, because the majority of my tape-recordings were made in informants' homes and under less than ideal conditions with a wide variety of background noises, such recordings could not be accurately scrutinized on so sensitive an instrument as the melograph.[1]

In many instances, during the rendition of the first one or two melody stanzas, the melody did not become sufficiently fixed in the informant's mind. This curious situation indicates the perceptive manner in which the folk have striven to achieve an acceptable norm for certain melodies within the established répertoire. This important aspect of ballad recitation has, to my knowledge, not been studied seriously. In those areas where we must rely upon the elders for renditions of traditional ballads, it becomes obvious that the tradition is already on the decline. When a répertoire is not practiced constantly, it is usual that a number of stanzas must be rendered before melodic stability is attained.

The individual ballad studies are grouped according to the number of melody sections comprising their musical strophes, beginning with the smallest. At the end of each study I have plotted geographically, with the aid of symbols, the centers which in my opinion played an important rôle in fostering the musical traditions of the Jerusalem *Romancero*. I have also indicated those centers where versions and variants of the ballad themes have been reported to exist.[2]

---

[1] For fundamental knowledge of the melograph and its application to the study of folk music, see Charles Seeger's "Toward a Universal Music Sound-Writing for Musicology," *Journal of the International Folk Music Council*, IX (1957), 63-66, and "Prescriptive and Descriptive Music Writing," *The Musical Quarterly*, XLIV, No. 2 (April, 1958), 184-195.

[2] I refer the reader to the map (p. 22 *supra*) for the locations of the various Sephardic communities.

Key to the symbols used:
- ▼ Published texts only.
- ■ Tape-recorded items.
- ☐ Published notations.
- ⊗ Published texts and notations.
- ⊕ Tape-recorded items and published notations.
- ⓨ Published texts, notations, and tape-recorded items.
- ⟶ Direct influence upon the musical tradition.
- ---- Textual link with major centers.
- ——— Musical link with major centers.

A. *Arbolero* or *La vuelta del marido* (*i*), MP 58

The *romance*, of *La vuelta del marido* (*i*) [*'The Husband's Return'*] or *Arbolero* as the Eastern Sephardim call it, is without doubt the most popular ballad in the Jerusalem répertoire. Only very rarely does one encounter a *Sabra* informant who cannot recite it. The ballad has Peninsular analogs in the Portuguese, Catalan, and Castilian traditions.[1] The ballad's popularity in the Levantine region is already attested in a seventeenth-century MS collection of *piyyutim*, שארית ישראל [*'Songs of Israel'*], composed by the Hebrew poet, Israel Najara (1555-1628). Najara's collection documents the *incipit*: *Arbolera arbolera tan gentil* as a contrafact melody, using the ballad as a model for a hymn in which the Spanish is replaced with similar sounding Hebrew words. Avenary states that Najara composed this hymn "sous la forme d'un villancico élargie."[2]

> In Sephardic versions Amadí's lady sits, combing her hair with an ivory comb, on the highest branch of a marvelous tree, which "has golden roots and a base of ivory." The knight Amadí passes by and asks what she is looking for. She answers that she is looking for her beloved Amadí. He asks what she would give in exchange for Amadí. She offers him her three mills. He asks for something more. She offers her three daughters, but he will only settle for sleeping with the wife of Amadí. She answers: "Accursed be the knight who allows himself to say such a thing." Having tested her fidelity, the knight identifies himself as Amadí.[3]

The six variants collected for *Arbolero* exhibit a marked similarity in their structural, melodic, and modal features which is attributable to the ballad's

---

[1] For Peninsular counterparts see Samuel G. Armistead and Joseph H. Silverman, "A New Sephardic *Romancero* from Salonika," *Romance Philology*, XVI, No. 1 (August, 1962), 71, n. 44.

[2] Hanoch Avenary, "Études sur le cancionero judéo-espagnol (XVIe et XVIIe siècles)," *Sefarad*, XX (1960), 12.

[3] Cf. Samuel G. Armistead and Joseph H. Silverman, "A New Collection of Judeo-Spanish Ballads," *Journal of the Folklore Institute*, III, No. 2 (Bloomington, 1966), 141.

high esteem among the *Sabra* informants of Jerusalem. A glance at the melodic skeletons of our six examples will reveal these similarities:

Example 26:

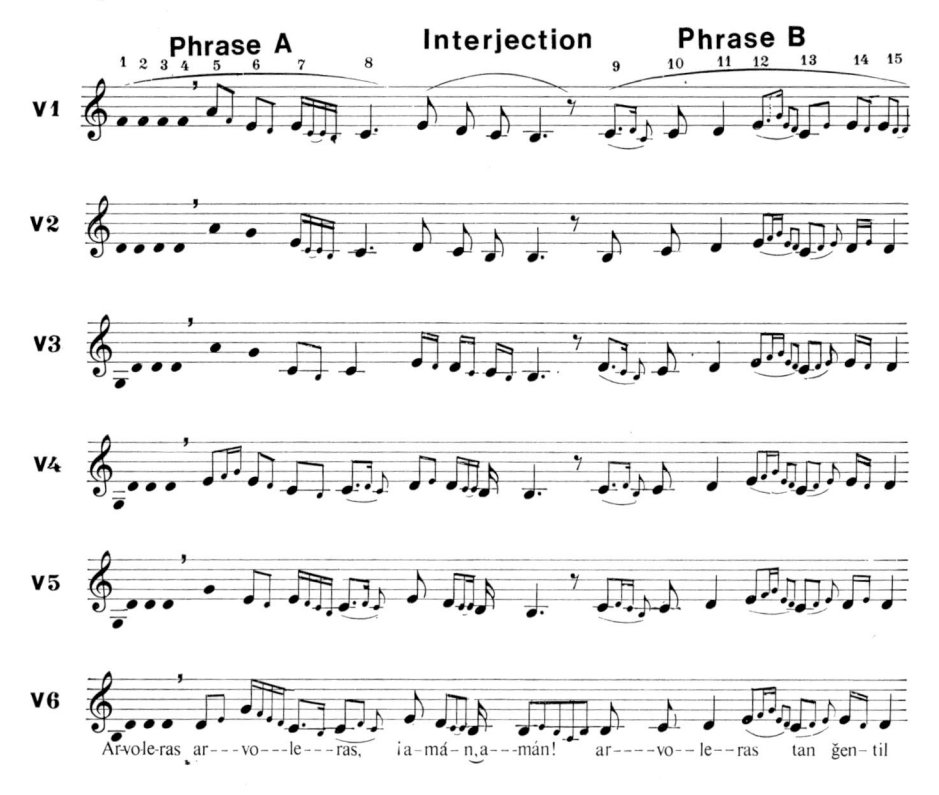

[Musical notation: Six variants (V1–V6) of the melody showing Phrase A (beats 1–8), Interjection (beat 9), and Phrase B (beats 10–15). Lyrics under V6: "Ar-vole-ras ar---vo---le---ras, ia-má-n,a---mán! ar----vo--le--ras tan ğen-til"]

The elements unifying all the variants can be outlined in the following manner:

1. *Formal*
a. A strophic distich, divided into hemistichs of eight and seven syllables, which corresponds musically to respective *ouvert* and *clos* cadences. (See also taped items A, B, C, and F and the published sources 1, 6 and 7).
b. The inclusion of an interjection, *amán* (Turkish *aman* 'alas, mercy!') which forms a bridge between the first and second hemistich. (See also taped items A, B, and C and the published sources 6 and 7).[1]

---

[1] The taped and published sources for *Arbolero* can be found in Appendix II. On the use of *amán* and *a ğanim* in Eastern Sephardic Ballads, see S. G. Armistead and J. H. Silverman, "Exclamaciones turcas y otros rasgos orientales en el Romancero Judeoespañol," *Sefarad*, XXX (1970), 177-193.

2. *Melodic*
a. The declamatory opening of phrase A, with its reïteration of the first four sung syllables. (See also taped items A through F and the published sources 1, 2, 6, and 7).
b. A cæsura after the first four syllables. (See also taped items A through F and published source 6).
c. The confinement of the interjection within a descending tetrachord *e* to *b*. (See also taped items A, B, and C and the published sources 6 and 7).
d. The melodic profile of phrase B is rigidly maintained. (See also taped items A, B, C, and D and the published sources 6 and 7).

3. *Modal*
a. A modal structure based upon the *finalis d*. (See also taped items A through F and the published sources 2, 6, and 7).
b. The final notes for phrase A, the interjection, and phrase B are *c, b*, and *d*, respectively. (See also taped items A, B, C and the published sources 6 and 7).

4. *Rhythmic*
a. Most characteristic is the establishment of a fixed tempo after the declamation of the first four syllables which is most often rendered in *parlando-rubato*. (See also taped items A through F).

5. *Ornamentation*
a. Due to the improvisatory nature of phrase A, there are more opportunities to use varied ornamental figurations while those for the interjection and phrase B appear to be more stereotyped, especially after the melodic stanza becomes established.

A possible connection between the formal aspects of *Arbolero* and those of the *chanson de geste* was discussed in an earlier article.[1] There I pointed out that the distich was also the most popular form for Greek songs since the Byzantine period. This point is significant in view of the possible adaptation of the ballad's tune from earlier Greek models.

Other formal structures for *Arbolero* have been reported by Stanley, Algazi, and Levy. Stanley offers the following transcription:

---

[1] Israel J. Katz, "Toward a Musicological Study of the Judeo-Spanish *Romancero*," *Western Folklore*, XXI (April, 1962), 83-91.

Example 27: [Stanley (Rhodes, Text A, p. 223)]

[musical notation with lyrics:]
Ar–bo–le– –ros, ar– –bo–le– ros, ar– –bo–le– –ros, tan ğen–til, la ra–iz ti– – – – – –
e– – – ne de o– – –ro, y la si– –mien– te de mar–fil.

While this notation has the appearance of a quatrain strophe, a closer look will reveal that it subscribes to a distich division. If we take as our clue the initial sixteenth-note pattern of the second and fourth melody sections, then it will readily be seen how this pattern alludes to the skeletal pattern of phrase B. Had Stanley attempted a complete notation of the ballad, it is most likely that Mrs. Cohen's rendition would have been seen to stabilize according to the traditional norm. From Stanley's transcriptions, we can only surmise that Mrs. Cohen's recollection of the traditional ballads as she knew them was not immediately framed at the onset of her renderings.

Algazi and Levy, on the other hand, present *Arbolero's* structure as a quatrain strophe. Their tunes are radically different from those of the *Sabra* ballads. One of the melodies, collected by both Algazi and Levy, can be described as A^{x+y} B C D, of which Levy's notation may be considered the simpler, if not the older. Levy's other tune, a third version, is also cast in the form: A^{x+y} B C D.

From among the supplemental taped items, still other formal structures emerge. The example D, depicted as A B C B, while presenting a good case for the quatrain with its melodic alternation of the first and third melody sections, must be considered as a distich in view of the singer's rigid adherence to phrase B together with her own personal touch, the alteration of phrases A and C. The taped example E is definitely a quatrain, A B C D, with the added interjection *a ğanim* (Turkish *a canım* 'Oh, my soul!') forming the last three cadential notes of phrase D.

A prominent feature of the recorded items of *Arbolero* is the declamatory rendition of the initial syllables in phrase A. A perusal of this phrase, as rendered in the *Sabra* variants, reveals that this declamatory feature includes a break in the melodic line, usually occurring after the fourth syllable. This may well be regarded as a dramatic element enhancing the dialogue between the knight Amadí and his wife. Again, it must be pointed out that such an extra-musical feature as regards the manner of performance is difficult to describe in terms of our notational system without having to resort to elaborate symbols. While we have had to accept the cruel economic impossibility of printing elaborate and complete notations, there is simply no excuse for the transcriber's lack of annotated explanations as an aid to learning more about a particular tradition. Although the interjection *amán* may seem to be a foreign addition, its musical sense is most compatible to the essence of the tune; because here, functioning as a bridge, it has the added rôle of establishing the thematic transition between the first and second melody sections, particularly as it provides the rhythmic impulse necessary for the steady melodic-rhythmic reiteration of phrase B.

The remarkable melodic stability of phrase B deserves special comment. Although all the skeletal variants vigorously maintain the melodic profile of phrase B (with some minor variation), it is possible that both, the interjection and phrase B, were intended to be sung by a chorus, while phrase A, which is more improvisatory by nature, was sung by a solo singer who continued in this manner until the end.[1]

A close scrutiny of the modal attributes of *Arbolero* clearly indicates the Dorian mode, with the uniform cadential patterns of phrase A, the interjection, and phrase B, falling upon the *sub-finalis*, the lower 3rd, and the *finalis*, respectively. However, the occurrence of certain peculiarities among the variants forms an interesting adjunct in the discussion of modality. Another look at Example 26 will reveal these peculiarities, particularly for phrase A in each of the variants. Immediately one will see for the fifth sung syllable, the note a^1 for V̌1, V̌2[2], and V̌3, and the note g for V̌5. Furthermore, it will be seen that while the note e is indicated for V̌4, the singer continues to g with the stereotyped figure . And, in V̌6 the attainment of g is postponed until the sixth sung syllable. Add to these features the pronounced use of the note G as the first note, or pair of notes, for V̌3, V̌4, and V̌5.

With these peculiarities in mind, the question arises as to whether the characteristics of phrase A can truly be considered as Dorian. The preponderant use of G, forming the interval of a 5th with d, or, at times, the interval of a major 6th with e (see the transcription for V̌3), appears as a strange occurrence from the standpoint of modality although it is more convincing that the note a, if one would suspect it to start with a. At any rate, the problem is most peculiar to V̌3. In the examples V̌4 and V̌5, the picture is quite different, because here the relationship between the initial G and its octave

---

[1] On the numerous occasions when I heard *Arbolero* sung by two or more informants, it appeared that they seldom agreed with phrase A but were in complete agreement with the interjection and phrase B. I had inquired about the possibility of the soloist-chorus rendition, but received no positive response. While the rule is for a solo recitation, my experience with the tradition has led me to believe otherwise because of the overwhelming urge by all present to participate in the performance of the ballad.

[2] V̌ stands here for tune variant.

occurrence on the fifth syllable is more readily understood. While it could also be construed to be in the Mixolydian mode with the repeated *d*'s considered as dominant tones, the shift at the end of phrase A to the transition (or bridge) is characteristically the same as that of the other *Sabra* renditions, which come to a close in the Dorian mode.

Considered as a melody type, the varied intoned inflections of certain notes, namely the lower third degree and second degree, place this melody in the mode of the *Bayat* maqam, with the key signature: [musical notation] .[1]

The taped items from Monastir, Aïden, and Rhodes are likewise in the Dorian mode, with features attributed to *Bayat*. Stanley and Gerson-Kiwi came to the same modal conclusions to judge by their transcriptions. Although Stanley's is in the *d* mode, his last measure (see Example 27 above) needs clarification. By transposing the last measure of Stanley's transcription to conform to our skeletal notations we have [musical notation], that is, *d* as
 fil.
our *finalis* extending down to *a*. Our taped example E, also from Rhodes, immediately solves this problem. While the piece does, in fact, end on the *finalis*, the three note extension carries the interjection *a ğanim*:

[musical notation]
¡A ga-nim!

Algazi, Jungić, and Levy (published source 4) are in major, while published source 5, also in Levy's collection, is Aeolian.

While we may designate the performance of this ballad as *parlando-rubato*, there are, nevertheless, definite rhythmic pulses which underlie the interjection and phrase B. From what we have already inferred above, together with other important observations, we can describe the ballad in the following manner:

Phrase A
a. Declamatory by nature.
b. Sung in *parlando-rubato* style.
c. Improvisatory-embellishments occur around the opening reiterated tones.
d. Cadence on the *sub-finalis*.
e. The last four syllables assume a more melodic character, with an implied rhythmic feeling.

---

[1] See A. Z. Idelsohn, *Gesänge der orientalischen Sefardim* (Jerusalem-Berlin-Vienna, 1929), pp. 75-78, and Dalia Carmi-Cohen, "An Investigation into the Tonal Structure of the *Maqamat*," *Journal of the International Folk Music Council*, XVI (1964), 102-106.

Interjection
f. Acts as a melodic and rhythmic bridge. Figuration may vary, but outline is apparent. Tradition-bound to the tetrachord.
g. Stimulates the rhythmic impulse of phrase B.
h. Cadence on *b*.

Phrase B
i. Rigidly fixed within the tradition.
j. Highly rhythmic.
k. The modality is established, ends on *finalis*.
l. Ornamental figures appear to remain quite constant throughout the performance.

The proper placement of the textual accents occur for phrase A, on the third and seventh (penultimate) syllables, while in phrase B, the accents fall on the third and last (ultimate) syllable. Because the rhythmic feeling of phrase B is indeed pronounced, the following scheme is offered (for phrase B of V̌4), which takes these textual accents into account:

Example 28:

It is interesting to note that the informant of V̌5 mimicked an instrumental interlude after every fourth verse. This was one of the few instances when an informant divulged the use of instrumental accompaniment as she recollected the days of her youth when the ballad was performed "that way." I give the rendition of the informant of V̌5 (Example 29a), followed by the same interlude sung by her daughter, Malka Dar, Age 50 (Example 29b).[1]

---

[1] Both informants were recorded at the same session; however, Mrs. Cabeli was asked to sing the instrumental interlude first, and her daughter immediately followed. For instrumental accompaniment of Sephardic ballads, see Michael Molho's *Usos y costumbres de los sefaradíes de Salónica* (Madrid- Barcelona, 1950), pp. 76-77; Menéndez Pidal, *Romancero Hispánico* (Madrid, 1953), II, p. 213; Idem, *Cómo vivió y comó vive el Romancero* (Valencia, n.d.), pp. 66-67 (including a photograph).

Example 29a:

la-la lai-la lai-la etc.

Example 29b:

la-la lai-la lai-la lai etc.

With the aid of the rather numerous published and recorded versions and variants of the *Arbolero* tune, we have been able to point out those salient features which the Jerusalem variants share with the taped examples from Monastir, Aïden, and Rhodes (item C). These three widely separated Sephardic communities have provided us with the necessary clues to consider this musical link. We submit the following map as an indication of the predominant musical influences which have been brought to bear upon the Jerusalem tradition of the *Arbolero* ballad:

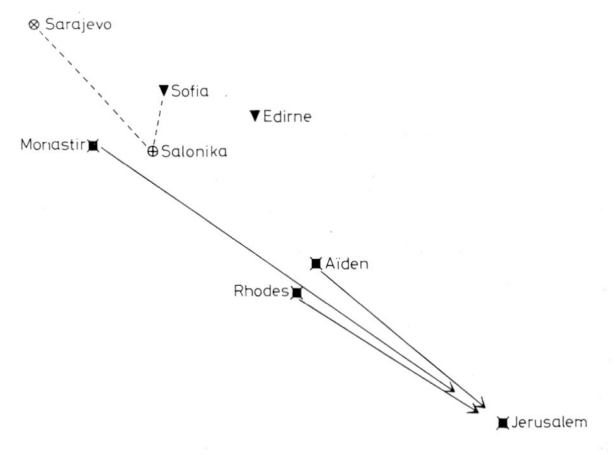

B. *La adúltera (á-a)*, MP 80

The numerous published texts of *La adúltera* (*á-a* assonance) attest to the ballad's great popularity among the Sephardim of the Eastern Mediterranean area. The ballad theme had also been found in the Moroccan tradition and in many Peninsular areas as well.[1] Among the *Sabra* informants of Jerusalem, the *romance* is designated by its first hemistich, *Un lunes por la mañana*.

The ballad deals with a wanton lover who rises early on a Monday morning, takes his bow and arrow, and goes to the house of his beloved. He knocks at her door and pleads with her to let him in, saying that his feet are in the snow and his head is covered with frost. She explains that she can not let him in because her husband is in her bed and her son is in her arms. Their conversation is interrupted by the husband, who wants to know with whom his wife is conversing. She replies that it is the boy from the bakery who has come to ask her for flour. In the same breath, she begs her husband to arise and go out hunting. When her husband leaves through the front door, her lover enters through a window. However, the husband has forgotten his lance and immediately returns home. Witnessing his arrival, the wife proceeds to hide her lover in a large chest containing pepper. As the husband enters the house, he hears a sneeze from the pepper chest. "Who is sneezing?" he asks. "It is the neighbour's cat," she answers. Uncovering the box, the husband then invites his neighbors in to see the "bearded cat."

La adúltera, as sung in the Jerusalem tradition, comprises three melody sections, with which the accompanying text is rendered abb, cdd, eff, etc. For the first six strophes taken from each of the five Sabra variants, I give the following skeletal forms:

Example 30

[1] Samuel G. Armistead and J. H. Silverman, "A New Sephardic *Romancero* from Salonika," *Romance Philology*, XVI, No. 1 (August, 1962), p. 78; Id., *The Judeo-Spanish Ballad Chapbooks of Yakob Abraham Yoná* (Berkeley and Los Angeles, 1970), No. 16.

The features common to all the variants are as follows:

1. *Formal*
a. A musical strophe based upon three melody sections, for which the predominant designation appears to be $A^{x+z}\ A^{y+z}\ B$. (See also the taped items A through D and the published sources 4 and 6).[1] $\dot{V}4$ resembles the other variants in the "z" portion of its A sections and the B section.
b. The main cæsura occurs after the second melody section. (See also the taped items A through D and the published sources 4 and 6).

2. *Melodic*
a. The skeletal outlines for the first two melody sections appear to be the most consistent, excluding $\dot{V}4$. (See also the taped items A through D). The B section of $\dot{V}2$ and $\dot{V}5$ bear the closest resemblance.

3. *Modal*
a. A modal structure based on the *finalis e*. (See also the taped items A through D and the published sources 1 and 6).
b. The cadences of each melody section end on *f, c*, and *e*, respectively. Notice particularly the cadential patterns formed on the four syllables of each variant. (See also the taped items A through D and the published source 6).

4. *Melodic-textual*
a. The distich forms the textual basis for each strophe, with the latter hemistich repeated in the manner abb, cdd, eff, etc., throughout the performance. (See also the taped items A through D and the published sources 4 and 6).

Stanzas containing three melody sections were also found in the taped examples from Monastir, Izmir, and Istanbul. However, in the Rhodes tradition it is the melodic couplet, AB, which predominates, and also its appearance in the Salonikan tradition is attested by Bordachar's transcription (see published source 2). Algazi (published source 3) and Levy (published sources 5 and 6) give further musical versions which are based on the quatrain ABCD*E*, the *E* representing a recurrent refrain, *También de la madrugada*. The latter three melodies are closely related. Hemsi's notation (published source 1), also from Salonika, appears to comprise an elaborate formal scheme, ABCDBC, with the text of the first strophe rendered as abbbcd, and the second strophe, deffgh.

---

[1] The taped and published sources for *La adúltera (á-a)* can be found in Appendix II.

Example 31: [Hemsi XVII, Op. 13-5]

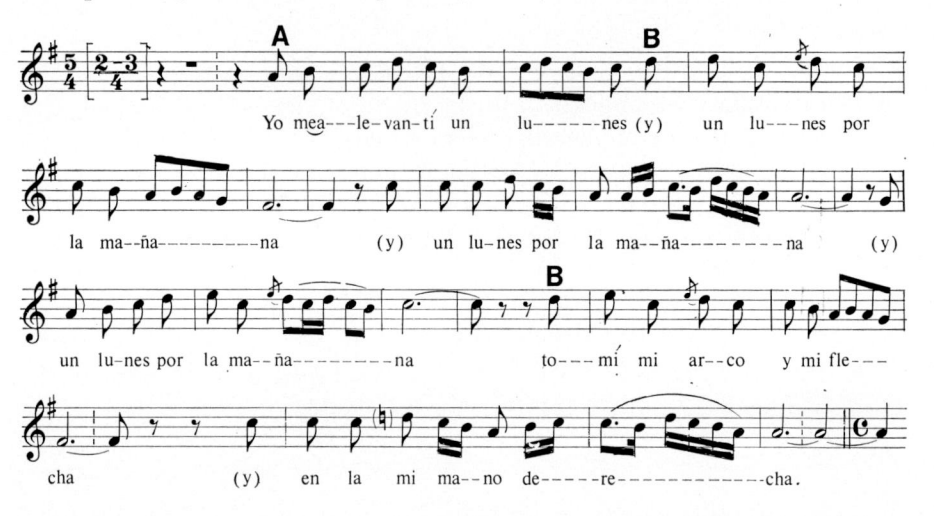

[musical notation with lyrics:]
Yo mea---le-van-tí un lu------nes (y) un lu---nes por la ma--ña---------na (y) un lu-nes por la ma--ña------na (y) un lu-nes por la ma--ña---------na to----mí mi ar--co y mi fle---cha (y) en la mi ma--no de-----re-----------cha.

By placing Hemsi's notation alongside our skeletal melodies, it becomes clear that Hemsi not only transcribed the tune as a tri-partite form, ABC, but that he gave two complete melody stanzas, ABC, A'BC, with A' representing a rather elaborate variation of A. Even Isaac Levy's tune (published source 4) was cast in the same form:

Example 32: [Levy (Eastern Mediterranean, No. 25, p. 30)]

[musical notation with lyrics:]
Un lu nes por la ma-----ña-------na Un lu---nes por la ma--ña-------na Y un lu---nes por la ma---ña---------------na.

With the exception of certain deviations in V̇4, the contours of the three-melody sections bear a remarkable resemblance to each other. Concerning each of the variants: V̇1 is consistent particularly in its third melody section; V̇2, V̇3, and V̇4 have stabilized their melodic stanzas, and V̇5 exemplifies the most varied rendition.

With regard to modality, the variants display features of the Phrygian mode, which is especially pronounced in the final melody section as indicated by the characteristic descending Phrygian cadence. The variants are not entirely free from certain chromatic alterations, particularly the note *g*, the third tone above the *finalis*, which is constantly subject to being raised a quarter-

or semi-tone. As a melody type, the *Sabra* variants can be placed in the mode of the *Siga* maqam; however, because of the raised qualities of *g*, as seen in all the variants except ℣5, the question arises as to whether influences of the *Hidjaz* maqam are present.[1] The two taped examples from Rhodes are in the Dorian mode. Of the published examples, items 2 and 6 are also in the Phrygian mode, 1 and 4 are in the Aeolian, while 3 and 5 are in major.

The tempo, taken as a whole for the *Sabra* renditions, ranges between M.M. 106 and 120. All but one ballad was transcribed with the underlying *tactus* given as an eighth note, the exception being ℣4, which was based on the quarter-note. The time signature which would best suit the performance of the ballad is the simple 2/4 designation. While certain informants tend to maintain longer pauses between melody sections, which is undoubtedly tradition bound, a rigid rhythmic performance is more likely the norm though hardly maintained in the oral tradition.

Ornamentation is particularly noticeable in the cadential sections for the penultimate syllable. The remaining accents merely coincide with the melodic accents in duple time.

Considering the sources at hand the diffusion of *La adúltera* may be plotted as follows:

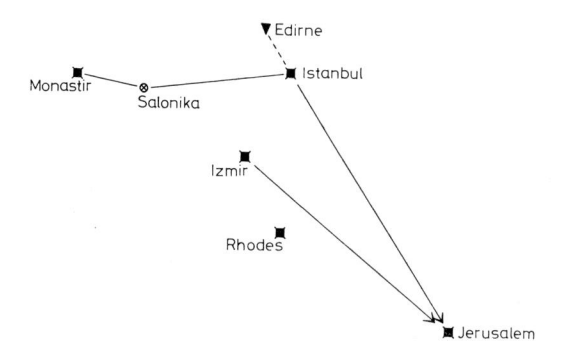

C. *Landarico*, MP 82

Landarico is one of the most widely diffused Sephardic ballads. This *romance* also deals with the theme of the adulteress. The narrative describes how a king, who arises early one morning, makes his way to the queen's quarters where he finds her intent on grooming her disorderly tresses. Realizing that

---

[1] See A. Z. Idelsohn, *Gesänge der orientalischen Sefardim* (Jerusalem-Berlin-Vienna, 1929), pp. 82-84, 92-101. See also P. José Antonio de Donostia "El modo de *mi* en la canción popular española," *Anuario musical*, I (1946), 170.

his presence is unexpected, the king decides to jest with his wife and proceeds to tap her gently, three times, on her waist. Without turning around, the queen calls out the name of her lover and begs him to cease his pranks.[1] However, to the amazement of the king, she does not stop with these endearing words, but continues uninhibitedly to reveal that of her four sons, her favorite two are those of her lover. It is they who are treated better during their meals, who are more elegantly dressed, and who are more properly equipped for the hunt. When the queen finally turns around to look at her supposed lover, lo and behold, the king stands enraged before her. While she pleads for forgiveness, trying to explain that it was nothing but a dream ("Pedrón, pedrón, señor reyes, ke un eshueño m'a soñado"),[2] he draws his sword and chops off her head.

The three *Sabra* variants collected for *Landarico* represent a unique display of formal, modal, and rhythmic characteristics. However, the published analogs and tape-recorded items provide us with further clues which point toward a unilateral Balkan genesis for the tune.[3] Let examine carefully the melodic skeletons of these tape-recorded variants in the order obtained:

Example 33:

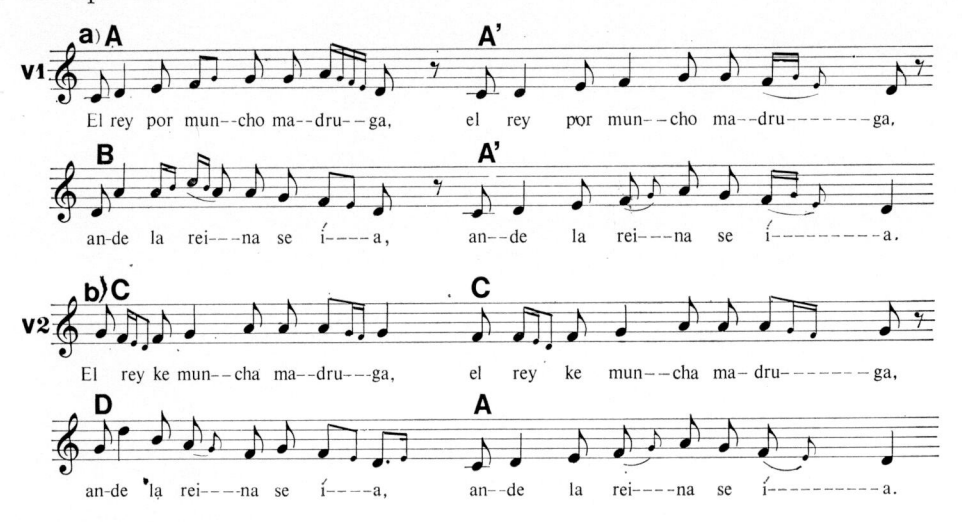

---

[1] *Landarico*, the lover's name, is used as the title of this *romance* theme. In the Eastern Mediterranean tradition, a variety of names are applied to the lover, but all consist of four syllables. These variations are discussed in S. G. Armistead and J. H. Silverman, *Diez romances hispánicos en un manuscrito sefardí de la Isla de Rodas* (Pisa, 1962), pp. 57-58.
[2] See verse 17 from the rendition of V1 in Volume II.
[3] The taped and published sources are listed in Appendix II.

El rey ke mun--cho ma—dru-- ga, el rey ke mun--cho ma-dru------- ga,

on-de la rei----na se i-----a, on-de la rei---na se i--------a.

From this preliminary examination, we find certain features that are common to all:

1. *Formal*
a. A quatrain strophe divided into four melody sections, each corresponding to a hemistich composed of eight syllables. (See also: Taped sources A through L, and the published notations 1, 3, 5, 6, 7, and 8).
b. The first two melody sections are repeated exactly or with slight variation. (See also: Taped sources A, C through L, and the published notations 3, 4, 5, 6, 7, and 8).
c. The textual repetition of each hemistich continues throughout each rendering in the scheme aa, bb, cc, dd, etc., causing the assonance to fall at the final cadence of each melodic stanza. (See also: Taped sources A through L, and the published notations 3, 5, 6, 7, and 8).

2. *Modal*
a. A modal structure based upon the *finalis d*. (See also: Taped sources A through L, and the published notations 2, 3, 4, and 7).

3. *Textual-melodic*
a. The lengths of the sung syllables, *ornamentation included*, are distinctly maintained. (See also: Taped sources A through L, and the published notations 4, 5, 6, 7, and 8).

Under normal conditions, we would depict the formal structure of each variant as: V̇1 = AA′BA′; V̇2 = AABC; and V̇3 = AABA. However, these designations are misleading, especially when attempting to describe variants as manifestations of an evolutionary process inherent in ballad transmission. A more accurate description should take into account all the melody sections as components of a broader structural context. By assigning "A" only to those melody sections whose initial motive is , we can proceed convincingly toward an objective description of their melodic stanzas. Thus, V̇1 remains AA′BA′; V̇2 becomes CCDA; and V̇3, AAEA.

Four taped examples (D, F, G, and H) from Istanbul subscribe to the outline given for V̇2. The taped example (I) from Rhodes, is very similar to V̇1. Of the remaining taped items, it is interesting to note that three examples from Rhodes (J, K, and L) are similar to the melody which Hemsi notated (see published source 3) and may be described as FFA′A′, in terms of the above explanation.[1]

The occurrence of A as the final melody section in all the variants outlined above is obvious indeed. Moreover, moving beyond the initial motive, A's rôle as the closing section is even more significant in that it displays cadential features which are necessary for determining its modal structure. The closing sections of the three skeletal variants would indicate a Dorian mode. However, due to their limited ambitus, in which no sixth degree is given, an Aeolian classification is also possible:

Example 34

This is also true for the taped items B through L. Even a closer look at the printed sources 2, 3, 4, and 7 will immediately reveal how tradition-bound this occurrence is:

Example 35:

Bordachar (measures 5-9) (Salonika)

Hemsi (measures 8-12, 13-16) (Rhodes)

[1] Stanley's notation was explained on pp. 97-98, *supra*.

Stanley (measures 7-9)
(Rhodes)

Levy (measures 4-6)
(Eastern Mediterranean)

Here, particularly, the question of modality must be handled individually for each of the *Sabra* versions, since they carry their own modal devices. Of the three variants, V̇1 poses a number of problems partly because of the informant's inconsistent fixation of an ambitus for succeeding repetitions of the melody stanza and partly because of her poor sense of pitch, undoubtedly a consequence of her age (seventy-two years). While the b-flat^1 in the third melody section places the melody in the Aeolian mode, a perusal of the complete transcription shows that the b-flat^1 occurs, not only in the phrase B, but occasionally in phrase A (first and fourth melody sections only). Also, the lowering of the second degree, almost by a quarter-tone, can be seen particularly before the *finalis* in the second and fourth melody sections, and only spasmodically in the third melody section. This latter idiosyncrasy plus the use of b^1-flat is most essential to its classification in the mode of the *Bayat* maqam, which may be indicated as: .[1]

The modal aspects of V̇2 clearly establish the Aeolian mode with its almost consistent use of b-flat^1 in phrase D. But, there are scattered instances of the flattened second degree, however slight, which still point out a strong influence of maqamat practices.

V̇3 may be considered a curiosity. Judging by its skeletal outline (Example 33c), it seems possible that, in view of its hexachordal line, this variant may be chronologically the earliest form of the three variants. In this instance, the skeletal outline is misleading, because the sole occurence of b-flat^1 takes place at the very onset in phrase E, and does not reappear again.[2] It is all the more startling that this informant continues the skeletal outline after having sung a b-flat^1 in the initial strophe; particularly, when the b^1-flat is common to all the taped items (save that of source A from Sofia). Even the flattened 2nd, which plays a small rôle here, is not entirely free from its culturally attuned environment.

The Aeolian modality for *Landarico* is also pronounced in Hemsi, Levy, Laning, and Stanley. However, Stanley also considered the flattened 2nd

---

[1] See Dalia Carmi-Cohen, "An Investigation into the Tonal Structure of the *Maqamat*," *Journal of the International Folk Music Council*, XVI (1964), 102-106.
[2] See verse 1, third melody section, of V̇3 in Volume II.

at certain cadential points. It is interesting that Bordachar notated the melody in its hexachordal form which could presuppose either Dorian or Aeolian modality. Although Gerson-Kiwi's notation (see published source 8) was transcribed in the Phrygian mode, consensus definitely attributes the Aeolian mode to the *Landarico* tune.

Entering into the realm of rhythmic structure, we come to a particularly striking phenomenon, which, unfortunately, had been overlooked by previous collectors. Here is a case where the melodic consideration overrules the textual, with the added peculiarity that certain accents in the *romance* line have been rigidly fixed. Admittedly, the first impression gained from the published notations would make us yield unquestionably to the varied rhythmic interpretations offered by individual transcribers. However, such is not the case when the tradition as preserved on tape is scrutinized. Here one has the advantage of experimenting with a goodly number of rhythmical possibilities from the transcriptions of which the prototype that governs *all* the variants emerges. As pointed out above, where we abstracted the common elements from our three variants, the lengths of the sung syllables were distinctly maintained. We will illustrate this feature by aligning the rhythmic values employed for the first two hemistichs of our *Sabra* variants including the published sources 4 through 8:

Example 36:

El réy que mu------cho ma--drú--------ga, el réy que mu------cho ma--drú------ga,

A clue for establishing a metrical base for the varied though essentially uniform distichs, outlined in Example 36, is furnished by the proper placement of accents above the *romance* line. Thus, for the first octosyllabic hemistich, *El rey que mu-cho ma-dru-ga*, the accents fall on the seventh (penultimate) and second syllable, functioning as the primary and secondary accents, respectively, though subject to intermittent changes brought about by individual nuances in the course of the performance. With this fact in mind, we can readily observe the delineation of accents, utilizing the text and rhythm of

Example 37:

El réy por muncha ma-drú---ga,   el réy por muncha ma-drú---ga.

Adding the values for *tactus* — in this case, an eighth-note — we obtain for both divisions, 7/8 and 5/8, which totals 12/8 per hemistich. However, we have yet to incorporate those accents inherent in the melodic line whose underlying pulsations in the 12/8 scheme carry the characteristic pattern $\frac{3\text{-}2\text{-}2\text{-}2\text{-}3}{8}$, and reïterated in the following manner:[1]

Example 38:

El rey por mun--cha ma-dru------ga,· el rey por mun-cha ma--dru--- ga

While five of the published examples contain an up-beat (2, 3, 4, 5, and 6), the transcribers, cognizant of the underlying *tactus*, relegated the entire melodic strophe to a simple triple meter. Yet, Hemsi, Stanley, and Laning failed to coördinate the main textual accent with the musical accent. In published source 3, Rodrigo utilizing Manrique de Lara's MS notation, maintained the proper accents within the triple time designation. Bordachar's notation (published source 2), on the other hand, contained two additional beats for the first hemistich, which, seemingly awkward, was altered by him to read:

Example 39:

El rey que mu----cho ma-┘---dru------ga,

---

[1] See Boris Kremenliev, *Bulgarian-Macedonian Folk Music* (Berkeley, 1952), pp. 23 and 37 and "Extension and its Effect in Bulgarian Folk Song," *Selected Reports* (Los Angeles, 1966), p. 4.

Isaac Levy (published source 7) was able to indicate the main stress in his duple-time notation, but forced the secondary stress on *rey* to appear as a syncopated accent. Again, Gerson-Kiwi claimed that the rhythm of *Landarico* "truly reflects the poetic meter with its units of :3-3-4-2:," which completely disregards the textual stresses of the traditional line, even though her textual underlay bears the stress indications.[1]

Considering the total number of taped and published sources, we can plot the geographical distribution for *Landarico* in the Eastern tradition as follows:

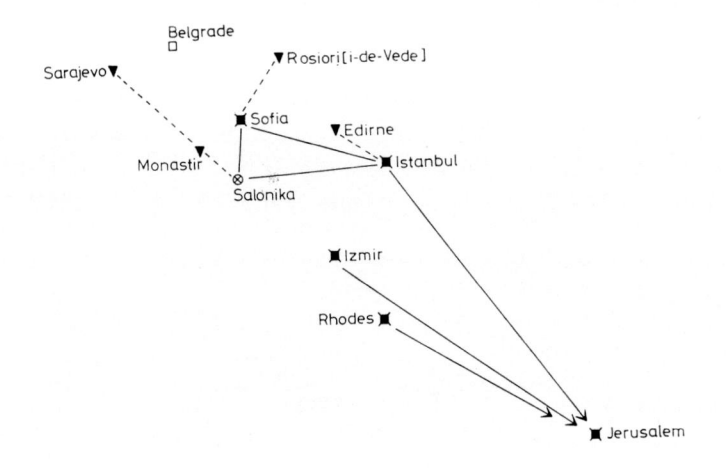

D. *Don Bueso y su hermana*, MP 49

The ballad of *Don Bueso y su hermana* is widely diffused in the Eastern Mediterranean tradition. One might expect it to figure prominently in the Jerusalem répertoire. However, only scant fragments of the ballad survive among the aged *Sabras*. The ballad's origin dates back to the thirteenth-century German epic poem *Kudrun*.[2] Its popularity on the Peninsula still continues to the present day and ample musical sources are available.[3] It is

---

[1] "On the Musical Sources of the Judaeo-Hispanic *Romance*," *The Musical Quarterly*, L (Jan., 1964), 40.

[2] See R. Menéndez Pidal, "Supervivencia del 'Poema de Kudrun'," *Los godos y la epopeya española* (Madrid, 1956), pp. 103-104, and "Los romances de Don Bueso," *De primitiva lírica española y antigua épica* (Buenos Aires, 1951), pp. 103-112. See also Moshe Attias, "הרומנסה של דון בואיזו ['The *romance* of Don Bueso']," *Edoth*, I (Jerusalem, 1946), 235-38, 260-61 (In Hebrew.)

[3] Juan Tomás Parés made a study of twenty-one tunes found in the Peninsular tradition of *Don Bueso* in "Las variantes en la canción popular: El romance popular *Los dos hermanos*," *Anuario musical*, XIV (1959), 195-205.

known in two different traditional forms among the Sephardim of Morocco.[1]

The ballad tells how Don Bueso, a Christian knight traveling through Moorish territory, pauses at a river to water his horse. As he dismounts, he notices a beautiful girl washing clothes. Bueso learns that she is a Christian being held in captivity by a Moorish queen. He persuades her to accompany him. As they reach Christian lands, they pass through the fields of Oliva. The young woman then reveals that she remembers these fields and how she was carried off by the Moors when she was a small child. At this astonishing revelation, Bueso realizes that he has rescued his long-lost sister.

Our *Sabra* variants are mere fragments of the ballad. Their melodies bear no resemblance to the Peninsular or to the Moroccan melodies cited above. The Sephardic variants share, with the archaïc Peninsular texts from Asturias, quatrain strophes and hexasyllabic (rather than the more modern octosyllabic) verses. In presenting the melodic outlines for each variant, I have attempted to derive the individual lines from the total (contextual) melodic profile. A mere skeletal outline would not suffice here, as it would suppress the animation so vital to the inherent beauty of this melody. Furthermore, it may readily be seen, in Example 40, how these melodies lend themselves to the common 4/4 designation together with their emphatic display of the Dorian modality. Perhaps here, we can add that the tune's basic tempo taken from the oral tradition, falls between M.M. 82 and M.M. 90, taking the quarter-note as our *tactus*. With these basic remarks, I give the three variants:

Example 40:

[1] The melodies for *Don Bueso* found in Bénichou's and Larrea Palacín's collection are musically connected to the Peninsular tradition.

V3 De la‑‑sal‑‑tas ma‑‑‑‑‑‑res tra‑‑‑ye‑‑‑nà la ni‑‑‑‑‑‑ña

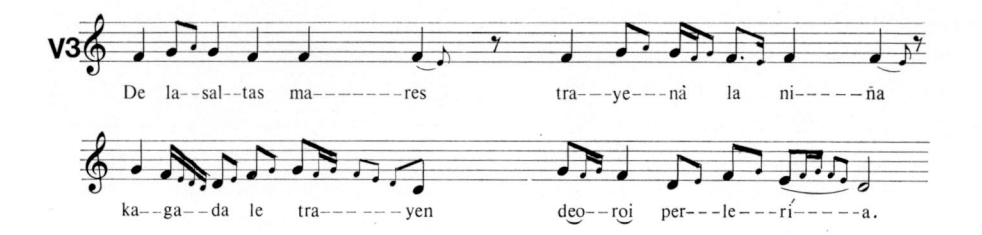

ka‑‑ga‑‑da le tra‑‑‑‑‑‑‑yen deo‑‑roi per‑‑‑le‑‑‑rí‑‑‑‑‑a.

Let us now take a closer look at our variants with special regard for those features which are common to all:

1. *Formal*
a. A quatrain strophe composed of four melody sections each containing a hemistich of six syllables. (See also taped items A through G and the published notations 1 and 3).[1]
b. The first two melody sections are repeated with slight variations. (See also taped items A through G and the published notations 1 and 3).

2. *Modal*
a. A modal structure based upon the *finalis d*. (See also taped items A through G).

3. *Textual-melodic*
a. The lengths of the sung syllables, *ornamentation included*, is distinctly maintained. (See also taped items A through G).

Having displayed the melodic outlines in Example 40, we must now explain in more detail the formal aspects in terms of their performance. The outline given for V̍1 was based primarily on the stabilizing lines of the second and third strophe. The fourth melody section presented problems because it was varied in all three strophes up to the cadential figure beginning on the penultimate syllable. In this instance, the outline was reconstructed from elements common to V̍2 and V̍3.

In the case of V̍2, all but the third melody section remained consistent throughout the performance; however, the outline given for the questionable fourth phrase was derived mainly from the first, fourth, and fifth strophes. Since the formal structure for V̍3 was established from the outset, I have transcribed only the first six strophes.

Taken as a whole, it would be more realistic to designate the *Sabra* outlines as A A′ B C, judging by their completed transcriptions rather than A A′ B B′ as shown for V̍2 and V̍3 in Example 40. The former scheme, A A′ B C

---

[1] The taped items and published sources can be found in Appendix II.

holds true for all the taped items A through C as well as the published notations 1 and 3.

Whereas the first two melodic sections have been shown to be similar in melodic content, that which is sung in the actual tradition brings to light a very interesting feature. While the first melody section of V̇1 and V̇2 conforms to the basic outline of Example 40, its movement in V̇3 is quite different. Here we encounter a peculiarity in the first and second melody sections which can best be described in terms of its performance. The informant renders the beginning of each phrase in a strict rhythmic pulse up through the fifth syllable — in this case the penultimate — after which she makes an abrupt break in the melodic line and continues in *rubato* with elaborate melismatic figurations to the cadential note *e*. However, this is not repeated for the second melody section. Thus the *tactus* is again maintained until the end of each strophe, and the performance is continued throughout in this manner. This rendition agrees with the taped item F from Çanakkale, Turkey, while V̇1 and V̇2 agree with the taped items B, C, and D from Rhodes. In addition, it should be pointed out that in the taped items A, E, and G, the informants often sang the ballad in the manner A A′ B C B C, repeating the last who hemistichs.

A closer look at the notations of Manrique de Lara (published source 1) and Levy (published source 3) will reveal how similar their melodies are, even though they appear different at the first glance. Although both conform to the A A′ B C structure as do our Jerusalem variants, they may be considered as additional versions, melodically speaking. Hemsi's melody (published source 2) is but another version, with the formal structure A B A′ C.

The modal features of *Don Bueso* clearly indicate the Dorian mode in spite of the fact that the ambitus of the tune is founded upon the traditional hexachord (*c* to a^1). Moreover, the consistent use of the flattened 2nd, seen particularly in the final cadential section of each strophe, is undoubtedly an environmental influence which places it in the mode of the *Bayat* maqam. It is curious indeed, that in one instance, in the third melody section of the third strophe of V̇2, the informant did in fact sing above the ambitus passing through b^1, in this case flattened by a quarter-tone, which would have implied the

Aeolian:

The final notes of the melody sections for V̇1 and V̇3 are in agreement with the cadential tones *e, e, c,* and *d*. All the taped examples concur with this; however, in the case of V̇2, where the opening melodic phrase ends on *e*, its cadential pattern is altered to conform with cadences ending on *f, f, c,* and *d*, respectively.

Hemsi's example (from Izmir) is in the Aeolian mode, while Manrique de

Lara's (from Istanbul) is in major. Levy's geographically unidentified rendition is a mixture of major and minor.

The tempo indication for the three *Sabra* variants are remarkable in that they remained within the range M.M. 80 to M.M. 90. The taped items are somewhat slower ranging from M.M. 68 to M.M. 80, though the rendering appears quite uniform in the Eastern tradition.

There is no doubt about the main accent in the hexasyllabic lines of *Don Bueso*. Here it falls on the penultimate syllable, which carries the elaborate ornamental figures of each melody section. This is also true for all the tape-recorded items, and for the published notations as well. Taking all the above comments into consideration, we plot the following distribution:

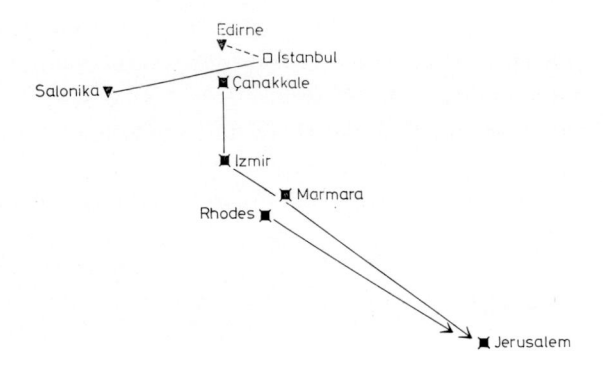

E. *La choza del desesperado*, MP 140

Another widely diffused ballad among the Eastern Mediterranean Sephardim is *La choza del desesperado*.[1] Known to the informants by its first hemistich, *Ir me kero, la mi madre*, the ballad "reflects a profound sense of tragedy and the circumstances of the narrative are sufficiently ambiguous in their implications as to be almost universally acceptable."[2] Its content is as follows:

> Oh, mother, I shall go wandering through the fields. For my bread I shall eat grass and for drink I shall have my tears. In the midst of those fields, I shall build myself a tower. I shall build it of mortar and stone and paint it on the outside. And every wayfarer who passes by, I shall take up into my tower to tell me of his woes and I in turn shall tell him mine. If his be greater, I shall patiently accept my fate. But if mine be greater, I shall throw myself down from my tower.[3]

---

[1] See Samuel G. Armistead and J. H. Silverman, "A New Sephardic *Romancero* from Salonika," *Romance Philology*, XVI (Aug., 1962), 77.
[2] S. G. Armistead and J. H. Silverman, "Hispanic Balladry among the Sephardic Jews of the West Coast," *Western Folklore*, XIX (Oct., 1960), 241.
[3] *Op. cit.*, p. 240.

Ir me kero is exceptional in its strophic form in that its constituent melody sections carry the textual burden of the traditional distich for which the following five skeletal melodies are given:

Example 41:

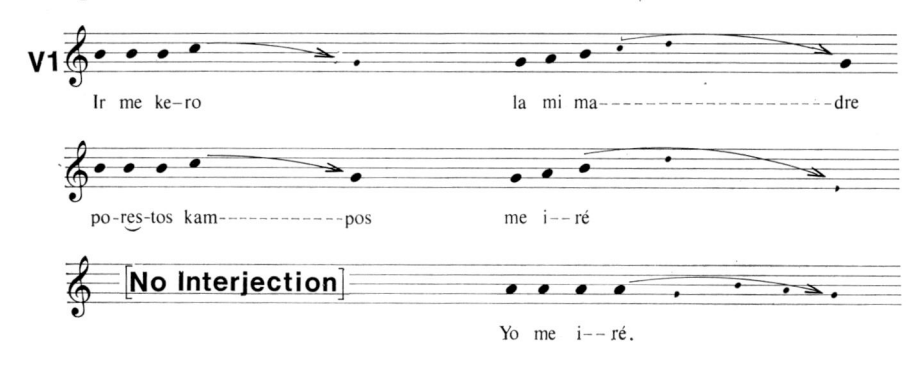

159

[V4]

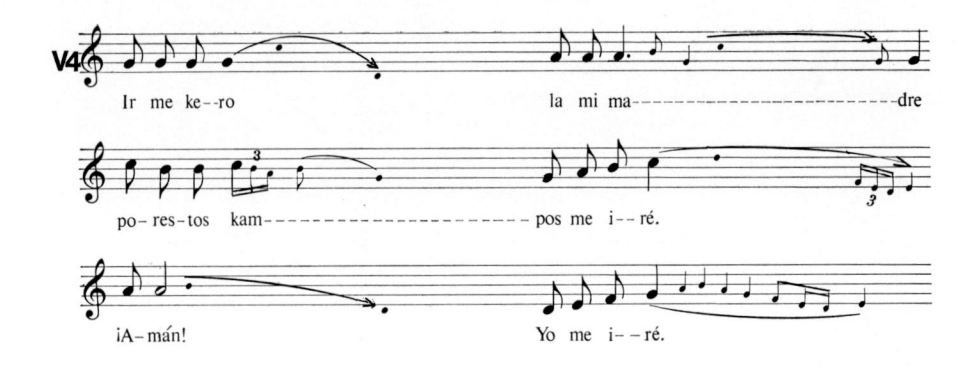

Ir me ke--ro la mi ma----------dre
po-res-tos kam------------ pos me i--ré.
¡A--mán! Yo me i--ré.

[V5]

Ir me ke-ro la mi ma-dre
po--res-tos kam-------------- pos me i--ré
¡A-mán! Yo me i--ré

While each of the variants display nuances peculiar to its individual rendition, the similarities become obvious upon closer examination. Let us first extract the following common features:

1. *Formal*
   a. A melodic stanza based upon six melody sections, with the exception of V̇1 which is based upon five melody sections. (See also taped items A. B, D, E, and G, and the published sources 2 and 3).[1]
   b. The inclusion of an interjection, ¡amán! (Turkish *aman* 'alas, mercy!') which acts as a bridge between the fourth and sixth melody sections. (See also taped items A, B, D, E, and G, and the published sources 2 and 3).
   c. The main cæsuræ follow the second and fourth melody sections. (See also taped items A, B, D, E, and G, and the published sources 2 and 3).

2. *Melodic*
   a. The initial three or four sung syllables of the first, second, and third melody sections are rendered in a declamatory manner before proceeding to rather

[1] The tape-recorded and published sources are listed in Appendix II.

elaborate melismata, whose final notes are usually sung syllables. (See also taped items A, B, D, E, and G. The published sources have rendered one stanza only).
b. The initial three or four sung syllables of the fourth and sixth melody sections are also rendered in a declamatory manner and also proceed to elaborate melismata but this time, they continue up through the cadential sections. (See also the taped items A, B, D, E, and G, and the published sources 2 and 3).
c. For the interjection or fifth melody section, only the first two syllables are sung and continue to their respective melismata. (See also the taped items A, B, D, E, and G and the published sources 2 and 3).
d. The initial sung syllable for the first four melody sections, taken as a whole, are confined within the tetrachord, g to c^1. The sung syllables of the last two melody sections as seen particularly in $\text{V}3$, $\text{V}4$, and $\text{V}5$, are not bound to such limitations. (The former condition also exists in the taped items A, B, D, E, and G and in the published sources 2 [making an exception for the opening note e] and 3).
e. The *ambitus* falls between d and d^1. (See also taped items A, B, D, E, and G and the published sources 2 and 3). $\text{V}3$, however, ranges from c to e^1.

3. *Modal*
a. A modal structure based on the *finalis* e. (See also taped items A, D, and E, and the published sources 2 and 3).
b. The final tones for the second, third, and fourth melody sections are g, g, and e, respectively. (See also taped items A, D, and E and the published source 3).

4. *Rhythmic*
a. The *parlando-rubato* style is exemplified in the performance of this ballad. A *tactus* may be discernible particularly in the ornamental portions of each melody section. (See taped items A through G).

5. *Ornamentation*
a. While ornamental features of each ballad abound in characteristic figurations, their relationship among the ballads is attested by their diatonic character, descending quality, and cadential patterns. (See also taped items A, B, D, E, and F, and the published sources 2 and 3).

6. *Textual-melodic*
a. The ballad is based on the distich which is broken up into phrases of four syllables each, with a reïteration of the last four syllables. (See also taped items A, B, D, E, G and the published sources 2 and 3).

b. The division of the distich into four four-syllable phrases corresponds to the first four melody sections. The interjection ¡amán! constitutes the fifth melody section; and finally, the reïteration of the last four syllables follows which comprises the sixth melody section. ℣1 is exceptional in that it does not have the interjection. (See also taped items A, B, D, E and the published sources 2 and 3).

c. The primary textual accents occur on the penultimate syllable of the first hemistich — the third syllable of phrase B — and on the ultimate syllable of the second hemistich — the last syllable of phrase D. (See also taped items A, B, D, E, F, G and the published sources 2 and 3).

Regarding other formal structures of *Ir me kero*, the taped item F from Rhodes rendered the melodic stanza as a quatrain, ABCD, whose melodic outline bears a marked resemblance to the melody of the ballad *La misa de amor* collected from a Salonikan informant residing in Los Angeles.[1] The taped item C from Salonika agrees with the first four melody sections of Bordachar's notated example (published source 1). Judging from Donostia's setting of the Bordachar tune, $\frac{ABCDCEB}{abcdeff}$ (the minuscule letters representing hemistichs), I am inclined to believe that the rendition of taped item C is more traditionally acceptable. Bordachar's transcription is as follows:

Example 42: Bordachar-Donostia (Salonika, No. 4, pp. 15-18)

It is also interesting to note that Bordachar's tune bears some resemblance to the popular Ladino folksong *Alta alta va la luna*, of which I give the transcription by Levy:[2]

---

[1] Recorded by Armistead and Silverman in Los Angeles, 22nd August 1957. The text appears in "Hispanic Balladry among the Sephardic Jews," *Western Folklore*, XIX (October 1960), 238.

[2] Isaac Levy, *Chants judéo-espagnols* (London, 1959), p. 27. A variant can be found in Léon Algazi, *Chants séphardis* (London, 1958), p. 44.

Example 43:

♪ Al--ta al----ta es la lu----na Quan-do em pe---sa es cla--re--- cer.

♪ Hi-jaher mo---za sin ven-tu----ra Nun-ca lle----que a na---cer.

The melodic sections of the *Sabra* variants require further elucidation. Especially when investigating their full transcriptions [in Volume II], one will immediately notice the wide individual divergence of phrase lengths, due particularly to their vocal ornamentations which are rendered in a free rhythmical style. While it is possible to designate the first four melody sections of each rendition as ABCD, such a designation does not provide an accurate description of these melody sections nor those which follow. In all the *Sabra* variants, the second, third, and fourth melody sections are doubtless the most rigid to judge by their notations. Therefore, by assigning the letters ABC to these sections, we can depict the *Sabra* variants in the following manner: ♭1 = BABC-A; ♭2 = DABCA′C; ♭3 = D′ABCEE; ♭4 = D″ABCA′E; and ♭5 = FABCGA. Of the taped items, A, D, and E resemble ♭5 and B resembles ♭2.

The modality of *Ir me kero* has Phrygian characteristics, yet its microtonal inflections, especially those found for the notes e and b^1, point to the Arab mode E of the *Siga* maqam. Thus, while the cadential tones of the three rigid melody sections discussed above are g, g, and e, respectively, those of the remaining melody sections show greater variance. The taped example G is an excellent example in the Lydian mode, while the taped example F is in Dorian. Bordachar's melody alternates between a Major and Aeolian modality resulting from the chromatic alterations of the major and minor 3rd.

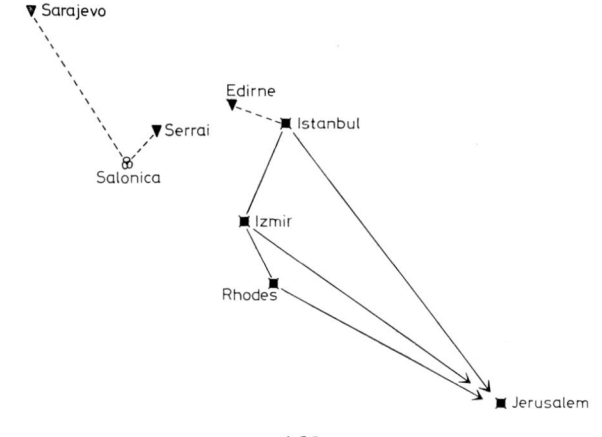

The *parlando-rubato* style is attested by all the *Sabra* and taped items, although Bordachar and Levy have given time designations. The declamatory beginnings of each phrase followed by lengthy ornamental melismata are most characteristic to all the renditions, excepting those given by Bordachar and Levy. One will certainly agree that *Ir me kero* is a fine example of a ballad which displays improvised melodic variations from stanza to stanza.

Having discussed the broad aspects of the ballad as it has been maintained in oral tradition, we can conclude that our musical analogs, although sparse, furnish us with evidence that the ballad had migrated from Turkish sources. The diffusion of *Ir me kero* can be charted in the manner as shown on page 163.

CONCLUDING STATEMENT

The varied speculations concerning the musical origins of the Judeo-Spanish ballad tradition have never been fully challenged. The fact that these ballads were sung in a language exhibiting many of the lexical and phonological features of fifteenth-century Spanish is not proof that the ballad's original melodies have survived in oral tradition. The evolution of the Sephardic *Romancero* is inextricably related to the history of the Spanish Jews after their expulsion from Spain. These exiles, who travelled to a great variety of Mediterranean centers, strove to maintain their Hispanic culture. In their new environments, which were often remote from Hispanic influences, they lived together in closely-knit communities, remaining loyal to their mother tongue and proud of their ennobled past. By 1700, the Sephardic communities of the Eastern and Western Mediterranean undoubtedly comprised two distinct cultural groups. The latter, because of its proximity to Spain, was able to maintain contact with the Peninsula, while the former was subject to alien influences.

The Sephardim who settled in the Eastern Mediterranean communities founded two important centers, namely Salonika and Istanbul, around which numerous ancillary communities clustered. It was primarily from these two centers and their subordinate communites that the Sephardic immigrants made their way to Jerusalem. Thus Jerusalem became a Sephardic center whose culture and language were an amalgam of features drawn from the various Balkan communites.

The numerous ballad themes which have persisted in the oral tradition of the Eastern Mediterranean basin provide us with an opportunity to study the diffusion of their melodies. Having compared the Jerusalem ballad melodies with analogs from other Eastern Mediterranean centers, we have attempted to prove that the *Sabra* tunes did not originate on Palestinian soil, but were indeed those brought over from the other major Balkan centers.

BIBLIOGRAPHY

Abrahams, Israel. *Jewish Life in the Middle Ages*. Philadelphia: The Jewish Publication Society of America, 1896.

Alatorre, Margit Frenk. "El antiguo cancionero sefardí," *Nueva Revista de Filología Hispánica*, XIV (1960), pp. 312-318.

Albeck, Šalom. "יסודות משטר הקהילות בספרד עד השנה הרמ"ה (1180–1244)" "Yisodot mištar ha-kehilot be-Sefarad ad ha-me'ah ha-šaloš esre (1180-1244) ['The Principles of Government in the Jewish Communities of Spain until the 13th Century']," ציון [*Zion*], XXV (Jerusalem, 1960), pp. 85-121.

Algazi, Léon. *Chants séphardis*. London: World Sephardi Federation, [c. 1958].
Algazi, Léon. "Chants traditionnels et populaires juifs," *Évidences*, No. 16 (Paris, Jan., 1951), pp. 12-15.
Algazi, Léon. "La Musique religieuse israélite en France," *La Reuvue Musicale*, No. 222 (1953-1954), pp. 157-166.
Algazi, Léon. "Le Folklore séphardi," *Judaïsme Séfardi*, (Paris-London, March, 1956), pp. 421-424.
Algazi, Léon. "Les Juifs dans la musique française," *Cahiers Juifs*, II, No. 4 (Paris, 1933), pp. 55-64.
Algazi, Léon. "Musique biblique," *L'Univers Israélite*, XLII (Paris, July 13, 1923), pp. 395-396.
Algazi, Léon. "Musique juive de Russie," *Évidences*, No. 33 (Paris, 1953), pp. 24-30.
Algazi, Léon. "Premier Congrès de musique orientale et Sefardie," *Kol-Sepharad*, II, No. 8 (June, 1959), pp. 117-118.

Alhony, A. H. "המלחין יהודה ליאון אלגאזי" "Ha-malḥin yehuda Léon Algazi ['The Jewish Composer Léon Algazi']," שבט ועם [*Ševet v'Am*], IV (Jerusalem, 1959), pp. 130-132.

Alvar, Manuel. "Amnón y Tamar en el romancero marroqui," *Vox Romanica*, XV, No. 2 (1956), pp. 241-258.
Alvar, Manuel. *Cantos de boda judeo-españoles*. Con notación de melodías tradicionales por María Teresa Rubiato (Madrid, 1969).

Alvar, Manuel. *Endechas judeo-españoles*. Colección filológica. Granada: Universidad de Granada, 1953. See also the newly revised and augmented second edition with musical notations by María Teresa Rubiato of the traditional melodies (Madrid, 1969).

Alvar, Manuel. *Poesía tradicional de los judíos españoles*. México D.F.: Editorial Porrúa, S.A., 1966.

Alvar, Manuel. "El romance de *Gerineldo* entre los sefarditas marroquies," *Boletín de la Universidad de Granada*, XXIII (1951), pp. 124-144.

Alvar, Manuel. "Los romances de *La bella en misa* y de *Virgilios* en Marruecos," *Archivum*, IV (Oviedo, 1954), pp. 264-276.

Amador de los Ríos, José. *Historia social, política y religiosa de los judíos de España y Portugal*. Madrid: Impr. de T. Fortanet, 1875-1876. 3 vols.

The Ancient Melodies of the Liturgy of the Spanish and Portuguese Jews. Harmonized by Emanuel Aguilar. Preceded by "An Historical Essay on the Poets, Poetry and Melodies of the Sephardic Liturgy," by the Rev. D. A. de Sola. London: Wessel and Co., 1857; reprinted later as *Sephardi Melodies being The Traditional Liturgical Chants of the Spanish and Portuguese Jews' Congregation London*. Part I 'The Ancient Melodies' by Emanuel Aguilar and The Rev. D. A. de Sola. London: Oxford University Press, 5691/1931.

Anglès [Anglés], Higini [Higinio]. "Hispanic Music Culture from the Sixth to the Fourteenth Centuries," *The Musical Quarterly*, XXVI (1940), pp. 498-528.

Anglès [Anglés], Higini [Higinio]. *La Música en la Corte de los Reyes Catolicos*, II: *Polifonía profana — Cancionero musical de Palacio*. Vol. I. Barcelona: Instituto España de Musicología, 1951. (Monumentos de la música española V).

Anglès [Anglés], Higini [Higinio]. "La Musique juive dans l'Espagne médiévale," *Yuval: Studies of the Jewish Music Research Centre* (Jerusalem, 1968), pp. 48-64.

Anglès [Anglés], Higini [Higinio]. "El Primer Congreso Internacional de Música Judía," *Sefarad*, XVIII (1958), pp. 211-213.

Anglès [Anglés], Higini [Higinio]. "Relations of Spanish Folk Song to the Gregorian Chant," *Journal of the International Folk Music Council*, XVI (1964), pp. 54-56.

Anglès [Anglés], Higini [Higinio]. "Das spanische Volkslied," *Archiv für Musikforschungen*, III, No. 3 (Leipzig, 1938), pp. 331-362.

Anonymous. "El arte de Yitsjak Levy," *Kol-Sepharad*, II, No. 10 (Oct., 1959), pp. 158-159.

Anonymous. "בעולם הספרות של מוסיקה הספרדים" "Ba-olam ha-sefrut šel ha-musika ha-sefardim ['In the Literary World of Sephardic Music']," ידיעות [*Yidiot*], II (Jerusalem, 1961), pp. 145-147.

Ansejo, S. de. Review of P. José Antonio de S[an] Sebastián, *Canciones sefardíes para canto y piano* in *Sefarad*, VIII (1948), pp. 228-230.

Apel, Willi. *Harvard Dictionary of Music*. Cambridge: Harvard University Press. [Ninth Printing, 1955].

Armistead, Samuel G. and Joseph H. Silverman. "A Judeo-Spanish Derivative of the Ballad of *The Bridge of Arta*," *Journal of American Folklore*, LXXVI (1963), pp. 16-20.

Armistead Samuel G. and Joseph H. Silverman. "A Judeo-Spanish *Kompla* and its Greek Counterpart," *Western Folkore*, XXIII (1964), pp. 262-264.

Armistead, Samuel G. and Joseph H. Silverman. "A New Collection of Sephardic Ballads" (Concerning M. Molho, *Literatura sefardita de Oriente*, Madrid-Barcelona, 1960), *Journal of the Folklore Institute*, III (1966), pp. 133-153.

Armistead, Samuel G. and Joseph H. Silverman. "A New Sephardic *Romancero* from Salonika," *Romance Philology*, XVI (Aug., 1962), pp. 58-82.

Armistead, Samuel G. and Joseph H. Silverman. "Algo más para la bibliografía de Yacob Abraham Yoná," *Nueva Revista de Filología Hispánica*, XVII (1963-1964: published in 1966), pp. 315-337.

Armistead, Samuel G. and Joseph H. Silverman. "Christian Elements and De-Christianization in the Sephardic *Romancero*," *Collected Studies in Honour of Américo Castro' Eightieth Year* (Oxford, 1965), pp. 21-38.

Armistead, Samuel G. and Joseph H. Silverman. *Diez romances hispánicos en un manuscrito sefardí de la Isla de Rodas*. Con un prólogo de R. Menéndez Pidal. Pisa: Istituto di Letteratura Spagnola e Ispano-americana dell' Università di Pisa, 1962.

Armistead, Samuel G. and Joseph H. Silverman. "Dos romances fronterizos en la tradición sefardí oriental," *Nueva Revista de Filología Hispánica*, XIII (1959), pp. 88-98.

Armistead, Samuel G. and Joseph H. Silverman. "El romance de *Celinos y la adúltera* entre los sefardíes de Oriente," *Anuario de Letras*, II (1962), pp. 5-14.

Armistead, Samuel G. and Joseph H. Silverman. "Exclamaciones turcas y otros rasgos orientales en el Romancero judeo-español" *Sefarad*, XXX (1970), pp. 177-193.

Armistead, Samuel G. and Joseph H. Silverman. "Hispanic Balladry among the Sephardic Jews of the West Coast," *Western Folklore*, XIX (October, 1960), pp. 229-244.

Armistead, Samuel G. and Joseph H. Silverman. "Jud.-Sp. *alazare*: An Unnoticed Congener of Cast. *alazán*," *Romance Philology*, XXI (1968), pp. 510-512.

Armistead, Samuel G. and Joseph H. Silverman. "Judeo-Spanish Ballads in a MS by Salomon Israel Cherezli," *Studies in Honor of M. J. Benardete* (New York, 1965), pp. 367-387.

Armistead, Samuel G. and Joseph H. Silverman. "*La Dama de Aragón*: Its Greek and Romance Congeners," *Kentucky Romance Quarterly*, XIV (1967), pp. 227-238.

Armistead, Samuel G. and Joseph H. Silverman. "*La sanjuanada*: ¿Huellas de una harğa mozárabe en la tradicion actual?," to appear in *Nueva Revista de Filología Hispánica*.

Armistead, Samuel G. and Joseph H. Silverman. "*Las Complas de las flores* y la poesía popular de los Balcanes," *Sefarad*, XXVIII (1968), pp. 395-398.

Armistead, Samuel G. and Joseph H. Silverman. "Review of Isaac Levy, *Chants judéo-espagnols* (London, 1959), in *Nueva Revista de Filología Hispánica*, XIV (1960), pp. 345-349.

Armistead, Samuel G. and Joseph H. Silverman. "Review of Manuel Alvar, *Poesía tradicional de los judíos españoles*, (México D.F., 1966) in *Romance Philology*, XXII (1968), pp. 235-242.

Armistead, Samuel G. and Joseph H. Silverman. "*Selví*: Una metáfora oriental en el romancero sefardí," *Sefarad*, XXVIII (1968), pp. 213-219.

Armistead, Samuel G. and Joseph H. Silverman. "Sobre unos romances del Cid recogidos en Tetuán," *Sefarad*, XXII (1962), pp. 385-396.

Armistead, Samuel G. and Joseph H. Silverman. "Sobre unos versos del cantar de gesta de las *Mocedades de Rodrigo* conservados tradicionalmente en Marruecos," *Anuario de Letras*, IV (1964), pp. 95-107.

Armistead, Samuel G. and Joseph H. Silverman. *The Judeo-Spanish Chapbooks of Yakob Abraham Yoná*. Berkeley: University of California Press, 1970.

Armistead, Samuel G. and Joseph H. Silverman. "Un romancerillo de Yacob Abraham Yoná," *Homenaje a Rodríguez-Moñino*, II (Madrid, 1966), pp. 9-16.

Armistead, Samuel G. and Joseph H. Silverman, eds. With the collaboration of Biljana Šljivić-Šimšić. *Judeo-Spanish Ballads from Bosnia*. Philadelphia: University of Pennsylvania Press, 1971.

Ashtor, Eli. קורות היהודים בספרד המוסלמית *Korot ha-yehudim be-Sefarad ha-Muslamit* ['*A History of the Jews in Moslem Spain*']. Jerusalem: Kiryat-Sepher, 1960.

Ashtor, Eli. "מספר היהודים בספרד המוסלמית" "Mispar ha-yehudim be-Sefarad ha-Muslamit ['The Number of Jews in Moslem Spain']," ציון [*Zion*], XXVIII (Jerusalem, 1963), pp. 34-56.

Attal, Robert. רשימה בבליוגרפיה על יהודות צפון־אפריקה [Rešimah b'bliografia al yehudot Tzafon-afrika, 'Bibliography on North African Jewry'], בתפוצות הגולה *Bitfutzot ha-golah* (Jerusalem, 1961), pp. 1-38.

Attias, Moshe. "הרומנסה של דון בואיזו" "Ha-romansa šel Don Buezo ['The *romance* of Don Bueso']," עדות [*Edoth*], I (Jerusalem, 1946), pp. 235-238, 260-261.

Attias, Moshe. רומנסירו ספרדי *Romancero sefaradí: romanzas y cantes populares en judeo-español*. Jerusalem: Kiryat-Sepher, 1961. (In Hebrew with a Spanish translation of the Introduction.)

Attias, Moshe. "A Sephardic Romancero," *Studies and Reports, Ben Zvi Institute*, I (Jerusalem, 1953), pp. 21-26.

Aubrun, Charles V. "Inventaire des sources pour l'étude de la poésie castillane au XVe siècle," *Estudios dedicados a Ramón Menéndez Pidal*, IV (Madrid, 1953), pp. 297-330.

Avenary, Hanoch. "Études sur le cancionero judéo-espagnol (XVIe et XVIIe siècles)," *Sefarad*, XX (1960), pp. 377-394.

Avenary, Hanoch. "השיר הנכרי כמקור השראה לישראל נג׳ירה" "Ha-šir ha-nakri k'makor hašra'ah l'Yisrael Najara ['The Foreign Song as a Source of Inspiration for Israel Najara']," *Papers of the Fourth World Congress of Jewish Studies*, II (Jerusalem, 1968), pp. 383-384.

Avenary, Hanoch. "Jüdische Musik," *Die Musik in Geschichte und Gegenwart*, VII (1958), col. 224-261.

Avenary, Hanoch. "מנגינות קדומות לפזמונים ספרדיים (המאה הט״ז)" "Manginot kadumot la-pizmonim sefaradim ha-me'ah šeš esre ['Ancient Melodies for Sephardic Hymns of the Sixteenth Century']," אוצר יהודי ספרד [*Tesoro de los judíos sefardíes*], III (Jerusalem, 1960), pp. 149-153.

Avenary, Hanoch. "The Sephardic Intonation of the Bible; Amsterdam 1699," *Le Judaïsme Séphardi*, No. 21 (Oct., 1960), pp. 911-913.

Bacher, W. "Les Poésies inédites d'Israël Najara," *Revue des Études Juives*, LVIII (1909), 241-269; LIX (1910), 96-105, 231-238; LX (1910), pp. 221-234.

Baer, Yitzhak. *A History of the Jews in Christian Spain*. Philadelphia: The Jewish Publication Society of America, 1961-1966. 2 vols.

Bal y Gay, Jesús. "Espagne," *Folklore Musical* (Paris, 1939), pp. 64-84.

Barbieri, Francisco Asenjo. *Cancionero musical de los siglos XV y XVI*. Madrid: Tip. de los Huérfanos, 1890.

Barnett, Richard D. and Frederico Pérez Castro. "Institute of Sephardic Studies, Madrid," *Kol-Sepharad*, II, Nos. 3-4 (London, 1966), pp. 18-19.

Baron, S[alo] W. "מתחילת המאה ה–19 עד ראשית ההתיישבות החדשה (1882–1880)" "Metehilat ha-me'ah ha-19 ad rašit ha-hityašvot ha-hadašah 1800-1882: ha-yešuv ha-yehudi ['From the Beginning of the 19th Century to the Beginning of the First Settlement']," *Encyclopaedia Hebraica*, VI (Jerusalem, 1957), pp. 504-508.

Bartók, Béla, and Albert B. Lord. *Serbo-Croatian Folk Songs*. With a Foreword by George Herzog. New York: Columbia University Press, 1951.

Baru[c]h, Kalmi. "Španske romanse bosanskih Jevreja," *Godišnjak* (Sarajevo-Belgrade, 1933), pp. 272-288.

Baud-Bovy, Samuel. "The Strophe of Rhymed Distichs in Greek Songs," *Studia Memoriae Belae Bartók Sacra*. Third edition (London, 1959), pp. 359-376.

Beinart, H. "Judiós y conversos en España después de la expulsión de 1492," *Hispania*, XXIV (1964), pp. 291-301.

Ben-Meir, Gad. "The World Sephardi Federation: Activities and Future Plans," *Kol-Sepharad*, I (London, 1965), pp. 16-20.

Ben-Zvi, Yitzhak. ארץ־ישראל ויישובה בימי השלטון העותמאני *Eretz-Yisrael v'yišuva b'yemai ha-šilton ha-ottomani* ['The Land of Israel under Ottoman Rule: Four Centuries of History']. Jerusalem: Bialik Institute, 1962.

Ben-Zvi, Yitzhak. *The Exiled and the Redeemed*. Translated from the Hebrew by Isaac A. Abbady. Philadelphia: The Jewish Publication Society of America, 5721/1961.

Benardete, Mair José. *Hispanic Culture and Character of the Sephardic Jews*. New York: Hispanic Institute in the United States, 1953.

Benardete, Mair José. *Los romances judeo-españoles en Nueva York*. Unpublished Master's thesis. New York: Columbia University, 1923.

Bendahan, Blanche. "Les Sephardim et le romancero judéo-castillan," *Cahiers de l' Alliance Israélite Universelle*, No. 107, (Paris, March-April 1957), pp. 4-11.

Benharoche-Baralia, J. *Chants traditionnels hébraïques en usage dans la communauté séphardie de Bayonne* (Biarritz-Paris, 1961).

Bénichou, Paul. "Le «romancero» castillan chez les Juifs espagnols," *Évidences*, No. 17 (Paris, 1951), pp. 17-22.

Bénichou, Paul. "Nouvelles explorations du romancero judeo-espagnol marocain," *Bulletin Hispanique*, LXIII (July-December, 1961), pp. 217-248.

Bénichou, Paul. "Romances judeo-españoles de Marruecos," *Revista de Filología Hispánica*, VI (1944), pp. 36-76, 105-138, 255-279, 313-381; thoroughly revised 2d ed., *Romancero judeo-español de Marruecos*. Madrid: Castalia, 1968.

Benveniste, Irving. "The Glory and Tragedy of Rhodes," *Kol-Sepharad*, II, Nos. 3-4 (London, 1966), pp. 9-11.

Bericht über den neunten internationalen Kongress, Salzburg 1964. Band II. Basel: Bärenreiter, 1966.

Bernfeld, Samson. "נעים זמירות ישראל (ר. ישראל נגירה)" "Ne'im Zemirot Yisrael (R. Yisrael Najara) ['Pleasant Hymns of Israel (R. Israel Najara)']," ה־מאסף [*Ha-Me'aset*], No. 2 (Warsaw, 1887), pp. 18-25.

Bernheim, Lucien. "Chansons populaires judéo-espagnoles," *Pages d'Art* (Geneva, August, 1920). [N.B.: This work was never published.]

Bernheim, Lucien. *Cinq Chansons populaires judéo-espagnoles du XVIe siècle* (*Smyrne*). Zagreb: Ed. Omanut, 1939.

Besso, Henry V. "Bibliografia sobre el Judeo-español," *Bulletin Hispanique*, LIV (1952), pp. 412-422.

Besso, Henry V. "Don Ramón Menéndez Pidal and the *Romancero sefardí*," *Sefarad*, XXI (1961), pp. 343-374.

Besso, Henry V. "Muestras del judeo-español con ilustraciones en cinta magnetofónica de canciones y romances sefardíes," *Actas y labores del IV Congreso de Academias de la Lengua Española* (Buenos Aires, 1966), pp. 410-432.

Book of Prayer of the Spanish and Portuguese Jews' Congregation, London. With an English translation based principally on the editions of the Rev. D. A. de Sola and Haham Moses Gaster. Revised under the authority of Solomon Gaon. London: Oxford University Press, 5718/1958.

Borrel, Eugène. "La Musique turque," *Revue de Musicologie*, IV, No. 4 (December, 1922), pp. 149-161; VII, No. 5 (February, 1923), pp. 26-32; VII, No. 6 (May, 1923), pp. 60-70.

Borrel, Eugène. "Mélodies israélites. Recueillies à Salonique," *Revue de Musicologie*, VIII, No. 12 (November, 1924), pp. 164-168.

Braïloïu, Constantin. "Le giusto syllabique. Un système rhythmique populaire roumain," *Anuario musical*, VII (1952), pp. 117-158.

Braïloïu, Constantin. "Sur une mélodie russe," *Musique russe*, II (Paris, 1953), pp. 329-391.

Bulletin of the International Folk Music Council, No. XXIII (London, April, 1963).

Burstein, Moshé. *Self-Government of the Jews in Palestine since 1900.* Tel Aviv: Hapoel Hatzair, 1934.

Cardozo, Abraham Lopez. "The Music of the Sephardim," *The World of the Sephardim* (Herzl Institute Pamphlet No. 15) (New York, 1960), pp. 37-71.

Cardozo, Abraham Lopez. "Some Sephardi Melodies and Customs," *Jewish Music Forum Bulletin*, X (January, 1956), pp. 20-22.

Carmi-Cohen, Dalia. "An Investigation into Tonal Structure of the *Maqamat*," *Journal of the International Folk Music Council*, XVI (1964), pp. 102-106.

Castrillo Hernández, Gonzalo. *Estudio sobre el canto popular castellano.* Palencia: Impr. de la Federación católico-agraria, 1925.

Castro, Américo. *The Structure of Spanish History*. Translated from the Spanish by Edmund L. King. Princeton: Princeton University Press, 1954.

Castro, Federico Pérez. "In Memoriam: Michael Molho," *Sefarad*, XXIV (1964), pp. 473-475.

Catalán, Diego. "A caza de romances raros en la tradición portuguesa." Reprinted from *III Colóquio Internacional de Estudos Luso-Brasileiros* (Lisbon, 1957), *Actas*, I (Lisbon, 1959), pp. 445-477.

Catalán, Diego. "El *motivo* y la *variación* en la trasmisión tradicional del romancero," *Bulletin Hispanique*, LXI (1959), pp. 149-182.

Catálogo de la Exposición Bibliográfica Sefardí Mundial. Biblioteca Nacional de Madrid, 18th November-19th December, 1959. Madrid: C. Bermejo, Impresor, 1959.

Chase, Gilbert. *The Music of Spain*. 1st edition: New York: W. W. Norton, Inc., [1941]. 2nd edition revised: New York: Dover Publications, Inc., [1959].

Cherezli, Salomon Israel. *Nouveau Petit Dictionnaire judéo-espagnol-français*. 2 vols. Jerusalem: A. M. Luncz, 1898-1899.

Chouraqui, André N. *Between East and West: A History of the Jews of North Africa*. Philadelphia: The Jewish Publication Society of America, 5728/1968.

Cirot, Georges. "Le mouvement quaternaire dans les romances," *Bulletin Hispanique*, XXI (1919), 103-142.

Clarke, Dorothy Clotelle. *A Chronological Sketch of Castilian Versification Together with a List of Its Metric Terms*. University of California Publications in Modern Philology (Berkeley and Los Angeles), Vol. 34, No. 3 (1952), pp. 279-382.

Cohen, Francis Lyon. "Folksong Survivals in Jewish Worship," *Journal of the Folk-Song Society*, I, No. 2 (London, 1900), pp. 32-38, 52-59.

Cohn, Hermann. *Mœurs des juifs et des arabes de Tetuan, Maroc*. Avec une lettre de S. Munk (Paris, 1927).

Cossío, J. M. de and T. Maza Solano. *Romancero popular de la Montaña* (Santander, 1933-1934). 2 vols.

Crews, Cynthia M. *Recherches sur le judéo-espagnol dans les páys balkaniques* (Paris, 1935).

Danon, Abraham. "La Communauté juive de Salonique au XVIe siècle," *Revue des Études Juives*, XL (1900), pp. 206-230; XLI (1900), pp. 98-117, 250-265.

Danon, Abraham. "Recueil de romances judéo-espagnoles chantées en Turquie," *Revue des Études Juives*, XXXII (1896), pp. 102-123, 263-275; XXXIII (1896), pp. 122-139, 255-268.

de Sola, D. A. and Emanuel Aguilar. *Sephardi Melodies: being The Traditional Liturgical Chants of the Spanish and Portuguese Jews' Congregation London*. London: Oxford University Press, 5691/1931.

Devoto, Daniel. "Nota adicional sobre las melodías de los «Romances de Tetuán»," *Bulletin Hispanique*, LXIII (1961), pp. 249-250.

Devoto, Daniel. "Poésie et musique dans l'œuvre des vihuélistes (Notes methodologiques)," *Annales Musicologiques*, IV (1956), pp. 85-111.

Devoto, Daniel. "Sobre el estudio folklórico del romancero español. Proposiciones para un método de estudio de la canción tradicional," *Bulletin Hispanique*, LVII (1955), pp. 233-291.

Devoto, Daniel. "Sobre la música tradicional española," *Revista de Filología Hispánica*, V (1943), pp. 344-366.

Díaz-Plaja, G. "Aportación al cancionero judeo-español del Mediterráneo Oriental," *Boletín de la Biblioteca de Menéndez Pelayo*, XVI (1934), pp. 44-61.

Dictionary Catalog of the Klau Library Cincinnati. Hebrew Union College — Jewish Institute of Religion. Boston: G. K. Hall and Co., 1964.

Donostia, P. José Antonio de. *Canciones sefardíes para canto y piano*. Tolosa: Gráficas Laborde y Labayen, S. L., [ca. 1945]. (See also San Sebastián, José Antonio de).

Donostia, P. José Antonio de. "El modo de *mi* en la canción popular española," *Anuario musical*, I (1946), pp. 153-180.

Durán, Agustín, ed. *Romancero general o colección de romances castellanos anteriores al siglo XVIII* (Madrid, 1828-1832). 2 vols.

Eisenstein, Judith K. *The Liturgical Chant of Provençal and West Sephardic Jews in Comparison to the Song of the Troubadours and the Cantigas*. Unpublished Ph. D. dissertation. New York: Hebrew Union College, 1966.

Emmanuel, Isaac Samuel. *Histoire des Israélites de Salonique* (Paris, 1936).

Entwistle, William J. "Ballads and Tunes which Travel," *Folklore*, L, No. 4 (London, 1939), pp. 333-341.

Entwistle, William J. *European Balladry*. Oxford: Clarendon Press, [1939].

Entwistle, William J. "Notation for Ballad Melodies," *Publications of the Modern Language Association*, LV (1940), pp. 61-72.

Espinosa, Aurelio M. "Spanish Ballad," *Standard Dictionary of Folklore Mythology and Legend*. New York: Funk & Wagnalls Co., 1950. Vol. II, pp. 1058-1061.

Estrugo, José María. *Los sefardíes*. Havana: Editorial Lux, 1958.

Farhi, Gentille. "La Situation linguistique du Sepharadite à Istanbul," *Hispanic Review*, V (1937), pp. 151-158.

Fernández, Africano. *España en Africa y el peligro judío: apuntes de un testigo desde 1915 a 1918*. Santiago: Tip. de "El Eco Franciscano", 1918. 328 pp.

Folklore Musical: Répertoire international des collections et centres de documentation avec notices sur l'état actuel des recherches: dans les différents pays et références bibliographiques. Départment d'art, d'archéologie et d'ethnologie. Paris: Institut international de coöperation intellectuelle, 1939.

Foss, George. "The Transcription and Analysis of Folk Music," *Folksong and Folksong Scholarship: Changing Approaches and Attitudes* (Dallas; 1964), pp. 39-71, 74.

Fraser, Norman, ed. *International Catalogue of Recorded Folk Music*. With a Preface by R. Vaughan Williams and Introduction by Maud Karpeles. London: Oxford University Press, 1954.

Friedländer, Max Hermann. *Pizmonim, Hymnum de R. Israel Najara* (Vienna, 1858).

Fuchs, Theodor. "Prilog muzici sefardskih zidova u Turskoj," with a resumé in German "Zur Musik der spaniolischen Juden in der Türkei," *Omanuth*, I (Agram = Zagreb] 1936-37), pp. 157-164.

Galante, Abraham. *Histoire des juifs d'Anatolie: Les Juifs d'Ismir (Smyrne)*. Vol. I. Istanbul: Imprimerie M. Babok, 1937.
Galante, Abraham. *Histoire des juifs d'Istanbul* (Istanbul, 1942).
Galante, Abraham. *Histoire des juifs de Rhodes, Chio, Cos, etc.* (Istanbul, 1935).
Galante, Abraham. *Le Juif dans le proverbe, le conte et la chanson orientaux* (Istanbul, 1935).
Galante, Abraham. "Quatorze romances judéo-espagnoles de Turquie," *Revue Hispanique*, X (1903), pp. 594-606.

Gaon, M. D. "ר. ישראל נגירה ז"ל וזמירותיו" "R. Yisrael Najara zikro livraha u-zmirotav ['R. Israel Najara — Le poète estimé du Judaïsme oriental']," מזרח ומערב [*Mizraḥ u-Ma'arav*], V, No. 3 (Jerusalem, July, 1930), pp. 145-163.

Garbell, Irene. "The Pronunciation of Hebrew in Medieval Spain," *Homenaje a Millás-Vallicrosa*, I (1954), pp. 665-669.

García-Barriuso, P. Patrocino. *La música hispano-musulmana en Marruecos*. Prólogo de D. Tomás García Figueras. Larache: Artes Gráficas Boscá, 1941.

García Blanco, Manuel. "El Romancero," *Historia general de las literaturas hispánicas*, II (Barcelona, 1951), pp. 3-51.

Gaster, Moses. *History of the Ancient Synogogue of Spanish and Portuguese Jews, the Cathedral Synogogue of the Jews in England, situate in Bevis Marks. A Memorial Volume to Celebrate the 200th Anniversary of its Inauguration, 1701-1901* (London, 5661/1901).

Gerson-Kiwi, Edith. "על המורשה המוזיקלית של העם היהודי" "Al ha-morašah ha-musikalit šel ha-am ha-yehudi ['On the Musical Legacy of the Jewish People']," בתפוצות הגולה [*Bitfutzot ha-golah*], IV (Jerusalem, Winter, 1963), pp. 52-71.
Gerson-Kiwi, Edith. "המוסיקולוגיה בישראל" "Ha-musikologia b'yisrael ['Musicology in Israel']," גשר [*Gešer*], III (Jerusalem, October, 1959), pp. 107-115.
Gerson-Kiwi, Edith. "Jerusalem Archive for Oriental Music," *Musica Hebraica*, I-II (Jerusalem, 1938), pp. 40-42.
Gerson-Kiwi, Edith. "Jüdische Volksmusik," *Die Musik in Geschichte und Gegenwart*, VII (1958), col. 261-280.
Gerson-Kiwi, Edith. "The Legacy of Jewish Music Through the Ages," *In the Dispersion*, III (Jerusalem, Winter 1963-64), pp. 149-172.
Gerson-Kiwi, Edith. "Musicology in Israel," *Acta Musicologica*, XXX (1958), pp. 17-26.

Gerson-Kiwi, Edith. "On the Musical Sources of the Judaeo-Hispanic *Romance*," *The Musical Quarterly*, L (January, 1964), pp. 31-43.

Gerson-Kiwi, Edith. Summary of the "Musical Sources of the Judaeo-Hispanic *Romance*," *Journal of the International Folk Music Council*, XIV (1962), p. 158.

Gerson-Kiwi, Edith. "Synthesis and Symbiosis of Styles in Jewish-Oriental Music," *Biblical and Jewish Folklore* (Bloomington: Indiana University Press, 1960), pp. 225-232.

Gerson-Kiwi, Edith. "Towards an Exact Transcription of Tone-Relations," *Acta Musicologica*, XXV (1955), pp. 80-87.

Geshuri, Me'ir Simeon. "Coplas sefardíes," *Le Judaïsme Séphardi*, III, No. 16 (January, 1934), p. 8.

Geshuri, Me'ir Simeon. "הרומנצים של יהודי ספרד (עם המנגינה של שלש אחיות)" "Ha-romantzim šel yehudai sefarad (im manginah šel «šaloš aḥiyot»)" ['The *Romances* of the Spanish Jews (with the Melody of *«Tres hermanicas»*)'], "כל-נוע" [*Kol-no'ah*], II (Tel Aviv, 1932), p. 7.

Geshuri, Me'ir Simeon. "חרומנצות הספרדיות ומנגינותיהן" "Ha-romantzot ha-sefardiot u-mangenotehen ['Sephardic *Romances* and their Melodies']," הציוני הכללי [*Ha-tzioni ha-klalli*], (Jerusalem, 1933), p. 6.

Geshuri, Me'ir Simeon. "Les romances sépharadites," *Le Judaïsme Séphardi*, I, No. 6 (January, 1933), pp. 92-93.

Gonzalo Maeso, D.' "Sobre la etimología de la voz «marrano» (Criptojudio)," *Sefarad*, XV (1955), pp. 373-386.

Goodblatt, Morris S. *Jewish Life in Turkey in the 16th Century: As Reflected in the Legal Writings of Samuel de Medina*. New York: Jewish Theological Seminary, [5712/1952].

Goodman, Paul. *Bevis Marks in History. A Survey of the External Influences of the Congregation Sahar Asamaim Bevis Marks, London.* With a Foreword by Lionel D. Barnett. London: Oxford University Press, 5694/1934.

Hassán, Iacob M. "El Simposio de Estudios Sefardíes," *Sefarad*, XXIV (1964), pp. 327-355.

Hemsi, Alberto. "Cancionero sefardí," *Sefarad*, XIX (1959), pp. 378-384.

Hemsi, Alberto, *Cancionero sefardi*. Unpublished MS. Contains 230 poems with 110 melodies.

Hemsi, Alberto, *Coplas sefardíes* (*Chansons judéo-espagnoles*). Alexandria: Édition Orientale de Musique, 1932-1938. 5 fascicles.

Hemsi, Alberto. *Coplas sefardíes* (*Chansons judéo-espagnoles*). Fascicles 6 to 9. Unpublished MS. Represents twenty-four additional melodies from Izmir.

Hemsi, Alberto. *El oriente a través de la música*. Alexandria: Édition Orientale de Musique, [n. d.].

Hemsi, Alberto. "המוסיקה העממית של הספרדים" "Ha-musika ha-ammamit šel ha-sefardim ['The Popular Music of the Sephardim']," [מזרח ומערב] *Mizraḥ u-Ma'arav*, II, No. 6 (Jerusalem, 1929), pp. 414-418.

Hemsi, Alberto. *Investigaciones folclóricas: sobre usos, costumbres y anécdotas sefardíes*. Unpublished MS.

Hemsi, Alberto. *La Musique de la Torah*. Alexandria: Édition Oriental de Musique, 1929. A synopsis of this work can be found in *Le Monde Musical*, XL (Paris, 31st July 1929), pp. 243-244.

Hemsi, Alberto. "Le Premier Congrès Internacional de Musique Juive à Paris, quelque réflexions," *Le Judaïsme Séphardi*, No. 16 (Paris-London, March, 1958), p. 733.

Hemsi, Alberto. *Maḥzor Sefardi*. Unpublished MS. Contains 200 liturgical melodies.

Hemsi, Alberto. "Sur le folklore séfardi," *Le Judaïsme Séphardi*, No. 18 (Paris-London, April, 1959), pp. 794-795.

Herculano, Alexandre. *Historia da origem e da estabelecimento da Inquisição em Portugal*. Lisbon: Antigua casa Bertrand, 1907.

Herschberg, Ḥaim Ze'ev. "מראשית שלטון העותמאנים עד מסע־נאפוליון" "Me-rašit šilton ha-Ottomanim ad masa-Napoleon ['From the Beginning of the Ottoman Rule to Napoleon's Expedition']," *Encyclopaedia Hebraica*, VI (Jerusalem, 1957), pp. 486-497.

Herzog, Avigdor. "Transcription and Transnotation in Ethnomusicology," *Journal of the International Folk Music Council*, XVI (1964), pp. 100-101.

Heskes, Irene. "Sephardi Music Featured in International Musicological Conference in Jerusalem," *Kol-Sepharad*, VII (January 1964), pp. 7-8.

Idelsohn, Abraham Zevi. *Gesänge der marokkanischen Juden*. Jerusalem-Berlin-Vienna: Benjamin Harz Verlag, 1929. (Vol. V of the *Hebräisch-orientalischer Melodienschatz*.)

Idelsohn, Abraham Zevi. *Gesange der orientalischen Sefardim*. Jerusalem-Berlin-Vienna: Benjamin Harz Verlag, 1923. (Vol. IV of the *Hebräisch-orientalischer Melodienschatz*.)

Idelsohn, Abram Zevi. *Hebräisch-orientalischer Melodienschatz* (Berlin-Vienna-Jerusalem, 1914-1933). 10 vols.

Idelsohn, Abraham Zevi. *Jewish Liturgy and Its Development*. New York: Sacred Music Press, [1932].

Idelsohn, Abraham Zevi. *Jewish Music in its Historical Development*. New York: Henry Holt and Company, Inc., 1929. Subsequently the work underwent two reprintings: the first, by the Tudor Publishing Company (New York, 1948); and the second, issued in paperback, by Schocken Books, Inc. (New York, 1967).

Idelsohn, Abraham Zevi. "Phonographierte Gesänge und Aussprachsproben des hebräischen der jeminitischen, persischen und syrischen Juden," *Sitzungsberichte der kaiserlichen Akademie der Wissenschaften in Wien*, 175, Band, 4. Abhandlung (Vienna, 1917), 119 pp.

Idelsohn, Abraham Zevi. "ר. ישראל נגירה ושירתו" "R. Israel Najara u-širatav ['R. Israel Najara and his Poetry']," [ה־שלוח] *ha-Šiloaḥ*, XXXVII (Berlin, 1919), pp. 25-36.

Jungić, B. "Tri sefardske romanse ['Three Sephardic *romances*']," *Godišnjak* ['*Yearbook*'] (Sarajevo-Belgrade, 1933), pp. 289-292.

Katz, Israel J. "A Judeo-Spanish *Romancero*," *Ethnomusicology*, XII (January, 1968), pp. 72-85.

Katz, Israel J. "The Enigma of the Bustelo Ballads in Manuel L. Ortega's *Los Hebreos en Marruecos*," to appear in the *International Folk Music Council, Yearbook*, (1970).

Katz, Israel J. "Toward a Musicological Study of the Judeo-Spanish *Romancero*," *Western Folklore*, XXI (April, 1962), pp. 83-91.

Katz, Solomon. *The Jews in the Visigothic and Frankish Kingdoms of Spain and Gaul*. Cambridge: The Mediæval Academy of America, 1937.

Kaufman, Nikolay. Summary of "Jewish and Gentile Folk Song in the Balkans and its Relation to the Liturgical Music of the Sephardic Jews in Bulgaria," *Journal of the International Folk Music Council*, XVI (1964), p. 63.

Keller, H., "The Music of British Jews," *The Jewish Quarterly*, III (London, 1956), pp. 21-23.

Kosover, Mordecai. "Ashkenazim and Sephardim in Palestine (A Study in Intercommunal Relations)," *Homenaje a Millás-Vallicrosa*, I (Barcelona, 1956), pp. 753-786. This article forms part of Kosover's recently published work, *Arabic Elements in Palestinian Yiddish* (Jerusalem, 1966).

Kraus, Karl. "Judeo-Spanish in Israel," *Hispania*, XXXIV (1951), pp. 261-270.

Kremenliev, Boris A. *Bulgarian-Macedonian Folk Music*. Berkeley: University of California Press, 1952.

Kremenliev, Boris A. "Extension and its Effect in Bulgarian Folk Song," *Selected Reports: Institute of Ethnomusicology* (Los Angeles: University of California Press, 1966), pp. 1-27.

Lachman, Robert. *Jewish Cantillation and Song in the Isle of Djerba*. Jerusalem: Hebrew University, 1940.

Lachmann, Robert. "Preserving Oriental Music," *Israel's Messenger* (Shanghai), XXXVII (20th December, 1940), p. 10.

Langas, Izaak and Barton Sholod, eds. *Studies in Honor of M. J. Benardete (Essays in Hispanic and Sephardic Culture)*. New York: Las Américas Publishing Company, 1965.

Larrea Palacín, Arcadio de. *Canciones rituales hispano-judías*. Madrid: Instituto de Estudios Africanos, 1954.

Larrea Palacín, Arcadio de. *Romances de Tetuán. Cancionero judío del norte de Marruecos*. Madrid: Instituto de Estudios Africanos, 1952. 2 vols.

Larrea Palacín, Arcadio de. "Romances hispánicos del medievo," *Mundo Hispánico*, V, No. 49 (1952), pp. 51-54.

Larrea Palacín, Arcadio de. "La saeta," *Anuario musical*, IV (1949), pp. 105-135.

Le Gentil, Pierre. *Le Virelai et le villancico. Le problème des origines arabes*. Paris: Société d'éditions «Les Belles Lettres», 1954.

Levi, Leo. "על היחס בין מוסיקה וחברה אצל הספרדים ובני עדות המזרח" "Al ha-yaḥas bayn musika v'ḥevra etzel ha-sefardim u-vnay edot ha-mizraḥ ['On the Relation of Music and Society among the Sephardim and the Jews of the Orient']," [שבט ועם] *Ševet v'Am*, V (Jerusalem, 1960), pp. 89-96.

Levi, Leo. "מוסיקה יהודית ומדינת ישראל" "Musika yehudit-u-medinat yisrael ['Jewish Music and the State of Israel']," [גשר] *Gešer*, III (Jerusalem, October, 1959), pp. 98-106.

Levy, Isaac. *Antología de liturgia judeo-española*. (Jerusalem, 1965-   ).

Levy, Isaac. *Chants judéo-espagnols*. London: World Sephardi Federation, 1959.

Levy, Isaac. "דפים מפנקסו של אספן" "Daphim mepinkaso šel asphan ['Pages from the Notebook of a Collector']," [תצליל] *Tatzlil* (*'The Chord'*), No. 5 (1965), pp. 127-129.

Levy, Isaac. "Rabbi Yitzhak Chlomo Algazi," *Le Judaïsme Séphardi*, No. 23 (December, 1961), p. 1007.

Lévy, Isaac Jack. *Sephardic Ballads and Songs in the United States: New Variants and Additions*. Tape recorded and edited by —. Unpublished Master's thesis. University of Iowa, 1959.

Levy, John. Notes for the Folkways Records Album No. FR 8961, *Music of the Spanish and Portuguese Synagogue*. New York: Folkways Records and Service Corp., 1960.

Llorca, Bernardino. "La inquisición española y los conversos judíos o «marranos», *Sefarad*, II (1942), pp. 113-152.

Llorca, Bernardino. "Los conversos judíos y la inquisición Española," *Sefarad*, VIII (1948), pp. 357-390.

Loeb, Isidore. "Le Nombre de juifs de Castille et d'Espagne au moyen âge," *Revue des Études Juives*, XIV (1887,) pp. 161-183.

López-Chavarri, Eduardo. *Música popular española*. 3rd edition. Barcelona: Labor, 1940.

Luncz, Abraham Moses., ed. לוח ארץ־ישראל *Luaḥ Eretz Yisrael* [*'Land of Israel Annual'*] (Jerusalem, 1895-1916).

MacCurdy, Raymond R. and Daniel D. Stanley. "Judaeo-Spanish Ballads from Atlanta, Georgia," *Southern Folklore Quarterly*, XV (December, 1951), pp. 221-238.

Malkiel, María Rosa Lida de. "Una colección de romances judeo-españoles," *Davar*, 10 (1947), pp. 5-26.

Mandel, Neville. "Turks, Arabs and Jewish Immigration into Palestine, 1882-1914," Albert Hourani, ed., *Middle Eastern Affairs*, No. 4 (London, 1965), pp. 77-108.

Manrique de Lara, Manuel. "Romances españoles en los Balkanes," *Blanco y Negro*, Año 26 (Madrid, Jan. 2, 1916), No. 1285.

Marcu, Valeriu. *The Expulsion of the Jews from Spain*. Translated from the German by Moray Firth. London: Constable & Co., Ltd., 1935.

Marcus, Jacob Rader. *The Jew in the Medieval World. A Source Book*: 315-1791. Philadelphia: The Jewish Publication Society of America, [1960].

Marcus, Simon. השפה הספרדית־יהודית *Ha-safah ha-sefaradit-yehudit* [*'The Judeo-Spanish Language'*]. Jerusalem: Kiryat Sefer, Ltd., [1965].

Marcus, Simon. "לתולדות היהודים ברודוס בימי שלטון מסדר אבירי יוחנן הקדוש" "Le-toldot ha-yehudim be-Rodas bemay šilton me-seder aviri yoḥanan ha-kaduš ['A History of the Jews of Rhodes during the Rule of the Order of the Knights of St. John']," אוצר יהודי ספר [*Tesoro de los judíos sefardíes*], II (Jerusalem, 1959), pp. 55-68.

Marranos in Portugal. Survey by the Portuguese Marranos Committee, London 1922-1938 (London, 1938).

Marx, Alexander. "The Expulsion of the Jews from Spain," *Jewish Quarterly Review*, XX (1908), pp. 240-271.

Mendoza, Vicente T. "El cancionero judío del norte de Marruecos," *Tribuna Israelita*, No. 107, (México D.F·, October 1953), pp. 23-24.

Mendoza, Vicente T. *El romance español y el corrido mexicano: estudio comparativo.* México D.F.: Ediciones de la Universidad Nacional Autónoma, 1939.

Menéndez Pidal, Gonzalo. "Ilustraciones musicales," Appendix to Vol. I of Ramón Menéndez Pidal's *Romancero Hispánico (hispano-portugués, americano y sefardí)* (Madrid, 1953), pp. 367-402.

Menéndez Pidal, María Goyri de. *Romances que deben buscarse en la tradición oral* (Madrid, n.d.).

Menéndez Pidal, Ramón. "Catálogo del romancero judío-español," *Cultura Española*, IV (1906), 1045-1077; V (1907), pp. 161-199. Reprinted with abbreviation of various *romances* in *El Romancero: teorías e investigaciones*, (Madrid, [1928]), pp. 101-183, and in *Los romances de América* (Buenos Aires-México D.F., 1948), pp. 121-188.

Menéndez Pidal, Ramón. *Cómo vivió y cómo vive el romancero.* Ilustraciones de Gonzalo Menéndez Pidal. Valencia: E. López Mezquida [1947?].

Menéndez Pidal, Ramón. "Poesía popular y romancero," *Revista de Filología Hispánica*, I (1914), 352-377; II (1915), 1-20, 105-136, 329-338; III (1916), 234-289.

Menéndez Pidal, Ramón. "Poesía popular y tradicional," *Los romances de América y otros estudios* (Buenos Aires, 1941), pp. 51-59.

Menéndez Pidal, Ramón. *El Romancero: teorías e investigaciones.* Madrid: Editorial Páez, 1928.

Menéndez Pidal, Ramón. *El Romancero Español.* Conferencias dadas en la Columbia University de New York los días 5 a 7 de abril de 1909. New York: The Hispanic Society of America, 1910.

Menéndez Pidal, Ramón. *Los romances de América y otros estudios.* Buenos Aires-México D.F.: Espasa Calpe, 1948.

Menéndez Pidal, Ramón. "Los romances de Don Bueso," *De primitiva lírica española y antigua épica* (Buenos Aires, 1951), pp. 103-112.

Menéndez Pidal, Ramón. "Los romances tradicionales en América," *Cultura Española*, I (Madrid, 1906), pp. 72-111.

Menéndez Pidal, Ramón. *Romancero Hispánico (hispano-portugués, americano y sefardí).* Madrid: Espasa-Calpe, 1953.

Menéndez Pidal, Ramón. *Romancero tradicional.* Vol. I: *Romanceros del Rey Rodrigo y de Bernardo del Carpio.* Madrid: Editorial Gredos, 1957.

Menéndez Pidal, Ramón. *Romancero tradicional.* Vol. II: *Romanceros de los Condes de Castilla y de los Infantes de Lara.* Madrid: Editorial Gredos, 1963.

Menéndez Pidal, Ramón. *Romancero tradicional.* Vol. III: *Romances de tema odiseico.* Edición a cargo de D. Catalán. Madrid: Editorial Gredos. 1969.

Menéndez Pidal, Ramón. "Romances y baladas," *Bulletin of the Modern Humanities Research*, I (Liverpool, 1927), pp. 1-17.

Menéndez Pidal, Ramón. "Sobre geografía folklórica: ensayo de un método," *Revista de Filología Española*, VII (1920), pp. 299-388.

Menéndez Pidal, Ramón. "Supervivencia del 'Poema de Kudrun'," *Revista de Filología Española*, XX (1933), 1-59; reprinted in *Los godos y la epopeya española* (Madrid, 1956), pp. 89-173.

Menéndez Pidal, Ramón. "Un viejo romance cantado por Sabbatai Çevi," *Mediæval Studies in Honor of J. D. M. Ford* (Cambridge, USA, 1948), pp. 183-190.

Menéndez y Pelayo, Marcelino. *Tratado de los romances viejos* (Madrid, 1903 and 1906). 2 vols. Vols XI and XII of his *Antología de poetas líricos castellanos* (Madrid, 1944-1945).

Michaëlis de Vasconcellos, Carolina. "Estudos sobre o romanceiro peninsular," *Cultura Española*, VII (1907), 767-803; VIII (1907), 1021-1057; IX (1908), 93-132; X (1908), 435-512; XI (1908), 717-758; XIV (1909), 434-483; XV (1909), 697-732.

Michaëlis de Vasconcellos, Carolina. "Estudos sobre o romanceiro peninsular," *Revista Lusitana*, II (1890-92), pp. 156-179, 193-240.

Millás, Francisca Vendrell de. "Los cancioneros del siglo XV," *Historia general de las literaturas hispánicas*, II (1951), pp. 55-70.

Milwitzky, William. "Judeo-Spanish Literature," *Encyclopedia of Literature*, ed. Joseph T. Shipley (New York, 1946), pp. 650-653.

Molho, Isaac R. ״אלברטו חמצי״ "Alberto Hemsi," אוצר יהודי ספר [*Tesoro de los judíos sefardíes*], II (Jerusalem, 1959), pp. 111-113.

Molho, Isaac R. ״מקורותיו וחוקריו של ח״רומאנסירו״ "Me-korotav v'ḥokrav šel ha «romancero» ['The Sources and Scholars of the *Romancero*']," מחברת [*Les Cahiers de l'Alliance Israélite Universelle*], IV (Paris, August 1955), pp. 108-112.

Molho, Isaac R. ״אוסף ה״רומאנסירו״ של יהודי־ספרד והבאלקאנים לשונו, מקורותיו וחוקריו״ "Osef ha «romancero» šel yehudim-sefarad v'ha-balkanim l'shono, mekorotav v'ḥokrav ['The *Romancero* Collection of Spanish and Balkan Jewry, its Language, Sources, and Scholars']," מחברת [*Les Cahiers de l'Alliance Israélite Universelle*], IV (Paris, 1955), pp. 60-62.

Molho, Isaac R. "Some Aspects of Sephardim and Ashkenazim," *Tesoro de los judíos sefardíes*, III (Jerusalem, 1960), pp. xvii-xxii.

Molho, Michael, "Cinq Élégies en judéo-espagnol," *Bulletin Hispanique*, XVII (1940), pp. 231-235.

Molho, Michael. "Consideraciones sobre folklore sefaradí," *Davar*, No. 76 (Buenos Aires, 1958-59), pp. 61-76.

Molho, Michael. *Histoire des Israélites de Castoria* (Salonika, 1938).

Molho, Michael. *Literatura sefardita de Oriente* (= Biblioteca Hebraicoespañola, VII). Madrid-Barcelona: Consejo Superior de Investigaciones Científicas, "Instituto Arias Montano," 1960.

Molho, Michael. "Tres romances de tema bíblico y dos canciones de cuna," *Comentario* (Buenos Aires, April-May-June, 1957), pp. 60-70.

Molho, Michael. *Usos y costumbres de los sefardíes de Salónica* (= Biblioteca Hebraicoespañola, III). Madrid-Barcelona: Consejo Superior de Investigaciones Científicas, "Instituto Arias Montano," 1950.

Montolíu, Plácido de. "*Coplas sefardíes (Judeo-Spanish Songs)*," *Hispanic Review*, VI (1938), pp. 166-168.

Morley, S. Griswold. "A New Jewish-Spanish *Romancero*," *Romance Philology*, I (August, 1947), pp. 1-9.

Morley, S. Griswold. "Are the Spanish *romances* written in Quatrains?" *Romanic Review*, VII (1916), pp. 42-82.

Morley, S. Griswold. *Spanish Ballad Problems. The Native Historical Themes*. University of California Publications in Modern Philology (Berkeley and Los Angeles), XIII, No. 2 (1925), pp. 207-228.

Muñiz Toca, D. Ángel. *Vida y obra de Eduardo M. Torner* (Musicólogo, folklorista y compositor). Contestación de D. José Fernández Buelta. Oviedo: Instituto de Estudios Asturianos, 1961.

Navon, Isaac Elijah. "המוסיקה בין יהודים המזרח" ['The Music among the Jews of the Near East']," הלל [*Hallel*], I, No. 3 (Jerusalem, 1930), pp. 55-57.

Nehama, Joseph. *Histoire des Israélites de Salonique*. Salonika: Libraire Molho, 1936. 3 vols., 5 fascicles.

Netanyahu, Ben Zion. *The Marranos of Spain from the Late 14th to the Early 16th Century According to Contemporary Hebrew Sources*. New York: American Academy for Jewish Research, 1966.

Netanyahu, Ben Zion. "The Marranos According to the Hebrew Sources of the 15th and Early 16th Centuries," *The American Academy for Jewish Research*, XXXI (1963), pp. 81-164.

Neuman, Abraham Aaron. "Some Phases of the Conditions of Jews in Spain in the 13th and 14th Centuries," *American Jewish Historical Society Publications*, XXII (1914), pp. 61-70.

Neuman, Abraham Aaron. *The Jews in Spain; Their Social, Political and Cultural Life during the Middle Ages*. Philadelphia: The Jewish Publication Society of America, 1942. 2 vols.

Ortega, Manuel L. *Los hebreos en Marruecos*. Estudio histórico, político y social. Madrid: Editorial Hispano Africana, 1919.

Pamphlet on the First International Congress of Jewish Music held in Paris, 4th-13th November 1957. [Contains program of events.]

Passy, Joseph, and J. Benaroya. "Spaniolisches Volkslied," *Der Urquell (Eine Monatschrift für Volkskunde)* (New Series) I, "Heft" 8 (Vienna, 1897), p. 206.

Patai, Raphael. *Israel between East and West: A Study in Human Relations*. Philadelphia: The Jewish Publication Society of America, 5713/1953.

Patai, Raphael. "Sephardi Folklore," *The World of the Sephardim*. Herzl Institute Pamphlet No. 15. (New York, 1960), pp. 22-36.

Pedrell, Felipe. *Cancionero musical popular español*. Valls, Cataluña: E. Castells, 1919-1922. 4 vols.

Pedrell, Felipe. "Folklore musical castillan du XVIe siècle," *Sammelbände der Internationalen Musikgesellschaft*, I (Leipzig, April-June, 1900), pp. 372-400.

Pedrell, Felipe. *Lírica nacionalizada. Estudios sobre folklore musical*. Paris, 1909.

Pena, Joaquín and Higinio Anglés. *Diccionario de la música «Labor».* Barcelona: Talleres Gráficos Ibero-Americanos, S.A., 1954.

Plá, Roberto. *Cuatro canciones sefardíes.* Madrid: Unión Musical Española, 1965.

Pope, Isabel. "The Musical and Metrical Form of the Villancico," *Annales Musicologiques,* II (1954), pp. 189-214.

Pope, Isabel. "The Musical Development and Form of the Spanish Villancico," *Papers of the American Musicological Society for 1940* (AMS, Inc., 1946), pp. 11-22.

Prescott, William H. *History of the Reign of Ferdinand and Isabella the Catholic.* Philadelphia: J. B. Lippincott Co., 1872.

Querol Gavaldá, Miguel. "Importance historique et national du romance," *Musique et poésie au XVIe siècle,* (Paris, 1953), pp. 299-327.

Querol Gavaldá, Miguel. "Romanze," *Die Musik in Geschichte und Gegenwart,* XI (1963), col. 845-848.

Ramos-Gil, C. "La lengua española en Israel," *Tesoro de los judíos sefardíes,* I (Jerusalem, 1959), pp. xxxii-xl.

Rodrigo, Joaquín. "Dos canciones sefardíes armonizadas," *Sefarad,* XIV (1954), 353-362. [Also published under the title *Dos canciones sefardíes del siglo XV para coro mixto.* Madrid: Grafispania, 1954.]

Rodrigo, Joaquín. *Triste estaba el Rey David.* Para coro mixto a capella. Madrid: Grafispania, 1952. [Also included in I. A. Langnas and B. Sholod, eds. *Studies in Honor of M. J. Benardete* (New York, 1965), pp. 389-398.

Rodrigo, Joaquín and Victoria Camhi. Review of "Chants séphardis recueillis et notés par Léon Algazi," in *Sefarad,* XVIII (1958), pp. 366-369.

Romances tradicionales y canciones narrativas existentes en el folklore español (Incipit y temas). Barcelona: Instituto Español de Musicología: Sección de folklore, 1945.

Roth, Cecil. *A History of the Marranos.* Philadelphia: The Jewish Publication Society of America, 1932.

Roth, Cecil. *A Life of Menasseh Ben Israel.* Philadelphia: The Jewish Publication Society of America, 1934.

Roth, Cecil. "The Bevis Marks Synagogue," *Le Judaïsme Séphardi,* No. 9 (London, Dec., 1955), pp. 392-394.

Roth, Cecil. "The European Age in Jewish History," in Louis Finkelstein's *The Jews: Their History, Culture and Religion* (New York: Harper, 1949), I, pp. 216-249.

Rubiato, María Teresa. "El repertorio musical de un sefardí," *Sefarad,* XXV (1965), pp. 453-463.

Rubiato, María Teresa. *Informe sobre los trabajos realizados en el tema musicología y folklore sefardí* (Madrid, 1966).

Rubiato, María Teresa. "Notas sobre el orientalismo de la música sefardí," *Sefarad,* XXVII (1967), pp. 421-428.

Rubiato, María Teresa. "Transcripción anatoda de seis canciones sefardíes," *Actas del Primer Simposio de Estudios Sefardíes,* (Madrid, 1969), Apéndice 2, pp. 559-567.

Salinas, Francisco. *De música libri septem* (Salamanca, 1577).

Saminsky, Lazare. *Music of the Ghetto and the Bible*. New York: Bloch Publishing Company, 1934.

S[an] S[ebastián], José Antonio de. *Canciones sefardíes para canto y piano*. Tolosa: Gráficas Laborde y Labayen, S. L., [ca. 1945]. (See also Donostia, P. José Antonio de).

Sánchez Moguel, A. "Un romance en el dialecto de los judíos de Oriente," *Boletín de la Real Academia de la Historia*, XVI (Madrid, 1890), pp. 497-509.

Sánchez Romeralo, Antonio. *El villancico (Estudios sobre la lírica popular en los siglos XV y XVI)*. Madrid: Editorial Gredos, S.A., 1969.

Schechter, Solomon. "Nachmanides," *Studies in Judaism*. Philadelphia: The Jewish Publication Society of America [1958], pp. 193-230.

Schechter, Solomon. "Safed in the Sixteenth Century," *Studies in Judaism*. Philadelphia: The Jewish Publication Society of America [1958], pp. 231-297.

Schindler, Kurt. *Folk Music and Poetry of Spain and Portugal*. With an introduction by Federico de Onís. New York: Hispanic Institute in the United States, 1941.

Schirmann, Jefim. "The Function of the Hebrew Poet in Medieval Spain," *Jewish Social Studies*, XVI (1954), pp. 235-252.

Schirmann, Jefim. "Hebrew Liturgical Poetry and Christian Hymnology," *The Jewish Quarterly Review*, XLIV (October, 1953), pp. 123-161.

Schlesinger, Emma Adatto. *Study of the Linguistic Characteristics of the Seattle Sefardi Folklore*. Unpublished Master's thesis. University of Washington, 1935.

Schmelz, Oscar. "The Development of the Jewish Population of Jerusalem During the Last Century," *Jewish Journal of Sociology*, XI (June, 1960), pp. 57-73.

Scholem, Gershom G. *Major Trends in Jewish Mysticism*. London: Thames and Hudson, [1955].

Schwarz, Samuel. "The Crypto-Jews of Portugal," *The Menorah Journal*, XII (April-May, 1926), 138-149; (June-July, 1926), pp. 283-297.

Seeger, Charles. "Prescriptive and Descriptive Music Writing," *The Musical Quarterly*, XLIV, No. 2 (April, 1958), pp. 184-195.

Seeger, Charles. "Singing Style," *Western Folklore*, XVII, No. 1 (January, 1958), pp. 3-11.

Seeger, Charles. "Toward a Universal Music Sound-Writing for Musicology," *Journal of the International Folk Music Council*, IX (1957), pp. 63-66.

Seeger, Charles. "Versions and Variants of the Tunes of 'Barbara Allen'," *Selected Reports: Institute of Ethnomusicology* (Los Angeles: University of California Press, 1966), pp. 120-167.

Šendrey, Alfred. *Bibliography of Jewish Music*. New York: Columbia University Press, 1951.

Šendrey, Alfred. *Music of the Jews in the Diaspora* (New York, 1970).

Shoḥet, E. "היהודים בירושלים במאה הי״ח" "Ha-yehudimb e-yerušalayim be-me'ah 18['The Jews in Jerusalem during the 18th Century']," ציון [*Zion*], I (1935), pp. 377-410.

Simmons, Merle E. *A Bibliography of the Romance and Related Forms in Spanish America*. Bloomington: Indiana University Press, 1963.

Simon, Walter. "Charakteristik des jüdenspanischen Dialekts von Saloniki," *Zeitschrift für romanische Philologie*, XL (1920), pp. 655-689.
Simon, Walter. "Judisch-spanisch," *Jüdisches Lexicon*, III (1929), pp. 464-466.

Simoni, Wolf. *Cuatro cánticas sefardies: chants populaires*. Paris: Éditions de la Sirène Musicale, [c. 1937]. 12 pp.

Smith, C. Colin. *Spanish Ballads*. London: Pergamon Press, [1964].

Sojo, V. E. *Nueve canciones de los safardies de Salonica*. Caracas: Editado por la dirección de la escuela de música "José Angel Lamas", 1964. 13 pp.

Sonne, I. "Relazione sul materiale achivistico e bibliografica della Comunità Israelitica de Rodi," *L'Idea Sionistica* (1931), pp. 4-5.

Spiegel, Shalom. "On Medieval Hebrew Poetry," *The Jews: Their History, Culture, and Religion*. Third edition. Edited by Louis Finkelstein (New York, 1960), pp. 854-892.

Starkie, Walter. *Spain: A Musician's Journey through Time and Space* (Geneva, 1958), 2 vols.

Subak, J. "Vorläufiger Bericht über eine im Auftrag der Balkan-Kommission der kais. Akademie der Wissenschaften zu Wien unternommene Forschungsreise nach der Balkanhalbinsel zur schriftlichen und phonographischen Aufnahme des Judenspanischen." *Anzeiger der philosophischen-historischen Klasse der kais. Akademie der Wissenschaften in Wien*, VI (Vienna, 1910).
Subak, J. "Zum Judenspanischen," *Zeitschrift für romanische Philologie*, XXX (1906), pp. 129-185.

Subirá, José. *Historia de la música española e hispanoamericana* (Barcelona, 1953).
Subirá, José. "Romances y refranes sefardíes," *Estudios dedicados a Menéndez Pidal*, V (Madrid, 1954), pp. 319-333.

Szold, Henrietta. *Recent Jewish Progress in Palestine*. Philadelphia: The Jewish Publication Society of America, 1915.

Tamar, David. צפת במאה הט״ז "Safed in the 16th Century," מחכרים ופעולות [*Studies and Reports*], Ben Zvi Institute, I (Jerusalem, 1960), pp. 12-13.

Thon, Hanna Helena. העדות בישראל *Ha-edot b'Yisrael* ['Ethnic Sub-groups in Israel, Their Origins and the Process of their Adjustment']. Jerusalem: Ruben Mass, 1957.

Tomás Parés, Juan. "Las variantes en la canción popular," *Anuario musical*, XIV (1959), pp. 195-205.

Torner, Eduardo Martínez. "El cancionero sefardí," *Temas folklóricos: Música y Poesía* (Madrid, 1935), pp. 51-58.

Torner, Eduardo Martínez. "El ritmo interno en el verso de romance," *Ensayos sobre estilística literatura española* (London: Dolphin Book Co., 1953), pp. 25-38.

Torner, Eduardo Martínez. "Ensayo de clasificación de las melodías de romance," *Homenaje ofrecido a Menéndez Pidal*, II (Madrid, 1925), pp. 391-402.

Torner, Eduardo Martínez. "Indicaciones prácticas sobre la notación musical de los romances," *Revista de Filología Española*, X (1923), pp. 389-394.

Torner, Eduardo Martínez. "La canción tradicional española," *Folklore y costumbres de España*, II (Barcelona, 1931), pp. 7-166.

Torner, Eduardo Martínez. "La rítmica en la música tradicional española," *Nuestra música*, III, No. 9 (January, 1948), Suplemento No. 3, pp. 55-68.

Torner, Eduardo Martínez. "Los vihuelistas del siglo XVI," *Temas folklóricos: Música y Poesía* (Madrid, 1935), pp. 21-31.

Torner, Eduardo Martínez. *Temas folklóricos: Música y poesía*. Madrid: Faustino Fuentes, 1935.

Trend, John Brande. *The Music of Spanish History to 1600*. London: Oxford University Press, 1926.

Uziel, Baruch. "הפולקלור של היהודים ספרדים" "Ha-folklor šel ha-yehudim ha-sefaradim ['The Folklore of the Sephardic Jews']," רשומות [*Rešumot*], (Tel Aviv, 1930), pp. 129-185.

Vicuña Cifuentes, Julio. *Instrucciones para recoger de la tradición oral romances populares*. Santiago: Imprenta E. Blanchard-Chessi, 1905. Reprinted in *Boletín bimestral de la Comisión Chilena de Cooperación Intelectual*, III:15 (Santiago, May-June, 1939), pp. 12-23.

Wagner, Max L. "Beiträge zur Kenntnis des Judenspanischen von Konstantinopel," *Kaiserliche Akademie der Wissenschaften. Schriften der Balkankommission. Linguistische Abteilung*. II *Romanische Dialektstudien*. Heft III (Vienna, 1914).

Webber, Ruth House. "Formulistic Diction in the Spanish Ballad," *University of California Publications in Modern Philology* (Berkeley and Los Angeles), Vol. 34, No. 2, (1951), pp. 175-278.

Webber, Ruth House. "Ramón Menéndez Pidal and the *Romancero*," *Romance Philology* V, No. 1 (1951), pp. 15-25.

Weisser, Albert. *Bibliography of Publications and Other Resources on Jewish Music*. New York: National Jewish Music Council — National Jewish Welfare Board, 1969.

Werner, Eric. *The Sacred Bridge*. The Interdependence of Liturgy and Music in Synagogue and Church during the First Millennium. New York: Columbia University Press, 1959.

Wholberg, Max. "The Music of the Sephardim," *Jewish Music Notes, JWB Circle* (Winter, 1961), 2; reprinted in *Le Judaïsme Séphardi*, No. 25 (December, 1962), 1058.

Wiener, Leo. "Songs of the Spanish Jews in the Balkan Peninsula," *Modern Philology*, I (1903-1904), pp. 205-216, 259-274.

Wolf, F. J. and C. Hofmann. *Primavera y flor de romances* (Berlin, 1856), 2 vols. Reprinted with additional appendices in M. Menéndez y Pelayo's *Antología de poetas líricos castellanos* (Madrid, 1945), Vols. VIII-IX.

Wünsch, Walter. "Der Jude im Balkanslavischen Volkstum und Volksliede," *Die Musik*, XXX (Stuttgart-Berlin, June, 1938), pp. 595-598.

ידיעות המכון הישראלי למוסיקה דתית *Yedi'ot ha-mahon ha-Yisraeli le-musika datit* ['*The Journal of the Israel Institute for Sacred Music*']. Edited by M. S. Geshuri (Jerusalem, 1959-   ).

Yehoshua, Jacob. ילדות בירושלים הישנה *Yaldot b'yerušalayim ha-yešenah* ['*Childhood in Old Jerusalem*: Description of Sephardic Life of the Past Century']. Jerusalem: Ruben Mass, 1965-1966. 2 vols.

Yurchenco, Henrietta. "Taping History in Morocco," *The American Record Guide*, XXIV, No. 4 (December, 1957), pp. 130-132.
Yurchenco, Henrietta. "The Music of the Jews in Morocco," *The American Philosophical Society Yearbook 1958* (Philadelphia, 1959), pp. 518-520.

Zenner, Walter P. "Sephardic Communal Organizations in Israel," *The Middle East Journal* (Spring, 1967), pp. 173-186.

Zimmels, H. J. *Ashkenazim and Sephardim*. Their Relations, Differences, and Problems as Reflected in the Rabbinical Responsa. With a Foreword by the Very Rev. The Chief Rabbi, Rabbi Israel Brodie. London: Oxford University Press, 1958.
Zimmels, H. J. *Die Marranen in der rabbinischen Literatur: Forschungen und Quellen zur Geschichte und Kulturgeschichte der Anussim* (Berlin, 1932).

APPENDIX I

Published Sources Containing Melodies of Judeo-Spanish *Romances*
Listed in Ramón Menéndez Pidal's *Catálogo*

1. Passy (1 ballad melody)
   Passy, Joseph. "Spaniolisches Volkslied (Aus Ostumelien)," *Der Urquelll: Eine Monatschrift für Volkskunde*, I (Vienna, 1897), p. 206.
2. Manrique de Lara #1 (2 ballad melodies)
   Manrique de Lara, Manuel. "Romances españoles en los Balkanes," *Blanco y Negro*, Año 26, Jan. 2, 1916, No. 1285. Reproduced in Vicente T. Mendoza, *El romance español y el corrido mexicano: estudio comparativo* (México D.F., 1939), pp. 36-37.
3. Manrique de Lara #2 (16 ballad melodies)
   Menéndez Pidal, Gonzalo. "Illustraciones musicales," Appendix to Vol. I of Ramón Menéndez Pidal's *Romancero Hispánico (hispano-portugués, americano y sefardí)* (Madrid, 1953), pp. 367-402.
4. Manrique de Lara #3 (2 ballad melodies)
   Rodrigo, Joaquín. "Dos canciones sefardíes armonizadas," *Sefarad*, XIV (1954), pp. 353-362.
5. Manrique de Lara #4 (1 ballad melody)
   Menéndez Pidal, Ramón. *Romancero tradicional*, (Madrid, 1957), Vol. I, p. 181.
6. Manrique de Lara #5 (3 ballad melodies)
   Catalán, Diego. "A caza de romances raros en la tradición portuguesa," reprinted from III Cologuio Internacional de Estudos Luso-Brasileiros (Lisbon, 1957), *Actas*, I (Lisbon, 1959), pp. 445-477. (Examples on Lam. I between pp. 464-465 and Lam. 2 between 448-449.)
7. Manrique de Lara #6 (2 ballad melodies)
   Katz, Israel J. "A Judeo-Spanish *Romancero*," *Ethnomusicology*, XII (January, 1968), pp. 78-81.
8. Bustelo (21 ballad melodies)
   Ortega, Manual L. *Los hebreos en Marruecos*. 1st and 2nd editions (Madrid, 1919), pp. 236-261; 3rd edition (Madrid, 1929), and 4th edition (Madrid, 1934), pp. 210-235.
9. Borrel (2 ballad melodies)
   Borrel, Eugène. "Melodies Israélites," *Revue de Musicologie*, VIII, No. 12 (Paris, 1924), p. 166.
10. Idelsohn (3 ballad melodies [of which two were taken from Borrel])
    Idelsohn, Abraham Zevi. *Gesänge der orientalischen Sefardim*, Vol. IV of the *Hebräisch-orientalischer Melodienschatz* (Jerusalem-Berlin-Vienna, 1923), pp. 275, 280.
11. Hemsi (15 ballad melodies)
    Hemsi, Alberto. *Coplas sefardíes (Chansons judéo-espagnoles)* (Alexandria, 1932-1938).

[Plá, Roberto. *Cuatro canciones sefardíes*. Madrid: Union Musical Española, 1965. Contains two ballad melodies from Hemsi's collection: MP 82 and 99.]

12. Jungić (2 ballad melodies)
    Jungić, B. "Tri sefardske romanse," *Godišnjak* (Sarajevo-Belgrade, 1933), pp. 289-291.
13. Torner (1 ballad melody)
    Torner, Eduardo Martínez. "La rítmica en la música tradicional española," *Música*, (Barcelona, Jan., 1938). Reprinted in *Nuestra música: Revista trimestral editada en México*, III (México D.F., 1948), p. 67.
14. Bénichou (Devoto, Berdichevsky de Arias, Algazi, and Bathori) (20 + 1 Ballad melodies)
    Bénichou, Paul. "Romances judeo-españoles de Marruecos," *Revista de Filología Hispánica*, VI (1944), pp. 374-381. The original article was revised, up-dated and re-issued in book form with additional material, under the title *Romancero judeo-español de Marruecos*. Madrid: Castalia, 1968. The original melodies were reset in much clearer type on pp. 293-303. N.B. In the new Castalia edition, there is an additional tune, *Siempre lo oyí yo dezir* [= *Vos labraré yo un pendón*, MP 120], p. 298.
15. Bordachar-Donostia (6 ballad melodies)
    S[an] S[ebastián], P. José Antonio de. *Canciones sefardíes para canto y piano*. (Tolosa, Spain [1945?].)
16. Molho (3 ballad melodies)
    Molho, Michael. *Usos y costumbres de los sefardíes de Salónica* (Madrid-Barcelona, 1950), pp. 328, 330.
17. Stanley (6 ballad melodies)
    MacCurdy, Raymond R. and Daniel D. Stanley. "Judaeo-Spanish Ballads from Atlanta, Georgia," *Southern Folklore Quarterly*, XV (1951), pp. 223-234.
18. Larrea (282 ballad melodies)
    Larrea Palacín, Arcadio de. *Romances de Tetuán* (Madrid, 1952), 2 vols.
19. Larrea (6 ballad melodies [taken from *Romances de Tetuán*])
    Larrea Palacín, Arcadio de. "Romances hispánicos del medievo," *Mundo Hispánico*, V, No. 49 (April, 1952), pp. 51-52.
20. Algazi (6 ballad melodies)
    Algazi, Léon. *Chants séphardis* (London, 1958).
21. Laning and Kruger (2 ballad melodies)
    Levy, Isaac Jack. *Sephardic Ballads and Songs in the United States*. Master's thesis (State University of Iowa, 1959).
22. Levy (23 ballad melodies)
    Levy, Isaac. *Chants judéo-espagnols* (London, 1959).
23. Katz #1 (3 ballad melodies)
    Katz, Israel J. "Toward a Musical Study of the Judeo-Spanish *Romancero*," *Western Folklore*, XXI (1962), pp. 86, 87, and 90.
24. Gerson-Kiwi #1 (1 ballad melody)
    Gerson-Kiwi, Edith. "The Legacy of Jewish Music through the Ages," *In the Dispersion* (Jerusalem, Winter, 1963-64), p. 160.
25. Gerson-Kiwi #2 (2 ballad melodies)
    Gerson-Kiwi, Edith. "On the Musical Sources of the Judaeo-Hispanic *Romance*," *The Musical Quarterly*, L (Jan., 1964), pp. 38-39.
26. Geshuri (1 melody)
    Geshuri, Me'ir Simeon. "(»שלש אחיות« הרומנצים של יהודי ספרד (עם המנגינה של [‏'The *Romances* of the Spanish Jews (with the Melody of «*Tres hermanicas*»)']," *Kol-no'ah*, II (Tel Aviv, 1932), p. 7. This is the melody for *Hero y Leandro*, MP 41.

27. Katz #2 (4 ballad melodies plus two Manrique de Lara MSS)
    Katz, Israel J. "A Judeo-Spanish *Romancero*," *Ethnomusicology*, XII (January, 1968), pp. 76-81.
28. Arm-Sil (U.S.)
    The field tapes of Professors S. G. Armistead and J. H. Silverman comprising some 550 ballad texts from Sephardic centers of the Eastern Mediterranean. The ballads were collected in the United States (1957-1966) from Sephardic informants residing in Los Angeles, San Francisco, Seattle, and New York. Approximately 80% of the ballads were sung.
29. Katz (Israel)
    The field tapes of Israel J. Katz which were recorded in Israel (1959-1961). This collection represents 250 ballad texts from the Judeo-Spanish *Romancero* traditions of the Eastern and Western Mediterranean including ballads gathered from the Sephardim of the Old City Jerusalem (see Appendix III). Approximately 95% of the ballads were sung.
30. Arm-Sil-Katz (Morocco)
    The field tapes of Armistead, Silverman, and Katz which were collected as a collaborative endeavor in the various Sephardic communities of Northern Morocco (Summer, 1962 and 1963). More than 550 ballad texts comprise the collection among which 95% were sung.

Addenda

31. Arnett (1 ballad melody) (*Catálogo* No. 124) Menéndez Pidal, Ramón. *Romancero tradicional*. Vol. III: *Romances de tema odiseico*. Edición a cargo de D. Catalán. Madrid: Editorial Gredos, 1969. (This ballad was collected by Isaac Jack Lévy.)
32. Berruezo de Mateo (2 ballad melodies) (*Catálogo* Nos. 12 and 49) Fernández, Africano. *España en Africa y el peligro judío: apuntes de un testigo desde 1915 a 1918* (Santiago, 1918).
33. Manrique de Lara (10 ballad melodies) (*Catálogo* No. 124) Menéndez Pidal, Ramón. *Romancero tradicional*. Vol. III: *Romances de tema odiseico*. Edición a cargo de D. Catalán.
34. Molho (3 ballad melodies) (*Catálogo* No. 15 plus two others) Sojo, V. E. *Nueve canciones de los sajardíes de Salonica* (Caracas, 1964). Sojo added piano accompaniments to the melodies given in Michael Molho's *Usos y costumbres de los sefardíes de Salónica* (Madrid-Barcelona, 1950).
35. Simoni (2 ballad melodies) (*Catálogo* Nos. 41 and 74) Simoni, Wolf. *Cuatro cánticas sejardíes: chants populaires*. Paris: Éditions de la Sirène Musicale, [c. 1937].

The following synoptic table lists published sources containing melodies of the Judeo-Spanish *romance* themes listed in Menéndez Pidal's *Catálogo*. Ballad themes not listed in the *Catálogo* have been omitted. They will appear in our projected Judeo-Spanish *Romancero* (see *Notes to Chapter Two*, page 9, note 1.)

Synoptic Table

- ◆ = Not considered a ballad.
  MP 29, 30, and 33 are religious songs.
  MP 131 and 138 are not ballad texts.
  MP 141 is an *endecha*.
- × = Ballad collected from informants representing the Western tradition.
- * = Ballad collected from informants representing the Eastern tradition.
- ⊗ = Ballad collected from informants representing both traditions.
- ▼ = Example taken from source indicated directly above it.
- T = Text (recited only).
- F = Fragment
- ❖ = Hemsi's examples which Plá rearranged for voice and guitar accompaniment.
- • = Identical to the published notation of Manrique de Lara.
- ✚ = Not listed in inventory, but found in Rodrigo's *Triste estaba el Rey David* (see bibliography).
- ? = May be the melody for MP 55, notated by Kruger.
- ↔ = May be considered a traditional melody since it employs a fragmentary text from *El conde Olinos*, MP 55.
- ≈ = Donostia set an accompaniment to this melody.

Menéndez Pidal Catálogo:	1. Passy	2. Manrique de Lara #1	3. Manrique de Lara #2	4. Manrique de Lara #3	5. Manrique de Lara #4	6. Manrique de Lara #5	7. Manrique de Lara #6	8. Bustelo	9. Borrel	10. Idelsohn	11. Hemsi [also Plá]	12. Jungić	13. Torner	14. Bénichou	15. Bordachar-Donostia	16. Molho	17. Stanley	18. Larrea Palacín #1	19. Larrea Palacín #2	20. Algazi	21. Laning and Kruger	22. Levy	23. Katz #1	24. Gerson-Kiwi #1	25. Gerson-Kiwi #2	26. Geshuri	27. Katz #2	28. Arm-Síl (U.S.)	29. Katz (Israel)	30. Arm-Síl-Katz (Morocco)
37																	×											×	×	
36																												×	×	
35◇																												⊗	×	
34																	×	×									*	×	×	
33																													×	
32																											*			
31																	×											×		
30◇																				*							*	×	×	
29◇																												×	×	
28														×			×			*	*						*	*	×	
27																												T		
26			*														×											×		
25																	× ▶										×	×		
24			*														×											×		
23																	×										T		T	
22																	×											×		
21			*														×											×	×	
20																											*			
19																	×												T	
18																	×													
17																														
16																												×		
15																	*											T		
14																	×										*	*	T	
13																											*	*		
12																	×				*						*	×		
11																												×		
10																												×		
9																	×										*	×		
8																														
7																	×													
6									×								×													
5																	×	×										×		
4																	× ▶													
3													×															×		
2			* ×														×											×		
1															×		×											×		

Menéndez Pidal *Catálogo*:

1. Passy
2. Manrique de Lara #1
3. Manrique de Lara #2
4. Manrique de Lara #3
5. Manrique de Lara #4
6. Manrique de Lara #5
7. Manrique de Lara #6
8. Bustelo
9. Borrel
10. Idelsohn
11. Hemsi [also Plá]
12. Jungić
13. Torner
14. Bénichou
15. Bordachar-Donostia
16. Molho
17. Stanley
18. Larrea Palacín #1
19. Larrea Palacín #2
20. Algazi
21. Laning and Kruger
22. Levy
23. Katz #1
24. Gerson-Kiwi #1
25. Gerson-Kiwi #2
26. Geshuri
27. Katz #2
28. Arm-Sil (U.S.)
29. Katz (Israel)
30. Arm-Sil-Katz (Morocco)

Menéndez Pidal *Catálogo*:	1. Passy	2. Manrique de Lara #1	3. Manrique de Lara #2	4. Manrique de Lara #3	5. Manrique de Lara #4	6. Manrique de Lara #5	7. Manrique de Lara #6	8. Bustelo	9. Borrel	10. Idelsohn	11. Hemsi [also Plá]	12. Jungić	13. Torner	14. Bénichou	15. Bordachar-Donostia	16. Molho	17. Stanley	18. Larrea Palacín #1	19. Larrea Palacín #2	20. Algazi	21. Laning and Kruger	22. Levy	23. Katz #1	24. Gerson-Kiwi #1	25. Gerson-Kiwi #2	26. Geshuri	27. Katz #2	28. Arm-Sil (U.S.)	29. Katz (Israel)	30. Arm-Sil-Katz (Morocco)
109																				×										
108bis																				×										×
108											*																	*	*	
107											*											*						*	*	
106											*				×			×									F	×	×	
105																				×									×	
104																														
103																														
102								×																					×	
101														×			×											×	×	
100																	×										*			
99								×			❖						×										*	⊗	×	
98																	×					*					*	*	×	
97																	×												×	
96																	×										*	⊗	×	
95									×		*						×										*		×	
94									×								×												×	
93																	×												×	
92																														
91																	×												×	
90																	×												×	
89																	×										*		×	
88																	×										*	×	×	
87																	×													
86									×								×										*		×	
85bis																														
85																	× × ×										*	*	×	
84																											*		×	×
83																											*		×	×
82		*	*								❖				*		*	× ×			*	*		*			*	*	×	×
81																		×											×	
80											*				*		*	× ×		*	*	*					*	*	*	×
79																				*										
78																		× × ×									*	*	×	×
77																											*	*	×	×
76																		×											×	
75																												×	×	×

143												
142												
141◆							×		*	*	*	×
140					≀						*	
139							*	×			*	
138◆							*	×			⊗	×
137												
136					*						*	
135								×			*	×
134				×							*	
133					*			×			*	T
132bis								×				
132								×			*	
131◆												
130								×			*	×
129				× ▶				×			* ×	×
128								×				×
127												×
126												×
125								×				
124					*			×	*		*	⊗ ×
123			×	×		× ×		×			×	× ×
122			⊗	×				×		T		× ×
121bis						×		×				
121	×			×		×	*	×			* *	
120				×	*	×		×	*		* ⊗	×
119bis		×						×			*	× ×
119			×					× ×				× ×
118								× ×				
117		×	×					× × ×			×	×
116								× ×				×
115								× ×			×	×
114	×	× ×	×				×		×		×	×
113							×				×	×
112												
111											× ×	
110											× ×	×

Menéndez Pidal *Catálogo*:

1. Passy
2. Manrique de Lara #1
3. Manrique de Lara #2
4. Manrique de Lara #3
5. Manrique de Lara #4
6. Manrique de Lara #5
7. Manrique de Lara #6
8. Bustelo
9. Borrel
10. Idelsohn
11. Hemsi [also Plá]
12. Jungić
13. Torner
14. Bénichou
15. Bordachar-Donostia
16. Molho
17. Stanley
18. Larrea Palacín #1
19. Larrea Palacín #2
20. Algazi
21. Laning and Kruger
22. Levy
23. Katz #1
24. Gerson-Kiwi #1
25. Gerson-Kiwi #2
26. Geshuri
27. Katz #2
28. Arm-Sil (U.S.)
29. Katz (Israel)
30. Arm-Sil-Katz (Morocco)

Judeo-Spanish *romance* themes listed in Ramón Menéndez Pidal's *Catálogo*

A. Romances históricos

1. Bernardo del Carpio
2. Las cabezas de los siete infantes de Lara
3. Ximena pide justicia
4. Don Sancho y doña Urraca [= Fernando I en Francia]
5. Destierro del Cid
6. Búcar sobre Valencia
7. La muerte del Maestre de Santiago
8. La pérdida de Antequera
9. El alcaide de Alhama
10. Abenámar
11. Portocarrero
12. La mujer de Juan Lorenzo
13. Expulsión de los judíos de Portugal
14. La muerte del duque de Gandía
15. La muerte del príncipe Don Juan
16. El Mostadí

H. Romances moriscos

17. Jarifa cautiva en Antequera
18. Abindarráez
19. Zaide

C. Asunto carolingio

20. Roncesvalles [= Almerique de Narbona]
21. El sueño de doña Alda
22. Cautiverio de Guarinos
23. Conde Claros y el Emperador
24. Conde Claros y la princesa acusada
25. Nacimiento de Montesinos
26. Rosa Florida y Montesinos
27. Miliselda y Don Gaifero
28. De la linda melisenda [= Melisenda insomne]

D. Asunto bíblico

    29. El pecado original
    30. Nacimiento y vocación de Abraham
    31. El sacrificio de Isaac
    32. El robo de Dina
    33. Nacimiento de Moisés
    34. Consagración de Moisés
    35. Las tablas de la Ley
    36. David y Goliat
    37. Amnón y Tamar
    38. David llora a Absalón
    39. Juicio de Salomón
    40. La tormenta calmada [= El idólatra]

E. Asunto clásico

    41. Hero y Leandro
    42. Juicio de Paris
    43. Robo de Elena
    44. Muerte de Alejandro
    45. Tarquino y Lucrecia
    46. Virgilios
    47. Amenaza a Roma

F. Romances de cautivos

    48. Hermanas reina y cautiva
    49. Don Bueso y su hermana
    50. Los cautivos Melchor y Laurencia
    51. El cautivo del renegado
    52. El cautiverio del príncipe Francisco
    53. Duque de Bernax
    54. Cabalgata de Peranzules

G. Amor fiel

    55. El Conde Olinos [= Amantes perseguidos]
    56. La aparición also: Alfonso XII
    57. ¿Por qué no cantáis la bella?
    58. Vuelta del marido (í) [= Arbolero]
    59. Vuelta del marido (é)
    60. La boda estorbada [= El Conde Dirlos]
    61. Moriana y Galván
    62. La esposa de Don García [= En busca de la esposa]
    63. Diego León

H. Amor desgraciado

    64. Conde Alarcos
    65. La novia del Conde de Alba
    66. El pájaro verde
    67. Catalina [= La novia abandonada]

I. Esposa desdichada

    68. El parto en lejas tierras [= Casada de lejas tierras] [= sueño profético]
    69. La mala suegra castigada
    70. La mala suegra
    71. Sufrir callando
    72. La malcasada del pastor
    73. La mujer del pastor
    74. La mujer engañada
    75. La muerte ocultada
    76. Mainés
    77. Isabel de Liar

J. Romances de la adúltera

    78. La adúltera (ó)
    79. Rachel Lastimosa (= La adúltera (ó)]
    80. La adúltera (á-a)
    81. La adúltera (é-a)
    82. Landarico [= Andarleto]
    83. Bernal Francés
    84. La infanticida

K. Venganzas femeninas y mujeres matadoras

    85. Rico Franco
    85. bis. La condesa traidora
    86. El veneno de Moriana
    87. Doña Antonia
    88. La envenenadora
    89. La Gallarda
    90. La fratricida por amor
    91. La calumnia

L. Romances de raptos y forzadores

    92. El raptor pordiosero
    93. El culebro raptor
    94. El rapto (a)
    95. Grandes bodas en Francia [= Rapto (í)]
    96. Los soldados forzadores
    97. Atrevimiento castigado
    98. Silvana
    99. Delgadina
    100. Blanca Flor y Felismena

M. Varias aventuras amorosas

    101. Gerineldo
    102. Aliarda
    103. Tiempo es, el caballero
    104. Espinelo

105. Flérida
106. La infanta deshonrada
107. Una ramica de ruda
108. Princesa y el segador [= Princesa enamorada de un segador]
108 bis. El mal encanto
109. Noche de amores
110. La guardadora de un muerto
111. Desilusión
112. El jugador
113. Generosidad de Narváez [= Generosidad]

N. Burlas y astucias

114. La infantina [= El caballero burlado]
115. Repulsa y compasión
116. Disfrazado de mujer
117. El capitán burlado
118. El molinero y el cura

N. Asuntos varios

119. La buena hija
119 bis. El hijo vengador
120. Vos labraré yo un pendón
121. Mujer guerrera [= Un capitán sevillano]
121 bis. El caballo robado
122. El huérfano
123. El rey envidioso de su sobrino
124. Vuelta del hijo maldecido
125. El encuentro del padre
126. Testamento del Rey Felipe
127. La pesca de truchas
128. El Polo [= Las siete guardas] [also: La guarda cuidadosa]
129. El sueño profético [= Pesadilla]
130. Buscando novia [also: Escogiendo novia]
131. Marido sin oficio
132. Díos los cría y ellos se juntan [= La cantiga del borrachón]
132 bis. Don Pedro Acedo

O. Romances líricos

133. La bella en misa
134. La lavandera de San Juan
135. Requiebros
136. Romance para bodas [= La galana y su caballo]
137. La semana del pretendiente
138. Otros tres, y son seis
139. El villano vil
140. La choza del desesperado
141. Endecha
142. El chuflete
143. El Conde Arnaldos

APPENDIX II

An Inventory of the Tape-Recorded Examples and the Published Notations Utilized for the Study of the Ballad Tunes from the Jerusalem Répertoire

This inventory includes musical examples taken from four sources:

I: My personal archives representing *Sabra* informants from Jerusalem. (Collected in Jerusalem, 1959-1961.)

II: My personal archives representing Sephardic informants from other Eastern Mediterranean areas who recently emigrated to Israel around the time I recorded them. (Collected in Jerusalem, 1959-1961.)

III: The archives of Professors S. G. Armistead and J. H. Silverman, which contain recorded examples of ballads from Sephardic informants of the Eastern Mediterranean. (Collected in the United States, 1957-1966).

IV: Published sources. (Taken from the pertinent sources listed in Appendix I.)

A. *Arbolero* or *Vuelta del marido (i)*, MP 58

The tape-recorded examples used for this study were taken from the following:

I: Katz (*Sabra* informants):
  Y1. Leah Pardo, Age 74. Recorded in Jerusalem, 17th August, 1960.
  Y2. Esther Maimara, Age 67. Recorded in Jerusalem, 29th June 1960.
  Y3. Rivka Shalom, Age 65. Recorded in Jerusalem, 8th November 1960.
  Y4. Sultana Parnass, Age 71. Recorded in Jerusalem, 12th November, 1960.
  Y5. Rivka Cabeli, Age 75. Recorded in Jerusalem, 20th November 1960.
  Y6. Schmuel Mizraḥi, Age 68. Recorded in Jerusalem, 31th January 1961.

II. Katz (Immigrants from other Sephardic centers residing in Israel):
  A. Monastir — now Bitolj — Yugoslavia (Female, Age 77). Recorded in Jerusalem, 12th January 1961.
  B. Aïden, Turkey (Female, Age 66). Recorded in Jerusalem, 25th April 1961.

III: Armistead/Silverman (United States collection):
  C. Rhodes (Female). Recorded in Los Angeles, 22th January 1958. [Leonore Halfon]
  D. Rhodes (Female). Recorded in Los Angeles, 11th June 1958. [Marie Russo]
  E. Rhodes (Female). Recorded in Seattle, 23rd July 1958. [Rebecca Peha]
  F. Rhodes (Female). Recorded in Seattle, 31st July 1958. [Leah Huniu]

Published notations can be found in the following sources:

(For the Eastern tradition):
1. Jungić (Sarajevo, pp. 290-291).
2. Stanley (Rhodes, Text A, p. 223).
3. Algazi (Eastern Mediterranean, No. 65, p. 52).
4. Levy (Eastern Mediterranean, No. 7, p. 10)
5. Levy (Eastern Mediterranean, No. 8, p. 12).
6. Katz #1 (Jerusalem, p. 87, which is the first verse of Sabra Variant 4).
7. Gerson-Kiwi #1 (Salonika, Example 13, p. 62).

B. *La adúltera* (á-a), MP 80

The tape-recorded items for this ballad were taken from the following:

I. Katz (*Sabra* informants):
   V1. Esther Maimara, Age 67. Recorded in Jerusalem, 29th June 1960.
   V2. Aura Ratan, Age 55. Recorded in Jerusalem, 17th September 1960.
   V3. Rivka Shalom, Age 65. Recorded in Jerusalem, 8th November 1960.
   V4. Josef Sasson, Age 60. Recorded in Jerusalem, 9th November 1960.
   V5. Gracia Hassán, Age 60. Recorded in Jerusalem, 12th November 1960.

II. Katz (Immigrants from other Sephardic centers residing in Israel):
   A. Monastir (Female, Age 77). Recorded in Jerusalem, 12th January 1961.
   B. Izmir (Female, Age 60). Recorded in Jerusalem, 6th February 1961.
   C. Istanbul (Female, Age 52). Recorded in Gezer Carmel, 4th May, 1961.
   D. Istanbul (Female, Age 65). Recorded in Safed, 4th May 1961.

III. Armistead/Silverman (United States collection):
   E. Rhodes (Female). Recorded in Brooklyn, 18th August 1959. [Julia Sadis]
   F. Rhodes (Female). Recorded in Seattle, 29th August 1958. [Rosa Alhadeff]

Published notations can be found in the following sources:

1. Hemsi (Salonika, XVII, Op. 13-5).
2. Bordachar-Donostia (Salonika, No. 7, p. 4).
3. Algazi (Eastern Mediterranean, No. 62, p. 50).
4. Levy (Eastern Mediterranean, No. 25, p. 30).
5. Levy (Eastern Mediterranean, No. 27, p. 32).
6. Levy (Eastern Mediterranean, No. 85, p. 78).
7. Katz #2 (Jerusalem). [This is the first strophe of Sabra, V1.]

C. *Landarico*, MP 82

The tape-recorded items used for the above observations were taken from the following:

I. Katz (*Sabra* informants);
   V1. Leah Pardo, Age 74. Recorded in Jerusalem, 17th August 1960.
   V2. Sultana Parnass, Age 71. Recorded in Jerusalem, 12th November 1960.
   V3. Rivka Cabeli, Age 75. Recorded in Jerusalem, 16th November 1960.

II. Katz (Immigrants from other Sephardic centers residing in Israel):
   A. Sofia (Female, Age 65). Recorded in Tel Aviv, 7th December 1960.
   B. Izmir (Female, Age 69). Recorded in Jerusalem, 25th April 1961.

    C.   Izmir (Female, Age 40). Recorded in Jerusalem, 11th April 1961.
    D.   Istanbul (Female, Age 70). Recorded in Jerusalem, 6th February 1961.
    E.   Istanbul (Female, Age 52). Recorded in Gezer Carmel, 3rd May 1961.
    F.   Istanbul (Female, Age 75). Recorded in Safed, 4th May 1961.
    G.   Istanbul (Female, Age 80). Recorded in Safed, 4th May 1961.
    H.   Istanbul (Female, Age 65). Recorded in Safed, 4th May 1961.

III. Armistead/Silverman (United States collection):
    I.   Rhodes (Female). Recorded in Seattle, 29th August 1958. [Esther Peha]
    J.   Rhodes (Female). Recorded in Seattle, 29th August 1958. [Rosa Alhadeff]
    K.   Rhodes (Female). Recorded in Los Angeles, 17th June 1958. [Rebecca Peha]
    L.   Rhodes (Female). Recorded in Los Angeles, 23rd July 1958. [Regina Hanan]

Published notations can be found in the following sources:

(For the Eastern tradition):
    1. Manrique de Lara #2 (Belgrade, p. 401).
    2. Bordachar-Donastia (Salonika, No. 10, p. 5).
    3. Hemsi (Rhodes, II, Op. 8-2).
    4. Stanley (Rhodes, Text F, p. 234).
    5. Manrique de Lara #4 (Near East, pp. 359-62).
    6. Laning (Rhodes, No. 90, p. 262).
    7. Levy (Eastern Mediterranean, No. 6, p. 9).
    8. Gerson-Kiwi (Jerusalem?, p. 39).

(For the Western tradition):
    9. Larrea (Tetuán, I, M119).
    10. Larrea (Tetuán, I, M120).

D. *Don Bueso y su hermana*, MP 49

The recorded examples used for this study were taken from the following:

I. Katz (*Sabra* informants):
    V̄1. Leah Candiel, Age 65. Recorded in Jerusalem, 20th June 1960.
    V̄2. Sultana Parnass, Age 71. Recorded in Jerusalem, 12th November 1960.
    V̄3. Rivka Cabeli, Age 75. Recorded in Jerusalem, 20th November 1960.

II. Armistead/Silverman (United States collection):
    A.   Rhodes (Female). Recorded in Los Angeles, 22nd January 1958. [Leonore Halfon]
    B.   Rhodes (Female). Recorded in Los Angeles, 31st July 1958. [Leah Huniu]
    C.   Rhodes (Female). Recorded in Seattle, 28th August 1958. [Tamar Tarika]
    D.   Rhodes (Female). Recorded in Los Angeles, 18th January 1959. [Perla Galante]
    E.   Rhodes (Female). Recorded in Brooklyn, 18th August 1959. [Bella Alhadeff]
    F.   Çanakkale (Male). Recorded in Los Angeles, 5th September 1957. [Salomon Abrevaya]
    G.   Marmara (Female). Recorded in Seattle, 29th August 1958. [Mrs. Sol Polichar]

Published notations can be found for the following:

(For the Eastern tradition):

1. Manrique de Lara #2 (Istanbul, p. 401).
2. Hemsi (Izmir, XXV, Op. 22-1).
3. Levy (Eastern Mediterranean, No. 10, p. 14).

(For the Western tradition):
1. Bénichou (Tetuán, XIV, p. 377).
2. Larrea (Tetuán, I, M53; also in "Romances hispánicos ...," p. 52).
3. Larrea (Tetuán, I, M54).
4. Larrea (Tetuán, I, M55).
5. Larrea (Tetuán, I, M56).
6. Larrea (Tetuán, II, M238).

E. *La choza del desesperado*, MP 140

The tape recorded items forming the basis of study for this ballad are the following:

I. Katz (*Sabra* informants):
 ℣1. Esther Maimara, Age 67. Recorded in Jerusalem, 29th June 1960.
 ℣2. Aura Ratan, Age 55. Recorded in Jerusalem, 17th September 1960.
 ℣3. Rivka Shalom, Age 65. Recorded in Jerusalem, 8th November 1960.
 ℣4. Josef Sasson, Age 60. Recorded in Jerusalem, 9th November 1960.
 ℣5. Gracia Hassán, Age 60. Recorded in Jerusalem, 12th November 1960.

II. Katz (Immigrants from other Sephardic centers residing in Israel):
 A. Izmir (Female, Age 55). Recorded in Jerusalem, 10th April 1961.
 B. Istanbul (Female, Age 75). Recorded in Safed, 4th May 1961.
 C. Salonika (Female, Age 85). Recorded in Jerusalem, 16th April 1961.

III. Armistead/Silverman (United States collection):
 D. Istanbul (Female). Recorded in Brooklyn, 19th August 1959. [Sarah Pavon]
 E. Istanbul (Female). Recorded in Los Angeles, 15th November 1959. [Virginia Behar]
 F. Rhodes (Female). Recorded in Los Angeles, 17th June 1958. [Perla Galante]
 G. Rhodes (Female). Recorded in Seattle, 26th August 1958. [Tamar Tarika]

Published notations can be found in the following sources:

1. Bordachar-Donostia (Salonika, No. 4, pp. 15-18).
2. Levy (Eastern Mediterranean, No. 9, p. 13)
3. Katz #1 (Jerusalem, p. 86, which is first verse of Variant 3 above).

APPENDIX III

Ballad Themes Collected from the Jerusalem Répertoire (1959-61)

A. Ballads listed in the Menéndez Pidal *Catálogo*:

1. MP 27: Don Gaifero y Miliselda
2. MP 41: Hero y Leandro
3. MP 43: Robo de Elena
4. MP 49: Don Bueso y su hermana
5. MP 58: Arbolero *or* Vuelta del marido (í)
6. MP 59: Vuelta del marido (é)
7. MP 68: El sueño profético [identical to MP 129]
8. MP 70: La mala suegra
9. MP 72: La malcasada del pastor
10. MP 74: La mujer engañada
11. MP 78: La adúltera (ó)
12. MP 80: La adúltera (á-a)
13. MP 82: Landarico
14. MP 85: Rico Franco
15. MP 96: Los soldados forzadores
16. MP 98: Silvana
17. MP 99: Delgadina
18. MP 107: Una ramica de ruda
19. MP 107 (Part II): La pedigüeña
20. MP 108: Princesa y el segador
21. MP 120: Vos labraré yo un pendén
22. MP 121: Mujer guerrera
23. MP 123: El rey envidioso de su sobrino
24. MP 124: Vuelta del hijo maldecido
25. MP 133: La bella en misa
26. MP 140: Choza del desesperado

B. Ballads not listed in the *Catálogo*:
27. Venganza de la novia rechazada
28. Niña de los siete enamorados
29. Princesa y el bozağí

UNSERE VERÖFFENTLICHUNGEN
OUR PUBLICATIONS

VERÖFFENTLICHUNGEN MITTELALTERLICHER MUSIKHANDSCHRIFTEN
PUBLICATIONS OF MEDIÆVAL MUSICAL MANUSCRIPTS

Vol. I	Madrid 20486	DM 32	$ 8.00
Vol. II	Wolfenbüttel 1099 Helmst. (1206)	DM 200	$ 50.00
Vol. III	Eine zentrale Quelle der Notre Dame-Musik. A Central Source of Notre-Dame Polyphony	DM 60	$ 15.00
Vol. IV	Paris, nouv. acq. frç. 13531 & lat. 11411	DM 30	$ 7.50
Vol. V	Worcester, Add. 68, Westminster 33327 & Madrid 192	DM 36	$ 9.00
Vol. VI	Oxford, lat. litur. d 20 & Chicago 654 App.	DM 48	$ 12.00
Vol. VII	Opera omnia Faugues	DM 60	$ 15.00
Vol. VIII	Sevilla, 5-I-43 & Paris, nouv. acq. frç. 4379	DM 72	$ 18.00
Vol. IX	Carmina Burana	DM 250	$ 62.50
Vol. X	Firenze, Pluteo 29,1 (Pars I)	DM 160	$ 40.00
Vol. XI	Firenze, Pluteo 29,1 (Pars II)	DM 160	$ 40.00

MUSICAL THEORISTS IN TRANSLATION

Vol. I	Anonymus IV	DM 30	$ 7.50
Vol. II	Robert de Handlo	DM 28	$ 7.00
Vol. III	Nivers, Treatise on the Composition of Music	DM 20	$ 5.00
Vol. IV	Huygens, Use and Nonuse of the Organ in the Churches of the United Netherlands	DM 20	$ 5.00
Vol. V	Bernier, Principles of Composition	DM 24	$ 6.00
Vol. VI	Loulié, Elements or Principles of Music	DM 50	$ 12.50
Vol. VII	Bacilly, A Commentary upon the Art of Proper Singing	DM 100	$ 25.00

GESAMTAUSGABEN - COLLECTED WORKS

Vol. I	Faugues (Gesamtausgabe, Collected Works)	DM 60	$ 15.00
Vol. II/1	A. Rener, Collected Works. I: The Motets	DM 48	$ 12.00
Vol. III/1	Goudimel, Collected Works. 1: Psalm Motets Vol. 1	DM 60	$ 15.00
Vol. III/2	Goudimel, Collected Works. 2: Psalm Motets Vol. 2	DM 60	$ 15.00
Vol. III/9	Goudimel, Collected Works. 9: 150 Psalms of 1564/1565 („Jaqui")	DM 60	$ 15.00
Vol. III/10	Goudimel, Collected Works. 10: 150 Psalms of 1568/1580 („St. André")	DM 120	$ 30.00
Vol. IV/1	Cabezón, Collected Works. 1: Duos, Kyries, Variations etc.	DM 64	$ 16.00

WISSENSCHAFTLICHE ABHANDLUNGEN - MUSICOLOGICAL STUDIES

Vol. I	L. Dittmer, Auszug aus The Worcester Music Fragments	DM 4	$ 1.00
Vol. II	G. Schuetze, An Introduction to Faugues	DM 42	$ 10.50
Vol. III	E. Trumble, Fauxbourdon, an Historical Survey, I	DM 30	$ 7.50
Vol. IV	L. Spiess, Historical Musicology	DM 32	$ 8.00
Vol. V	S. Levarie, Fundamentals of Harmony	DM 7,80	$ 1.95
Vol. VI	E. Southern, The Buxheim Organ Book	DM 60	$ 15.00
Vol. VII	L. Dittmer, Friedrich Ludwig, Repertorium organorum ... I, 1	vergriffen	O.P.
Vol. VIII	C. Jacobs, Tempo Notation in Renaissance Spain	DM 40	$ 10.00
Vol IX	E. Thomson, An Introduction to Philippe (?) Caron	DM 12	$ 3.00
Vol. X	H. Tischler, A Structural Analysis of Mozart's Piano Concertos	DM 72	$ 18.00
Vol. XI	V. Mattfeld, Georg Rhaw's Publications for Vespers	DM 60	$ 15.00
Vol. XII	E. Borroff, An Introduction to Elisabeth-Claude Jacquet de la Guerre	DM 48	$ 12.00
Vol. XIII	F. J. Smith, The Speculum Musicæ of Jacobus Leodiensis I	DM 24	$ 6.00
Vol. XIV	J. Travis, Miscellanea musica celtica	DM 40	$ 10.00
Vol. XV	C. W. Brockett, Antiphons, Reponsories, and Other Chants of the Mozarabic Rite	DM 120	$ 30.00
Vol. XVI	F. Crane, Materials for the Study of the Fifteenth-Century Basse Danse	DM 60	$ 15.00
Vol. XVII	L. Dittmer, Friedrich Ludwig, Repertorium organorum ... II	DM 80	$ 20.00

MIKROFILME - MICROFILMS

I Studies of Music in the Middle Ages	DM 72	$ 18.00
II U. Chevallier, Repertorium hymnologicum I-VI	DM 48	$ 12.00

Die Preise verstehen sich in DM; andere sind Richtpreise. Official prices are in German Marks.

THE INSTITUTE OF MEDIÆVAL MUSIC, LTD.

1653 West 8th Street, Brooklyn, New York 11223, U.S.A.